US Civil–Military Relations After 9/11

US CIVIL–MILITARY RELATIONS AFTER 9/11

Renegotiating the Civil–Military Bargain

Mackubin Thomas Owens

continuum

2011

The Continuum International Publishing Group
80 Maiden Lane, New York, NY 10038
The Tower Building, 11 York Road, London SE1 7NX

www.continuumbooks.com

Library of Congress Cataloging-in-Publication Data
Owens, Mackubin Thomas.
  US civil-military relations after 9/11 : renegotiating the civil-military bargain / Mackubin Thomas Owens.
     p. cm.
  Includes bibliographical references.
  ISBN-13: 978-1-4411-5748-5 (hardcover : alk. paper)
  ISBN-10: 1-4411-5748-4 (hardcover : alk. paper)
  ISBN-13: 978-1-4411-6083-6 (pbk. : alk. paper)
  ISBN-10: 1-4411-6083-3 (pbk. : alk. paper)
  1. Civil-military relations–United States. I. Title. II. Title: United States civil-military relations after 9/11.

  JK330.O84 2011
  322'.50973--dc22

                                                          2010019838

ISBN: HB: 978-1-4411-5748-5
       PB: 978-1-4411-6083-6

Typeset by Newgen Imaging Systems Pvt Ltd, Chennai, India
Printed and bound in the United States of America

For my children, Cynthia, Miranda, Mackubin, and Benjamin
And for my Muse, Doreen

Contents

Introduction

There is no more important question facing a state than the place of its military relative to civil society and the roles that the military exercises. The reason is simple: on the one hand, the coercive power of a military establishment, especially a strong and effective one, makes it at least a potential threat to the regime. On the other hand, a weak military establishment also threatens the regime because of the likelihood that the former will fail to protect the latter. This is the central paradox of Civil–military relations.

The United States has been fortunate in that its military has successfully defended the Republic on the battlefield while avoiding threats to civilian control, the most extreme and dangerous forms of which are coup d'état and praetorianism. But tensions have always existed and are manifestations of the fact that from the time of the Revolution to the present day, Civil–military relations in America essentially have constituted a *bargain* among three parties: the American people, the government, and the military as an institution.

The goal of this bargain is to allocate prerogatives and responsibilities between the civilian leadership on the one hand and the military on the other hand. From time to time throughout US history, certain circumstances— political, strategic, social, technological, etc.—have changed to such a degree that the terms of the existing Civil–military bargain become obsolete. The resulting disequilibrium and tension have led the parties to renegotiate the bargain in order to restore balance in the Civil–military equation.[1]

There are five questions that define the Civil–military bargain. First, who controls the military instrument? Second, what level of influence by the military is acceptable in a liberal society such as the United States? Third, what is the appropriate role of the military? Fourth, what pattern of civil–military relations best ensures the effectiveness of the military instrument? And finally, who serves? Clearly, there are many possible patterns of civil–military relations that provide different answers to these five questions. The purpose of this book is to flesh out the answers to these questions in the context of the post-9/11 era.

The various patterns of American civil–military relations have generally worked well, but have occasionally exhibited signs of stress as the civil–military bargain has been renegotiated. This has certainly been the case in the United States during the last two decades.

A substantial renegotiation of the civil–military bargain took place with the end of the Cold War. The change in the security environment occasioned by the collapse of the Soviet Union led to a lack of a consensus regarding what the US military was expected to do in the new security environment. The resulting period of drift had a substantial impact on civil–military relations. As the brief summary below suggests, the civil–military bargain is still being negotiated.

Civil–Military Relations from Clinton to Obama

During the decade of the 1990s, a number of events led observers to conclude that all was not well with civil–military relations in America. These events generated an often-acrimonious public debate in which a number of highly respected observers concluded that American civil–military relations had become unhealthy as best and were "in crisis" at worst. In the words of the distinguished military historian, Richard Kohn, the state of civil–military relations during this period was "extraordinarily poor, in many respects as low as in any period of American peacetime history."[2]

Nothing was more illustrative of the unhealthy state of civil–military relations during this period than the unprecedented instances of hostility on the part of the uniformed military toward President Bill Clinton, whose antimilitary stance as a young man during the Vietnam War years did not endear him to soldiers.[3] Many of the most highly publicized disputes between the uniformed military and the Clinton administration reflected cultural tensions between the military as an institution and liberal civilian society, mostly having to do with women in combat and open homosexuals in the military.

The catalog included the very public exchange on the issue of military service by open homosexuals between newly elected President Bill Clinton on the one hand and the uniformed military and Congress on the other hand, "Tailhook," the Kelly Flinn affair, and the sexual harassment scandal at Aberdeen, MD.[4] But civil–military tensions were not limited to social issue. Others included the charge that General Colin Powell, then-Chairman of the Joint Chiefs of Staff, was illegitimately invading civilian turf by publicly advancing opinions on foreign policy,[5] and the military's purported resistance to involvement in constabulary missions, motivated primarily by the fact that while the Clinton administration cut force structure by a third from the level of the "Base Force" of President George H. W. Bush, the pace of nonwarfighting deployments increased by 300 percent from 1989 to 1999.[6] Critics contended that such examples illustrated that the uniformed military had illegitimately expanded its influence into inappropriate areas and had succeeded in making military, not political, considerations paramount in the political-military decision-making process—dictating to civilians not only how its operations would be conducted, but also the circumstances under which the military instrument would be used.

This purported attitude reflected the post-Vietnam view dominant within the military that only professional military officers could be trusted to establish principles guiding the use of military force. Taking its bearings from the so-called Weinberger doctrine, a set of rules for the use of force that had been drafted in the 1980s, the US military did everything it could to avoid what came to be known—incorrectly—as "nontraditional missions": constabulary operations required for "imperial policing," e.g., peacekeeping and humanitarian missions.

The clearest example of a service's resistance to a mission occurred when the Army, arguing that its proper focus was on preparing to fight conventional wars, insisted that the plans for US interventions in Bosnia, Kosovo, and elsewhere reflect the military's preference for "overwhelming force." Many interpreted such hostility as just one more indication that the military had become too partisan (Republican) and politicized.[7]

Those who argued that US civil–military relations had become problematic during this period claimed to have identified serious systemic problems affecting the interaction between the uniformed military and civilians, both government leaders and the society at large. These individuals argued, among other things, that

- the US military had become more alienated from its civilian leadership than at any time in American history;
- there was a growing gap between the US military as an institution and civilian society at large;
- the US military had become politicized and partisan;
- the US military had become resistant to civilian oversight, as illustrated by the efforts to dictate when and under what circumstances it would be used to implement US policy;
- officers had come to believe that they had the right to confront and resist civilian policy makers, to insist that civilian authorities heed their recommendations; and
- the US military was becoming too influential in inappropriate areas of American society.[8]

The likely and very dangerous outcome of such trends, went the argument, was a large, semiautonomous military so different and estranged from society that it might become unaccountable to those whom it serves. Those who advanced this view worried about the expansion of the military's influence and were concerned about the possibility of a military contemptuous of American society and unresponsive to civilian authorities.

Most writers who took this line acknowledge that the crisis was not acute; it did not, for instance, involve tanks rumbling through the streets or soldiers surrounding the parliament building or the presidential palace. Instead, they said, it was subtle and subversive—like a lymphoma or termite infestation—destroying silently from within and appearing as mutual mistrust and misunderstanding, institutional failure, and strategic incapacitation.[9] If the problem had not yet reached the danger point, they contended that time was not too far off if something was not done soon.

Not all observers agreed with this assessment. Some argued that American civil–military relations were not in crisis but in transition as a result of the Cold War's end and changes in American society.[10] And others contended that the civil–military tensions of the 1990s were a temporary phenomenon, attributable to the perceived antimilitary character of the Clinton administration.

However, civil–military tensions did not disappear with the election and reelection of George W. Bush. If anything, civil–military relations became more strained as a result of clashes between the uniformed services and Bush's first secretary of defense, Donald Rumsfeld, over efforts to "transform" the military from a Cold War force to one better able to respond to likely future contingencies, and the planning and conduct of U.S. military operations in Afghanistan and Iraq. For one thing, the instances of military officers undercutting Secretary of Defense Donald Rumsfeld and his polices in pursuit of their own goals—what Peter Feaver has called "shirking," e.g., anti-Rumsfeld leaks to the press, "foot-dragging" and "slow rolling"—that had plagued the Clinton administration continued apace.[11]

But public criticism of civilian leaders by military officers accelerated, peaking with the so-called revolt of the generals in the spring of 2006, which saw a number of retired Army and Marine Corps generals publicly and harshly criticize Secretary Rumsfeld.[12] During this episode, much of the language they used was intemperate, indeed contemptuous. The seemingly orchestrated character of these attacks suggested that civil–military disharmony had reached a new and dangerous level.[13]

Although the critics in this case were retired general officers, observers of this episode believed that these retired flag officers were speaking on behalf of not only themselves, but many active-duty officers as well. As Richard Kohn has observed, retired general and flag officers are analogous to the Cardinals of the Roman Catholic Church. While there are no legal restrictions that prevent retired members of the military—even recently retired members—from criticizing public policy or the individuals responsible for it, there are some important reasons to suggest that the public denunciation of civilian authority by soldiers, retired or not, undermines healthy civil–military relations.

With Rumsfeld's departure and the apparent success of the "surge" in Iraq, some expressed hope that harmony might return to US civil–military relations. And to be sure, his successor as secretary of defense, Robert Gates, did a great deal to improve the civil–military climate. But subsequent events— including the decision by Gates to fire two service secretaries and a service chief and to force the retirement of a combatant commander, as well as a public disagreement on military strategy between President Obama and the ground commander in Afghanistan, General Stanley McChrystal and the latter's subsequent relief—make it clear that, while mutual suspicion and misunderstanding have abated to some degree since the Rumsfeld's departure, the state of US civil–military relations remains turbulent and potentially contentious.

Renegotiating the US Civil–Military Bargain After 9/11

The purpose of this book is to use these events as a way to examine the character of American civil–military relations since 9/11, but also to place them in their proper historical context. Civil–military tensions are not new. They have recurred periodically since the American Revolution.

Renegotiating the Civil–Military Bargain After 9/11 is primarily a work of synthesis. However, it is not simply a rehash of the debate about the Iraq War. Questions concerning the actual conduct of the war and who was responsible for this or that aspect of planning for the conflict have been addressed by a number of writers, e.g., Bob Woodward, Tom Ricks, Bing West, Michael Gordon, and Bernard Trainor.[14] The goal here is to examine the issues they raise from the perspective of the theory and practice of civil–military relations and to place them in the context of the ongoing renegotiation of the civil–military bargain in America.

The first chapter of *Renegotiating the Civil–Military Bargain After 9/11* discusses the content of civil–military relations, a term that refers broadly to the interaction between the armed force of a state as an institution and the other sectors of the society in which the armed force is embedded. The study of civil–military relations is an intensely interdisciplinary area of research, reflecting the work of political scientists, military sociologists, and historians. Accordingly, this chapter will review the various contending theories of civil–military relations, including such classic treatments of the topic by Sam Huntington and Morris Janowitz, as well as more recent offerings by Charles Moskos, John Allen Williams, Peter Feaver, Deborah Avant, Rebecca Schiff, Risa Brooks, and Michael Desch.

The next three chapters address the five questions raised at the beginning of this introduction. Chapter 2 discusses the questions of who *controls the military* and what *level of influence by the military* is acceptable and appropriate in the United States. Liberal societies often take civilian control for granted, but doing so begs several further questions: does civilian control refer simply to the dominance of civilians within the executive branch— the president or the secretary of defense? What is the role of the legislative branch in controlling the military instrument? Is the military establishment "unified," that is, does it speak with anything like a single voice vis-à-vis the civil government? What is the nature of military advice? Should military leaders "insist" that their advice be heeded? What courses of action are available to military leaders who believe the civilian authorities are making bad decisions?

The second question addressed in this chapter is closely related to the first. What degree of *military influence* is appropriate for a given society? The extreme form of military influence in society is a *coup d'état*. Another form of military intervention in domestic politics is *praetorianism*. While the United States, along with other advanced liberal societies have avoided these forms of military intervention, it is still necessary to ascertain the proper scope of military affairs. What constitutes military expertise? Does it go beyond what Samuel Huntington called in *The Soldier and the State*, his classic study of civil–military relations, the "management of violence?" Should it?

To what extent should the military influence foreign policy? Has American foreign policy become "militarized?" Do combatant commanders exercise too much power? Have they become the new "viceroys" or "proconsuls?" What is proper regarding the military and domestic politics? Should active-duty officers be writing op-eds in support of particular programs or policies? Should retired officers get involved in partisan politics? What is the military's proper role in influencing the allocation of resources?

Chapter 3 examines the questions regarding the *appropriate role* of the military and the *effectiveness of the military establishment*. Is the military establishment's role to fight and win the nation's wars or engage in constabulary actions? What kind of wars should the military prepare to fight? Should the focus of the military be foreign or domestic? The United States has answered this question differently at different times and under different circumstances. For example, throughout most of its history, the US Army was a constabulary force. It oriented itself toward large-scale conflicts against foreign enemies only in the 1930s. The end of the Cold War and the attacks of 9/11 have suggested new answers, e.g., a focus on "irregular warfare" (counterinsurgency and counterterrorism) as well as an openness to the use of the military in domestic affairs. What impact do such issues have on civil–military relations?

This chapter also addresses the relationship between a given pattern of civil–military relations and the effectiveness of the military instrument. All the other questions mean little if the military instrument is unable to ensure the survival of the state. If there is no constitution, the question of constitutional balance does not matter. Does effectiveness require a military culture distinct in some ways from the society it serves? What impact does societal structure have on military effectiveness? What impact does political structure exert? What impact does the pattern of civil military relations have on the effectiveness of strategic decision-making processes?[15]

Chapter 4 examines the character of military service in the post-9/11 era. Who serves? Is military service an obligation of citizenship or something else? How are enlisted members recruited and retained? How should the US military address issues of "diversity" in the force? What about reserves, racial and ethnic minorities, women, and homosexuals?

Obviously, such questions have been answered differently by Americans at different times under different circumstances. Through most of its early history, the United States maintained a small regular peacetime establishment that mostly conducted limited constabulary operations. During wartime, the several states were responsible for raising soldiers for federal service, either as militia or as volunteers.

Conscription was the norm in the United States from World War II until the 1970s. Today, the US military is a volunteer professional force. But even now the force continues to evolve, as debates over such issues as the role of the reserve components in the post-9/11 military force, women in combat, service by open homosexuals, and the recruitment of religious minorities— Moslems—make clear. The centerpiece of this chapter is the research of such writers as Charles Moskos and John Allen Williams on the question of the "postmodern" military.

The final chapter addresses the question of the future of US civil–military relations. Is there a crisis in civil–military relations or are the alleged problems merely the manifestation of yet another search for a new equilibrium based on changing factors? What are the particular problems arising from a "post-modern" military, a relatively small, highly educated and professional force, reared to conducting constabulary operations rather than conventional interstate wars? What impact will continued technological change have on American civil–military relations? What about social issues? What are the prospects for balanced, harmonious, and effective civil–military relations in the future?

Conclusion

The Prussian military theorist, Carl von Clausewitz, identified the essence of the problem that the study of civil–military relations seeks to address when he wrote: "The first, the supreme, the most far-reaching act of judgment that the *statesman and commander* have to make is to establish . . . the kind of war on which *they* are embarking; neither mistaking it for, nor trying to turn it into, something alien to its nature. This is the first of all strategic questions and the most comprehensive" (emphasis added).[16] This oft-quoted passage makes it clear that the decision for war and its subsequent conduct require the successful—if not always harmonious—collaboration of civilian policy makers and their military advisers, who will also be responsible for providing the instrument necessary for the conduct of war and the plans and decisions required to bring it to a successful conclusion.

However, the dysfunctional character of US civil–military relations during much of the period following 9/11 meant that the judgment that Clausewitz described was not properly made, especially with regard to the war in Iraq. For a variety of reasons, there was, in Colin Gray's formulation, "a black hole where American strategy ought to [have resided]."[17] The absence of strategy meant that all-too-often, military operations were not connected to policy considerations. Of course, this is not the first time that divided policy councils and dysfunctional relations between soldiers and statesmen have opened the door to strategic failure.

Thus, the most significant lessons of US civil–military relations since 9/11 are not concerned primarily with the question of civilian control. Instead, they raise such issues as how informed civilian leaders are when they choose to commit the military instrument, how well the civil–military pattern enables the integration of divergent and even contradictory views, and how this pattern ensures a practical military strategy that properly serves the ends of national policy.[18] The lessons of post-9/11 US civil–military relations also point to the issue of trust: the mutual respect and understanding between civilian and military leaders and the exchange of candid views and perspectives between the two parties as part of the decision-making process.

The emphasis on civilian control in much of the civil–military relations literature obscures that fact that the real lessons of the post-9/11 era are less about the civilian authorities dictating policy to the military than about the tenor of the dialog and the quality of the policy decisions and strategic plans that emerge from that dialog.[19]

Notes

1   I am indebted to Andrew Bacevich for this formulation of the problem in a comment on an early version of my proposal for a book tentatively titled *Sword of Republican Empire: A History of U.S. Civil-Military Relations*. See also Bacevich, "Elusive Bargain: The Pattern of US Civil-Military Relations Since World War II," in Andrew Bacevich, ed., *The Long War: A New History of US National Security Policy Since World War II* (New York: Columbia University Press, 2007) and Thomas S. Langston, "The Civil-Military Bargain," in Langston, *Uneasy Balance: Civil-Military Relations in Peacetime America Since 1783* (Baltimore: Johns Hopkins University Press, 2003).

2   Richard H. Kohn, "The Erosion of Civilian Control of the Military in the United States Today," *Naval War College Review*, vol. L, No. 3, Summer 2002, p. 10.

3   For examples of the hostility of the uniformed military toward President Clinton, see John Lancaster, "Accused of Ridiculing Clinton, General Faces Air Force Probe," *Washington Post*, June 8, 1993, p. 21; "A Military Breach?" *Seattle Post-Intelligencer*, June 11, 1993, p. 10; David H. Hackworth, "Rancor in the Ranks: The Troops vs. the President," *Newsweek*, June 28, 1993; Rowan Scarborough, "Marine Officer Probed for Blasting Clinton," *Washington Times*, November 11, 1998, p. 1 and "Major Gets Punished for Criticizing President," *Washington Times*, December 7, 1998; C.J. Chivers, "Troops Obey Clinton Despite Disdain," *USA Today*, November 18, 1998; and Jane Perlez, "For 8 Years, a Strained Relationship with the Military," *New York Times*, December 28, 2000, p. A13.

4   For instance, see Cragg Hines, "Clinton's Vow to Lift Gay Ban is Reaffirmed," *Houston Chronicle*, November 12, 1992, p. A1; Barton Gellman, "Clinton Says He'll 'Consult' on Allowing Gays in Military," *Washington Post*, November 13, 1992, p. A1; U.S. Department of Defense, Office of the Inspector General, *The Tailhook Report: The Official Inquiry into the Events of Tailhook '91* (New York: St. Martin's, 1993); William McMichael, *The Mother of All Hooks* (New Brunswick, NJ: Transaction, 1997); Elaine Sciolino, "B-52 Pilot Requests Discharge That is Honorable,"

New York Times, May 18, 1997, p. A1; and Bradley Graham, "Army Leaders Feared Aberdeen Coverup Allegations," *Washington Post*, November 11, 1996, p. A1.

5   See Chapter 2. Powell's pieces were, "Why Generals Get Nervous," *New York Times*, October 8, 1992 and "U.S. Forces: Challenges Ahead," *Foreign Affairs*, Winter 1992/93, pp. 32–42.

6   Edward Dorn and Howard Graves, *American Military Culture in the 21st Century: A Report of the CSIS International Security Program* (Washington, DC: Center for Strategic and International Studies, February 2000), pp. xvi and xix.

7   Andrew Bacevich and Richard Kohn, "Grand Army of the Republicans," *The New Republic*, December 8, 1997, pp. 22–25.

8   Cf. Kohn, "The Erosion of Civilian Control of the Military in the United States Today" and "Out of Control: The Crisis in Civil-Military Relations," *National Interest*, No. 35, Spring 1994; Russell Weigley, "The American Military and the Principle of Civilian Control from McClelland to Powell," *Journal of Military History*, special issue, October 1993; Edward Luttwak, "Washington's Biggest Scandal," *Commentary*, 97(5), May 1994; Charles Dunlap, "The Origins of the Coup of 2012," *Parameters*, Winter 1992/93; Dunlap, "Welcome to the Junta: The Erosion of Civilian Control of the Military," *Wake Forest Law Review*, Summer 1994; Gregory Foster, "Confronting the Crisis in Civil-Military Relations," *The Washington Quarterly*, 20(4), Autumn 1997; and Ole Holsti, "Of Chasms and Convergences: Attitudes and Beliefs of Civilians and Military Elites at the Start of a New Millennium," in Peter Feaver and Richard Kohn, eds., *Soldiers and Civilians: The Civil-Military Gap and American National Security* (Cambridge: MIT Press, 2001).

9   Foster, p. 15.

10 See, for instance, Douglas Johnson and Steven Metz, "American Civil-Military Relations: A Review of the Recent Literature," in Don M. Snider and Miranda A. Carlton-Carew, eds., *US Civil Military Relations: In Crisis or Transition?* (Washington, DC: Center for Strategic and International Studies, 1995), p. 201 and Michael Desch, *Civilian Control of the Military: The Changing Security Environment* (Baltimore: The Johns Hopkins University Press, 1999), p. 141.

11 Peter Feaver, *Armed Servants: Agency, Oversight, and Civil-Military Relations* (Cambridge: Harvard University Press, 2005).

12 See Frank G. Hoffman, "Dereliction of Duty *Redux*?: Post-Iraq Civil-Military Relations," *Orbis*, Spring 2008, pp. 217–235 and Bob Woodward, *The War Within: A Secret White House History, 2006–2008* (New York:

Simon and Schuster, 2008). As discussed in a later chapter, Woodard reveals that many senior military leaders—most notably General George Casey, the overall commander in Iraq (now Army chief of staff), and Admiral William "Fox" Fallon—not only did not buy into the surge but also actively resisted the president's policy in Iraq.

13 David S. Cloud and Eric Schmitt, "More Retired Generals Call for Rumsfeld Resignation," *New York Times,* April 14, 2006, p. A1.

14 Bob Woodward, *Bush at War* (New York: Simon and Schuster, 2002); Woodward, *Plan of Attack: The Definitive Account of the Decision to Invade Iraq* (New York: Simon and Schuster, 2004); Woodward, *State of Denial* (New York: Simon and Schuster, 2007); Woodward, *The War Within: A Secret White House History, 2006–2008* (New York: Simon and Schuster, 2008); Thomas Ricks, *Fiasco: The American Military Adventure in Iraq, 2003–2005* (New York: Penguin, 2007); Ricks, *The Gamble: General David Petraeus and the American Military Adventure in Iraq, 2006–2008* (New York: Penguin, 2009); Bing West, *The Strongest Tribe: War, Politics, and the Endgame in Iraq* (New York: Random House, 2008); Michael Gordon and Bernard Trainor, *Cobra II: The Inside Story of the Invasion and Occupation of Iraq* (New York: Pantheon, 2006).

15 See Risa Brooks, *Shaping Strategy: The Civil-Military Politics of Strategic Assessment* (Princeton: Princeton University Press, 2008); Michael Desch, *Power and Military Effectiveness: The Fallacy of Democratic Triumphalism* (Baltimore: Johns Hopkins University Press, 2008); and Suzanne C. Nielsen, "Civil-Military Relations Theory and Military Effectiveness," *Public Administration and Management,* Vol. X, No. 2, pp. 61–84.

16 Carl von Clausewitz, *On War,* Michael Howard and Peter Paret, eds. and trans. (Princeton: Princeton University Press, 1976), p. 88.

17 Colin Gray, *Another Bloody Century: Future Warfare* (London: Orion, 2005), p. 111.

18 Hew Strachan, "Making Strategy: Civil-Military Relations after Iraq," *Survival,* Autumn 2006, p. 60.

19 Richard Kohn, "Building Trust: Civil-Military Behaviors for Effective National Security," in Suzanne Nielsen and Don Snider, eds., *American Civil-Military Relations: The Soldier and the State in a New Era* (Baltimore: Johns Hopkins University Press, 2009), pp. 264–289; Bacevich, "Elusive Bargain," p. 210; Hoffman, "Dereliction of Duty Redux?" p. 219.

CHAPTER ONE

The Theory and Practice of
Civil–Military Relations

Civil–military relations are concerned with the interactions among the people of a state, the institutions of that state, and the military of the state. At the institutional level, there are "two hands on the sword."[1] The civil hand determines when to draw it from the scabbard and thence guides it in its use. This is the dominant hand of policy, the purpose for which the sword exists in the first place. The military's hand sharpens the sword for use and wields it in combat.[2]

The empirical domain of civil–military relations is vast, including the direct and indirect dealings of ordinary people and institutions with the military; interactions among the military, Congress, and the executive branch concerning the funding, regulation, and employment of the military instrument; and the complex bargaining between civilian and military elites to define and implement national security policy and strategy. For a variety of reasons, there is no single overarching theory of civil–military relations that can satisfactorily explain "the widely divergent patterns of conduct that occur throughout [the civil–military] domain under the whole range of imaginable conditions."[3]

For the most part, those who study civil–military relations take for granted that there are significant differences between the leaders, institutions, values, prerogatives, attitudes, and practices of, on the one hand, a society at large and, on the other hand, that society's military establishment.[4]

The basis of civil–military relations is a dilemma that Peter Feaver has called the civil–military *problematique*, which requires a given polity to balance two concerns. On the one hand, it must create a military establishment strong enough and effective enough to protect the state. On the other hand, it must somehow ensure that this same military establishment does not turn on the state that created it.[5]

As suggested in the Introduction, the response of a polity to the civil–military *problematique* can be seen as a *bargain* negotiated among three parties: the citizens, the civilian governmental authorities, and the uniformed military. The purpose of this bargain is to allocate prerogatives and respon-sibilities among the parties.

Obviously, the terms of the bargain and the bargain itself will vary from country to country and, even within a single polity, may vary across time. For instance, in the United States, the playing field is relatively balanced: all three parties have more or less of a say in negotiating the terms of the bargain. Although the citizenry may not be directly involved in drawing up the bargain, the bargain cannot be sustained without their acquiescence. For instance, during the period of the Early US Republic, important political and military leaders such as George Washington, Alexander Hamilton, and Henry Knox would have preferred a larger regular military establishment, but strong opposition to the idea of a standing army rendered such a prefer-ence moot. The fact is that during the Early Republic, military prowess was thought to reside in a "people numerous and armed"—the militia—rather than in a standing army.[6]

This is not to say that in the United States, the parties to the bargain are equal. The American civil–military bargain is the outcome of an "unequal dialogue." It is "a dialogue, in that both [the civilian and military] sides expressed their views bluntly, indeed, sometimes offensively, and not once but repeatedly—and unequal, in that the final authority of the civilian leader was unambiguous and unquestioned."[7] In the United States, the military, despite having a monopoly on coercive power, has generally accepted its position relative to the other parties.

In general, there are two lenses through which to examine civil–military relations. The first is the *institutional* lens, which focuses on how the actors in a polity, including the military as an organization, interact within the institutional framework of a given polity's government. The most influential institutional theory of civil–military relations was advanced 50 years ago by Samuel Huntington in his seminal work, *The Soldier and the State*.[8] In terms of the basic questions of civil–military relations, the primary concerns of institutional theorists are civilian control of the military, the proper role of the military, the level of the military's influence on society, and the ability of the military to maintain its effectiveness in protecting the interests of the state—in the face of a "societal imperative" that may be hostile to the military's "functional imperative."

The second lens is *sociological* or *cultural*. This lens focuses on the broad question of military culture vs. liberal society; the role of individuals and groups, e.g., women, minorities, enlisted servicemen and women within the military, and the relationships among them; the effectiveness of individual service members in combat; small-unit cohesion; the relationship between military service and citizenship (to include the civic republican tradition);

the nature of military service (occupation, profession, etc.); and the relationship of militaries and the societies from which they stem.

In terms of the five civil–military relations questions, the sociological lens looks primarily at who serves, the relationship between the military and civil society, and military effectiveness. The origins of the sociological perspective on military affairs can be traced to Morris Janowitz's 1960 book, *The Professional Soldier.*[9]

A variation of this latter perspective is "concordance theory," which rejects the idea that "healthy" civil–military relations necessarily require a distinct separation between the civilian and military realm. Israel, for instance, has little separation between the two and yet civil–military relations seem stable.[10]

Questions of civil–military relations are complex. It is unlikely that one analytical approach will provide anything close to the whole picture. There is no "general" or "unified field" theory that successfully explains all civil–military patterns.[11] Nor, given the variety and complexity of civil–military patterns, is one likely or desirable. A "central task of the political sociology of the military is to look at both the military institution and the political system and to determine how the special institutional characteristics of a particular military establishment shape its response to influences coming from the political system."[12]

Of course, an important reason for studying civil–military relations is to determine what constitutes "good" and "bad" relations. Such a determination is of more than merely academic interest. It has implications for the very survival of a polity. As the civil–military *problematique* would suggest, the worst-case consequences of dysfunctional civil–military relations would include catastrophic failure on the battlefield leading to the defeat of the state in a war or the seizure of the government by the military itself.

But dysfunctional civil–military relations may generate other adverse outcomes short of the catastrophic ones. For example, poor civil–military relations may lead to failures in strategic assessment.[13] This is true during both war and peacetime. In the case of war, poor strategic assessment may contribute directly or indirectly to defeat on the battlefield because strategic leaders, both political and military, fail to share information or cooperate in other ways.[14]

A case in point is the US war in Iraq. Many observers contend that most of the problems the United States faced in that conflict were the result of Secretary of Defense Rumsfeld's management style,[15] the insulated nature of the Bush administration,[16] or Rumsfeld's penchant for simply overruling advice that did not support his preferences. However, Risa Brooks has argued

persuasively that these problems, especially with regard to postconflict planning, resulted from civil–military pathologies created by earlier debates over
"transformation" in the Pentagon between Rumsfeld and the uniformed
military. These pathologies resulted in oversight mechanisms that weakened
strategic coordination.[17]

In the case of peacetime, poor strategic assessment may lead to an over-
estimation of an adversary's capabilities, resulting in the wasting of resources
on defense. On the other hand, underestimating adversaries' capabilities
leads to the allocation of too few resources to defense.

Criteria for judging the health of civil–military relations might include
the following: (1) relative harmony between civilians and the military;
(2) the effectiveness of the armed forces in executing their missions; and
(3) constitutional balance. "Good" civil–military relations would seem to
exhibit some combination of the following: (1) comity and a low number of
disagreements between civilian and military decision-makers; (2) success in
war and peace and the absence of policy-strategy "mismatches"; and (3) a
lack of encroachment by either party on to civil–military decisions on the
"turf" of the other.

Some authors dispute the notion that harmony and comity necessarily
make for "good" civil–military relations, arguing that tension between civilian authorities and the military is healthy. For instance, a low number of
disagreements between civilian and military decision-makers may simply
mean that the civilians have appointed "yes men" who can always be expected
not to "rock the boat."[18] This charge was frequently leveled against former
US Secretary of Defense Donald Rumsfeld.

Unfortunately, "except for the most obvious cases, there is no consensus
in the recent literature as to what constitutes 'good' civil–military relations
or 'effective' civilian control of the military."[19] In the case of the liberal
democracies, the absence of coups would seem to set the bar too low. Most
scholars focus on the extent to which civilian preferences prevail when there
are differences between the civilians and the military.[20]

Others equate healthy civil–military relations with the maintenance
of civilian values and the lack of military domination of society.[21] Of course,
a critical measure of good civil–military relations is success in war.
Paradoxically, this may require civilian intervention in military affairs,
generating significant civilian-military friction.[22]

Determining "bad" civil–military relations is less difficult. The two
polar extremes of bad relations are *militarism* and *de-bellicization*. The
former is the dominance of military institutions, values, prerogatives, attitudes
and practices, etc., within society.[23] The latter is the denigration or even

complete extirpation of military virtues from a society, the most dangerous consequence of which is defeat in war.[24] While some have suggested that the United States is moving toward one extreme or the other,[25] the evidence to support such claims is weak. The real issue of civil–military relations for the United States concerns the mutual influence of the civilian and military sectors of society. "The problem of the modern state is not armed revolt but the relation of the [military] expert and the politician."[26]

Influences on US Civil–Military Relations

A number of factors influence the civil–military relations of the United States. The first of these include its history and culture. All too often, students of civil–military relations treat history and culture as peripheral issues, "intervening variables" that lie between the "real" factor to be studied—the independent variable, whatever it may be—and the dependent variable, the state or pattern of civil–military relations.[27] But the substantial differences in patterns of civil–military relations between Prussia and Great Britain in the nineteenth century and between the United States and Israel today are directly attributable to differences in culture and history.[28]

The political institutions of a state also exert a strong influence on its civil–military relations by allocating relative power to civilian and military leaders. In the United States, civil–military relations are affected by the Constitution and the statutes and practices arising therefrom. As such, US civil–military relations are complicated by the vast array of players in both the civilian and military realms.

The former consists of the executive and legislative branches of government, both of which are further divided. The executive branch includes the president; the appropriate cabinet officers, especially the secretary of defense; advisory committees, e.g., the National Security Council in the United States; and noncabinet civilian appointees such as the service secretaries. The fact that the interests of political appointees and career civil servants are not always the same and that the interests of both may differ from those of the uniformed military has an important impact on civil–military relations. Nor is Congress monolithic, consisting of members from two political parties. Structure matters as well. Congress is bicameral and does most of its business in committees.

The same goes for the military realm, which includes a number of uniformed services. For many years in the United States, the services were the main players on the military side. The result was often a high degree of interservice rivalry, which reached its peak in the United States during the

"defense unification" debates after World War II. This extreme manifestation of interservice rivalry played out not only within the newly formed
Department of Defense, but also in Congress and the press.[29] While competition among separate services for mission and resources may contribute to
civil–military pathologies, such competition may also have some beneficial
effects, e.g., division of labor, a prudent focus on planning future forces, and
innovation.[30] But since the passage of the Goldwater-Nichols Defense Act in
1987, power has flowed from the services to the commanders of the "unified
commands," the joint regional and functional organizations that are tasked
with the actual conduct of operations and deployments.

Nonetheless, the individual services still exert a great deal of influence
on US policy. As Huntington observed, each military service is built around
a particular "strategic concept [. . .] which defines the role of the service in
national policy, public support which furnishes it with the resources to perform this role, and organizational structure which groups the resources so
as to implement most effectively the strategic concept."[31] These paradigms,
which the late Carl Builder called "masks of war," have shaped the services'
institutional approaches to influencing policy, especially in Congress.[32]

The power of the Chairman of the Joint Chiefs of Staff (CJCS) was also
enhanced by Goldwater-Nichols.[33] Previously, CJCS was merely the spokesman for the Joint Chiefs of Staff, a corporate body consisting of the four
service chiefs, who in their collective capacity were the source of military
advice to the president. But Goldwater-Nichols made the Chairman, not the
Joint Chiefs of Staff as a whole, the primary military adviser to the president
and the secretary of defense. Along with the large Joint Staff, the Chairman
per se has become a major player in civil–military affairs, despite the fact
that he is not in the chain of command.

Precedent is also important. In the case of the United States, the principle
of military subordination to civilian authority seems to have been internalized by each generation of officers based on the example set by George
Washington at the end of the American Revolution. Most analysts agree that
the likelihood of a coup d'état in the United States is low, but others wonder
if the power of this precedent has been weakened over the past few years.
However, the low likelihood of a coup in the United States does not mean
that military actors cannot still find other ways to undermine balanced
civil–military relations.[34]

Changes in the international security environment also influence civil–
military relations, although writers have disagreed about the direction of
that influence. Harold Lasswell contended that a greater level of external
threat would move civil–military relations in the direction of a "garrison

state."[35] Michael Desch, on the other hand, has argued that states facing high external threats and low internal threats have the most stable civil–military relations.[36]

Technology also clearly exerts an impact on patterns of civil–military relations. For instance, the destructive power of nuclear weapons not only increased the role of civilians in the development of strategy, but also reduced the leeway of the military in operational and even tactical matters.[37] The proliferation of information technology increases the potential for civilian involvement in operational details. Social forces play an important role as well in shaping civil–military relations, as illustrated by debates over racial integration, women in combat, and open homosexuals serving in the military.[38]

The character of conflict also affects civil–military relations. Changes in the kinds of war the military is expected to fight have potential implications for the process of strategic decision-making, the composition and operations of military organizations, and the interagency cooperation process during the course of a conflict. Patterns of civil–military relations during traditional interstate war may well differ from those during the conduct of a counterinsurgency.[39] For instance, heavy reliance on special operations forces has implications for congressional oversight.

Finally, there is the changing concept of "soldier-hood." In the case of the United States, the idealized model for military service throughout most of American history was the "citizen-soldier." A civilian most of the time, he answered his country's call at times of emergency, returning to civilian pursuits once the emergency had passed. Since the end of the draft in 1973, the citizen-soldier has given way to the long-term professional, a soldier akin to the Roman legionnaire.[40] In addition, the proliferation of civilian contractors carrying out tasks that were once the responsibility of soldiers has increased the complexity of US civil–military relations.[41]

Theories of Civil–Military Relations

As the Prussian "philosopher of war," Carl von Clausewitz, observed: "theory exists so that one need not start afresh each time sorting out the material and plowing through it, but will find it readily to hand and in good order."[42] A theory seeks to illuminate comprehensively and systematically the link between cause and effect.

At a minimum, a theory must be able to *describe* usefully the phenomenon or phenomena under investigation and explain it. This is the *empirical* function of theory. But theories often are employed to do two other things. First, based on its description and explanation of the phenomenon under examination, a theory may be used to *predict*, at least in a general way, what might happen under similar conditions in the future. A theory may also serve as the basis for *prescribing* policy, for translating "is" to "ought." This *normative* function links the descriptive and predictive qualities of the theory to the policy of the state.

Applied to civil–military relations, a workable theory would meet the minimum requirement to describe and explain the nature and characteristics of different patterns of civil–military relations. But most theories of civil–military relations are also used to specify general conditions either conducive or detrimental to healthy relations.[43] Finally, a theory of civil–military relations may prescribe what steps a state must take in order to achieve or maintain healthy relations.

Clearly this meaning of theory is less formal than that found in the physical sciences. It is based more on intuition, experience, and an understanding of the rules arising out of practice. What Michael Handel observed with regard to theory in war applies with equal force to theories of civil–military relations: "the development of the study and theory of war is (and probably will remain) in a pre-Newtonian, pre-scientific, or non-formal stage."[44]

The need for a theory of civil–military relations is driven by the aforementioned civil–military *problematique*. In order to ensure its security, society delegates the authority for the use of force to a subgroup within society. How does society ensure that this subgroup does what it is supposed to—protect society from its enemies, both foreign and domestic—without turning on society itself?

The *problematique* implies that there are two polar dangers for a society when it comes to civil–military relations. If the military is weakened in order to ensure that it will not turn on society itself, it may face defeat on the battlefield. But if the military is given everything it needs to ensure that it will prevail on the battlefield, it may be in a position of political dominance, able to dictate policy to the civilians. These extremes correspond to de-bellicization and militarism.

The extreme case of military dominance, of course, is a coup. But even short of a coup, there is always the possibility that the military will not do what civilian authorities want it to do. For instance, in the United States, the uniformed military has often employed such techniques as leaks to the press, lobbying the public and Congress, "foot-dragging," and "slow-rolling" to thwart the policy goals of civilian authorities.[45]

Samuel Huntington: An Institutional Theory of Civil–Military Relations

The theory of civil–military affairs prevalent in the United States is based on a distinction between the civil and military realms. This approach can be traced to the practice of eighteenth- and nineteenth-century European states and to the theory of war advanced by Clausewitz. Rebecca Schiff calls this approach "separation" theory.[46]

Although the Prussian state that Clausewitz served is often seen as the exemplar of militarism, his formulation of war as a continuation of politics or policy (*politik*) by other means[47] implies a distinction between political decision-makers and the military. "No one starts a war—or rather no one in his senses ought to do so—without first being clear in his mind what he intends to achieve by that war and how he intends to conduct it. The former is its political purpose; the latter its operational objective."[48]

Actual war as opposed to war in theory (absolute war) "is only a branch of political activity" that "is in no sense autonomous."[49] "The character and general shape of any war should mainly be assessed in light of political factors and conditions."[50] Since "absolute" war is theoretically unlimited, driven by its own logic to the extreme of violence and exhaustion, it is the political purpose of war that makes war "rational," providing war with a purpose beyond its own logic.

In keeping with this logic, the most influential theory of civil–military relations in the United States is the institutional theory advanced half a century ago by the eminent political scientist Samuel Huntington in his 1957 book, *The Soldier and the State*. This book has had a great and lasting effect on American thinking about the way the military interacts with civilian society, especially within the uniformed military. Indeed, the US military has come to endorse many of its general conclusions and has made it central to its civil–military relations education.

Huntington's main *descriptive* or *empirical* claim was that American civil–military relations were shaped by three variables: first, the external threat, which he called the *functional imperative*; second and third being the two components of what he called the *societal imperative*, i.e., "the social forces, ideologies and institutions dominant within the society."[51] The first component of the societal imperative is the constitutional structure of the United States, the legal-institutional framework that guides political affairs generally and civil–military affairs specifically. The second is *ideology*, the prevailing worldview of a state. Huntington identified four ideologies: conservative pro-military, fascist pro-military, Marxist antimilitary, and liberal antimilitary.[52] He argued that the fourth was the dominant ideology of the United States.[53]

Huntington contended that both components of the societal imperative—the constitutional structure and the American ideology of antimilitary liberalism—had remained constant throughout American history. Accordingly, the entire burden of explaining any change in civilian control or level of military armament would have to rest with the functional imperative, i.e., the external threat.[54] Huntington further contended that liberalism was "the gravest domestic threat to American military security."[55] "The tension between the demands of military security and the values of American liberalism," Huntington continued, "can, in the long run, be relieved only by the weakening of the security threat or the weakening of liberalism."[56] Thus, the requisite for military security would have to be a shift in basic American values from liberalism to conservatism. Only an environment that was sympathetically conservative would permit American military leaders to combine the political power, which society thrusts upon them with the military professionalism without which society cannot endure.[57]

According to Huntington, America's antimilitary liberal ideology produced "extirpation"—the virtual elimination of military forces—when the external threat was low and "transmutation"—the refashioning of the military in accordance with liberalism, which leads to the loss of "peculiarly military characteristics"—when the external threat was high. In Huntington's view, the problem for the United States in a protracted contest such as the Cold War was that while transmutation may work for short periods of time during which concentrated military effort is required, e.g., a world war, it would not assure adequate military capability over the long term.

In the context of the Cold War, Huntington argued that the ideological component of America's societal imperative—liberal antimilitary ideology—would make it impossible to build the forces necessary to confront the functional imperative in the form of the Soviet threat to the United States and to permit US military leaders to take the steps necessary to provide national security. Thus, the *predictive* element of Huntington's theory held that without a change in the societal imperative, the United States would never be able to build the military forces necessary to confront the USSR.

The *prescriptive* or *normative* element of Huntington's theory was to suggest a way for the United States to deal with the dilemma raised by Feaver's civil–military *problematique*: how to minimize the power of the military and thus make civilian control more certain without sacrificing protection against external enemies. His prescription, which he called "objective civilian control," has the virtue of simultaneously maximizing military subordination and military fighting power. Objective control guarantees the protection of civilian society from external enemies and from the military themselves.

In Huntington's prescriptive or normative theory, the key to objective control is "the recognition of autonomous military professionalism," i.e., respect for an independent military sphere of action. Interference or meddling in military affairs undermines military professionalism and so undermines objective control.[58]

This constitutes a bargain between civilians and soldiers. On the one hand, civilian authorities grant a professional officer corps autonomy in the realm of military affairs. On the other hand, "a highly professional officer corps stands ready to carry out the wishes of any civilian group which secures legitimate authority within the state."[59] In other words, if the military is granted autonomy in its sphere, the result is a professional military that is politically neutral and voluntarily subordinate to civilian control. Of course, autonomy is not absolute. Huntington argues that while the military has responsibility for operational and tactical decisions, civilians must decide matters of policy and grand strategy.

While objective control weakens the military politically, rendering it politically sterile or neutral, it actually strengthens the military's ability to defend society. A professional military obeys civilian authority. A military that does not obey is not professional.

At the opposite pole from objective control lay Huntington's worst-case situation, "subjective control," which constituted a systematic violation of the autonomy necessary for a professional military and produced transmutation. Huntington argued that subjective control was detrimental to military effectiveness and would lead to failure on the battlefield by forcing the military to defer to civilians in the military realm.[60]

Huntington's institutional theory remains the dominant paradigm for examining civil–military relations. First, it deals with the central problem of such relations: the relation of the military as an institution to civilian society. Huntington was the first to attempt a systematic analysis of the civil–military *problematique*. Second, despite the claims of many of those who look at US civil–military relations through the lens of sociology, analytically distinct military and civilian spheres do appear to exist.

But there are many problems with Huntington's argument. In 1962, Samuel Finer argued that Huntington had severely understated the problem of civilian control.[61] He contended that a professional military does not necessarily keep officers out of politics, but indeed might incline them to engage in politics.[62] He also observed that differences in national experience limit the applicability of Huntington's theory.

In addition, empirical studies have not confirmed some of Huntington's key assertions or predictions. For instance, his definition of "professionalism"—Lasswell's "management of violence"—seems too narrow. The American military traditionally has carried out tasks that go far beyond battlefield activities.[63] US officers have been and continue to be responsible for activities, e.g., diplomacy, stability operations, and nation-building, that require them to plan, coordinate, and execute "interagency" operations. Recent writers also have argued that by restricting the terms to active-duty officers, Huntington ignored other subgroups—senior noncommissioned officers (NCOs) and reserve officers—who do many of the same sorts of things that Huntington attributed only to active-duty officers. This is especially true of today's reserve force, which has been deployed to Afghanistan and Iraq nearly as often as the active force. In addition, Huntington postulated a distinctly "military mind," one informed by "conservative realism" in opposition to the dominant liberalism of America. Yet, surveys seem to indicate that for the most part, military officers hold a diverse range of ideas in keeping with the liberal tradition of the United States.[64] It is also the case that some of Huntington's historical arguments are questionable. For instance, the US Army in the late nineteenth century was not nearly as isolated as Huntington contended it was.[65] This particular problem illustrates the importance of keeping historical context in mind when examining civil–military relations. Historians such as Russell Weigley, Richard Kohn, and Lawrence Cress have made significant contributions to the study of civil–military relations.[66] Finally as Eliot Cohen, perhaps Huntington's most accomplished student, has pointed out, some of the most successful democratic war leaders have paid very little attention to the divide that Huntington's objective control demands.[67]

Morris Janowitz: The Sociological Response to Huntington

In his 1960 book, *The Professional Soldier*, Morris Janowitz offered an early critique of Huntington from the standpoint of sociology. The sociological perspective does not ignore the institutional question of civilian control. However, it focuses most of its attention on the relationship between individuals in the military and civilian society.[68]

James Burk argues that the civil–military relations theories of Huntington and Janowitz represent two contending theories of democracy: the former reflects the "liberal" theory of democracy and the latter the "civic republican." Liberal theory, flowing from the political philosophy of Thomas Hobbes and John Locke, is based on the idea that the primary responsibility of the democratic state is to protect the rights and liberties of individual citizens.

"To retain its authority, the state must protect its citizens from . . . foreign threats, not least of all by means of an effective military establishment."[69] The institutional issue associated with the liberal theory of democracy is creating a military strong enough to provide security but not inclined to threaten civilian control. As we have seen, Huntington's solution was "objective control."

In contrast to the liberal theory of democracy, civic republican theory, the origins of which may be found in the writings of Niccolo Machiavelli and Jean Jacques Rousseau, argues that the priority of the democratic state is to engage the citizens in the activity of public life. "Citizenship is based on participation in the rule and defense of the republic. It is a matter of civic and martial practice." Soldiering constructs civic virtues. "When citizen participation flags, the republic becomes corrupt. In addition, when citizens serve as soldiers to defend the republic, the interests of the military and the interests of the state overlap, and there is no reason to fear a military challenge to the republic."[70]

With regard to Huntington's civilian-military divide, Janowitz argued that the distinction between the civilian and military roles that lay at the heart of Huntington's theory had been blurred by the emergence of nuclear weapons and limited war. For Janowitz, this state of affairs was only the latest manifestation of the way in which emerging technologies and the political interaction between civilian and military elites were causing the two spheres to converge. This increasing "civilianization" of the military manifested itself in bureaucratization, the assimilation by the military of nonmilitary functions, the ascendancy of a managerial as opposed to a heroic ethos, and reduced physical isolation from the rest of society. But Janowitz also sought to preserve the ideal of the citizen-soldier at a time when the character of war no longer required mass participation in military service but did require the United States to maintain a large standing force of professional soldiers.[71]

Like Huntington, Janowitz focused on the meaning of a professional officer corps. But while Huntington saw military professionalism as a fixed standard, an "ideal-type" based on a strict division of labor between the uniformed military and civilians, Janowitz conceived professionalism as dynamic, changing in response to new sociological conditions. Part of this was the merging of the "hero-warrior" associated with the management of violence with the military manager. Janowitz argued that, given the central place of the US–Soviet rivalry in both international and domestic politics, even a professional military could not avoid some degree of politicization.

With regard to Huntington's functional imperative, Janowitz contended that in the nuclear age, the military needed to adopt a new military role and military self-conception—that of a constabulary force. According to Janowitz, "the military establishment becomes a constabulary force when it is continuously prepared to act, committed to the minimum use of force, and seeks viable international relations, rather than victory."[72] Obviously, the constabulary concept blurs the distinctions between peace and war. Accordingly, the soldier comes to resemble a police officer instead of a warrior. This leads to politicization of the military and raises a challenge to civilian supremacy, as the military attempts to use the political system to resist unwelcome policy direction.

Janowitz's solution to the new problems created by the constabulary concept was to reject Huntington's concept of objective control of the military. Instead of autonomy, he prescribed greater civilian oversight of the military at all levels. He pointed out that civilians possess three main mechanisms for controlling the uniformed military: the budget process; the allocation of roles and missions; and advice to the president concerning the use of the military to advance US interests in the international realm. But the military, Janowitz argued, had found ways to undermine civilian control.[73] Although Janowitz proposed a number of external mechanisms for strengthening civilian control, he, like Huntington, ultimately fell back on professionalism. But unlike Huntington's professional officer who eschews politics altogether, Janowitz's officer corps would be politically aware and possess functions and expertise that overlapped with those of its civilian counterpart.

Janowitz's heirs have taken military sociology far beyond his own conclusions, generating a vast and rich literature that examines how civil society and the military have each shaped the other. But when it comes to the critical issue of civilian control of the military, Janowitz did not really go much beyond Huntington. He merely concluded that to ensure civilian control, Huntington's "self-imposed professional standards," the basis of objective control, needed to be supplemented by a "meaningful integration" of military and civilian values.[74]

Janowitz and the military sociologists also provide useful insights, especially regarding the question of "who serves?" and related issues. The writers who take their bearings from Janowitz have indeed moved the question of demographics, ethnicity, and recruitment to center stage in a way that transcends the American experience.[75] But even as they argue that the concept of separation between the two spheres is theoretically and empirically flawed, these writers still maintain the analytical distinction between the military and civilians.

Despite Janowitz's sociological challenge to Huntington's institutional theory of civil–military relations, the latter still dominates the field. The reason for this continued dominance is its elegance as an ambitious treatment of civil–military relations and the fact that his prescriptions for how best to structure civil–military relations continue to find a very receptive ear within the American officer corps.[76]

Post–Cold War Theorizing: Desch, Avant, and Langston

Huntington and Janowitz wrote during the Cold War and some have suggested that their theories have been rendered moot by the collapse of the Soviet Union and the end of that conflict. But the power of the two theories is illustrated by the fact that, with few exceptions, most recent attempts to reconstruct the theoretical edifice of civil–military relations constitute refinements of the two rather than providing a new theoretical alternative.

For instance, Michael Desch emphasizes the impact of external and internal threats on civil–military relations. For Desch, the threat, both external and domestic, constitutes the independent variable in his analysis. Desch examines a number of cases to support his thesis that the structural threat environment affects the character of civilian leadership, the structure of the military institution, the cohesiveness of state institutions, the method of civilian control, and the convergence or divergence of civilian and military ideas and cultures.[77]

Desch argues that a state facing a high external threat and a low internal threat will exhibit the strongest civilian control. Conversely, a state facing low external but high internal threats will exhibit low levels of civilian control because the civilian leadership is less likely to attend to national security affairs. Desch's structural theory faces a more difficult situation when a state faces either of the following threat structure: (1) both low domestic and external threats; or (2) both high domestic and external threats.

But although structure tends to establish parameters, Desch argues that actual outcomes are sometimes determined by other factors, one of the most important of which is military doctrine. Military doctrine affects civilian control in at least three ways: first by determining the particular military resources that will be employed, how they will be employed, and where. Militaries that are oriented toward external threats are more amenable to civilian control than those that are oriented toward suppressing domestic threats.

Second, military doctrine affects civilian control by shaping the structure of military organizations as well as their cultures. Finally, military doctrine influences civilian control as a focal point for the convergence or divergence of civilian and military ideas about the use of force and the inter-national environment.[78] Following Louis Hartz, Huntington called these two perspectives civilian liberalism and military realism.[79] "In a challenging external security environment, civilian and military ideas will converge on realism. In a less threatening environment, civilian liberalism is more likely to emerge and come into conflict with military realism, weakening civilian control."[80]

Deborah Avant has followed a different tack. Employing a neoinstitu-tionalist theory and drawing on the principal–agent framework that origi-nated in economics, Avant placed her main emphasis on the structure of domestic institutions and their impact on military organizations and doc-trine. The underlying issue for her was why certain military institutions have been able to adapt to changing circumstances and others have not. She takes issue with the conventional narrative regarding Vietnam, which holds civilian leaders responsible for the defeat because they were more worried about re-election than producing good policy. But in fact, most of the failure can be traced to the inability of the US Army in particular to adapt to a different type of war.[81] Why this failure to adapt? According to Avant, it was a combination of the Army's doctrinal autonomy and the US domestic political institutions. ". . . [C]ivilian leaders in the United States, who had institutional incentives to act separately, found it harder to agree on policy goals and often chose more complex oversight mechanisms, which did not always induce the US Army to respond easily to change."[82]

The main institutional factors in the case of the United States, according to Avant, are divided government (Congress and the executive branch) and electoral politics—"doing what is necessary to say in power in a democracy."[83] Divided civilian institutions in the United States led to reliance on budgets to control military institutions, which in turn permitted a high degree of discretion on the part of the individual services with regard to doctrine, culture, and the meaning of military professionalism. In other words, civil-ian control of the military in the United States was a manifestation of Huntington's objective control.

Part of her explanation of the failure of the US Army to adapt to Vietnam is based on agency theory. The problem agency theory seeks to analyze is this: given different incentives, how does a principal ensure that the agent is doing what the principal wants him to do?

In the case of the United States, the terms of delegation required coordi-nation between Congress and the executive branch. This arrangement has permitted a great deal of autonomy, allowing the services to pay attention to whichever institution it wished to, depending on the circumstances. Military leaders have realized that political leaders will not employ control mechanisms that cause them to operate in ways detrimental to their electoral interests and will believe, accordingly, that the latter will not employ such control mechanisms. This belief may have been reinforced by the fact that, with rare exceptions, during the Cold War and post–Cold War eras, neither Congress nor the executive branch has interfered with service promotion policies. At the same time, presidents or secretaries of defense have rarely relieved commanders.[84]

Thomas Langston takes a different approach. To address the differing preferences of civilian elites and the military leadership after war, Langston uses Huntington's concepts of "extirpation" and "transmutation" as well as claim that American civil–military relations are influenced by an inherent conflict between the civilian liberal perspective and the military's "conservative realism." As noted above, Huntington argued that the liberal perspective of civilian elites inclines them to "extirpate" the military after a war, based on the recurring belief that with the end of conflict, the military is no longer needed.[85] Since extirpation is never truly achieved, the civilian settle for "transmutation," seeking to transform the military instrument into something that conforms more closely to the values of a liberal society.[86]

The source of the civil–military conflict in peacetime is that the military prefers to reform the military for the next war (the military's "functional imperative") while civilians would rather "tame" the military in order to serve the goals of the civilian elites (imposing a "societal imperative"). Langston takes issue with Huntington's contention that the civil–military bargain is a zero-sum game in which one side or the other gets its way. According to Langston, "the inevitable conflicts of civil–military relations . . . are best resolved when neither the civilianizers nor their opponents [the military reformers] win a complete victory."[87]

In this outcome, the military's need to reform is balanced against a society's need for a military responsive to its nonmilitary needs. On the basis of this framework, Langston argues that civil–military realignments were "good' after the American Revolution, the War of 1812, and the Spanish–American War; "fair" after the Mexican War and the two World Wars; and "poor" after the Civil War and Vietnam.[88]

Peter Feaver: Agency Theory and Civil–Military Relations

Feaver also has employed agency theory to address the reality of US civil–military relations, arguing that his more general theory subsumes

Huntington's argument. Feaver argues that although Huntington's theory is "elegant," it does not fit the evidence of the Cold War. For instance, one of Huntington's testable hypotheses was that a liberal society (such as the United States) would not produce sufficient military might to survive the Cold War. But in fact, the United States did prevail during the Cold War despite the fact that the country did not abandon liberalism.[89] The continued divergence between civilian and military preferences during the Cold War casts doubt on the predictive power of Huntington's empirical theory.

The same problems affect Huntington's prescriptive theory. During the Cold War, the military became more "civilianized," the officer corps more politicized, and civilians habitually intruded into the military realm.[90] Feaver concludes that the disjunction between Huntington's theory and the available evidence requires another theory. To provide such an alternative, Feaver turns to "agency theory."

Feaver poses the central question of agency theory as this: is the agent "working" or "shirking?" In Feaver's reasoning, the major question for the principal is the extent to which he will monitor the agent. Will monitoring be intrusive or nonintrusive? This decision is affected by the cost of monitoring. The higher the cost of monitoring, the less intrusive the monitoring is likely to be.

The agent's incentives for working or shirking are affected by the likelihood that shirking will be detected by the principal and that the agent will then be punished for it. The less intrusive the principal's monitoring, the less likely that the agent's shirking will be detected. Feaver argues that shirking by the military takes many forms: the most obvious is disobedience, but it also includes "foot-dragging" and leaks to the press designed to undercut policy or individual policy makers.

Feaver posits four general patterns of civil–military relations: (1) civilians monitor intrusively, the military works; (2) civilians monitor intrusively, the military shirks; (3) civilians monitor unintrusively, the military works; and (4) civilians monitor unintrusively, the military shirks. He then shows that Huntington's postulated outcomes are in fact special cases of his own more general agency theory of civil–military relations: Huntington's "objective control" corresponds to pattern (3); his "subjective control" corresponds to pattern (1).[91] Feaver uses the Cold War to test Huntington's prescriptive theory. Huntington had argued that the best way to ensure both military effectiveness and subordination to civilian control was through pattern (3)—objective control. However, it turns out that the civil–military relations pattern during the Cold War that most corresponds to the evidence is pattern (1)—Huntington's nightmare civil–military scenario—subjective control.[92] Indeed, agency theory predicts that pattern (1) will prevail when there is a wide gap between the preferences of the civilians and the military, when the costs of intrusive monitoring are relatively low and when the military thinks the likelihood of punishment for shirking are fairly high. Feaver argues persuasively that the evidence from this period supports these hypotheses. Yet according to Huntington's own criteria for professionalism—expertise, responsibility, and corporateness[93]—the US military remained highly professional despite extensive civilian intervention.

Of critical importance in establishing Cold War civil–military relations, says Feaver, was the firing of a popular military hero (MacArthur) by an unpopular president (Truman). This dramatic action shaped the expectations of the military concerning the likelihood of punishment for shirking during the Cold War period.[94] Feaver explains the post–Cold War "crisis" in civil–military relations in a way that integrates a number of features that arose in the 1990s—the end of the Cold War, a growing gap between civilian and military elites, the personal history of President Clinton, the creation of a powerful CJCS by the Goldwater-Nichols Defense Act of 1986, and the occupation of this office by a popular, politically savvy general—Colin Powell.[95]

Feaver argues that civil–military relations pattern (2) prevailed during the 1990s: civilians monitored intrusively, the military "shirked." First, the cost of intrusive monitoring went down. Second, the preferences of civilian and military elites diverged in many important ways, increasing incentives for the military to pursue its own preferences. Finally, the expectation of punishment for shirking decreased as a result of the election of Bill Clinton, whose equivocal relationship with the military made punishment unlikely. Combined with a powerful and popular military leader and an absence of consensus regarding security affairs across the executive and legislative branches, the civilian principals were in a relatively weakened position vis-à-vis the military agents.[96] Feaver observes that civil–military relations are obviously better when there are good civilian leaders and worse when civilian leadership is bad. One issue is how to hold civilians accountable to the same or greater degree than the military is held accountable. Bad policy, after all, presumably comes from civilian principals.

But Feaver's focus is on the military institution in a democratic polity. As he observes,

> [E]ven when the military is right, democratic theory intervenes and insists that it submit to the civilian leadership that the polity has chosen. Let civilian voters punish civilian leaders for wrong decisions. Let the military advise against foolish adventures, even advising strenuously

when circumstances demand. But let the military execute those orders faithfully. The republic would be better served even by foolish working than by enlightened shirking.[97]

After all, the claim that the military should not do what civilians want because what the latter wants is bad for the country shapes the rhetoric of every coup leader who justifies his seizure of power as the rescue of a state from the consequences of an inept government.

When it comes to the question of civilian control of the military, Feaver's agency theory corrects some of the flaws in Huntington's theory. Agency theory seems to do a better job of *describing* the problem of civilian control than Huntington's theory. It is also does better with regard to the *predictive* aspect of the theory. One reason for this is that agency theory does not depend on the nonrigorous and therefore problematic concepts of professionalism and autonomy to predict how and under what circumstances civilians will best be able to control the military instrument.

Finally, it follows that if agency theory fulfills both the descriptive and predictive functions of a theory better than Huntington's institutional theory, its *prescriptive* element will also be more useful than what Huntington laid down. Nonetheless, critics argue that as applied to civil–military relations, agency theory achieves analytical rigor by severely limiting its scope. The theory is too parsimonious; it fails to explain enough in the world.

Civil–Military Relations and the "Invitation to Struggle" Between the President and Congress

As the constitutional scholar Edwin Corwin once famously observed, the Constitution is an "invitation to struggle for the privilege of directing American foreign policy" between Congress and the president.[98] Charles Stevenson reminds us that a similar tension is at work with regard to civil–military relations. For Stevenson, those who neglect the congressional role in American civil–military relations provide defective descriptive models.

Stevenson contends that a more complete model would include the following testable propositions:

- The president and secretary of defense control the US military concerning the use of force, to include strategy and rules of engagement. Congress controls the military directly when it comes to force structure, equipment, and organization and indirectly regarding doctrine and personnel. The US military accepts both forms of civilian control, but insists on offering advice intended to maintain the organization's institutional and professional autonomy. On use of force, the US military is treated by the president as having a veto. However, instead of exercising that veto, the US military insists on, and is usually granted, terms and conditions for the planned use of force.

- By not resigning in protest, the US military implicitly agrees to support presidential decisions on the budget and use of force, but it also recognizes an obligation to provide alternative personal views in response to Congress. Congress exerts its control with less regard for military preferences than for the political considerations of individual members and committees.

- When the president and Congress are in agreement, the military complies. When the two branches are in disagreement, the military tends to side with the branch that most favors its own views, but never to the point of direct disobedience to orders of the commander in chief.[99]

Concordance Theory

Rebecca Schiff has argued on behalf of a theory that questions the assumptions underlying much of today's thinking about civil–military relations: that a theory of civil–military relations should be based on the physical and ideological separation of the military from the political institutions of a state.[100] Concordance theory is a version of Janowitz's sociological approach and is concerned with predicting and preventing military intervention in the domestic affairs of a state.

Schiff contends that the best way to avoid such an occurrence is to achieve concordance among three "partners" within a polity—the military, the political elites, and the citizenry—on four issues: the social composition of the officer corps; the political decision-making process; the method of recruiting soldiers; and "military style." Such a cooperative relationship may involve separation, but does not require it.

According to Schiff, concordance theory resolves two problems associated with separation theory. The first is the tendency of separation theorists to treat the particular institutional arrangements arising from the experience of the post–World War II United States as universal, applicable to all states regardless of their particular historical conditions and culture. This is especially relevant to the cases of developing states because it means that they "need not adopt the traditional Western model of civil–military relations in order to achieve greater political maturity."[101] The second problem is methodological. Separation theory's institutional analysis alone "fails to take into account the cultural and historical conditions that may encourage or discourage civil–military separation. We can see this deficit, for example, in the postrevolutionary US example—a stark contrast to the post–World War II United States from which separation theory is derived."[102]

For instance, Schiff argues that Huntington's theory is particular to the American experience and is therefore not applicable to other countries.[103] Indeed, she argues that it does not even apply to the United States during all historical periods.[104]

Criticism of concordance theory includes the charge that it is merely a variation of Huntington's concept of "fusion," the demand that "military leaders incorporate political, economic, and social factors into their thinking" and that "military leaders assume non-military responsibilities."[105] Critics also claim that the predictive aspect of concordance theory falls short with regard to the correlation between agreement among the three partners and military intervention on the one hand and to the likelihood of coup d'état on the other.[106] They also charge that the definition of military intervention sets the bar too low to be meaningful. The cooperative relationships that are necessary to avoid military intervention themselves look like intervention unless the standard for civilian control is merely the absence of a military coup. Finally, they criticize the idea of "concordance" for a lack of clarity regarding the degree of harmony among civilian and military leaders: is it a "good" or "bad" thing in terms of either political control or military effectiveness?

But, according to Schiff, these objections ask concordance theory to be something it is not: a theory capable of analyzing all facets and problems in the realm of civil–military relations. Its causal objective is more limited: to predict the likelihood of military intervention in domestic affairs, which, Schiff claims, it does successfully.[107]

Civil–Military Relations and Strategic Assessment

Risa Brooks argues that patterns of civil–military relations affect national security because of their impact on strategic assessment. Strategic assessment matters for at least four reasons. First, when done poorly, it can generate failure by undermining a state's net assessment of military capabilities and available resources. For example, overstating one's own military capabilities may lead to crisis escalation and war or the failure to terminate a war when actual conditions would dictate it. Conversely, underestimating one's own military capabilities may lead to appeasement or the granting of unwarranted concessions to an adversary.

Second, poor strategic assessment makes it more difficult to anticipate political constraints governing the use of force in an interstate dispute. After all, wars are fought to achieve political ends and not for their own (military) sake. For example, the failure to adopt a strategy consistent with diplomatic or other political constraints may incite external hostility and third-party intervention.

Third, poor strategic assessment can compromise a state's ability to integrate political goals and military strategy. For instance, the failure to integrate military means and political objectives may lead to defeat, long and costly wars, or a poor capacity to commit to a war effort. This in turn may lead to failed international agreements, crisis escalation, and war.

Finally, an ambiguous process for strategic assessment can complicate the peaceful resolution of disputes by increasing the chances that other states will miscalculate the first state's priorities and objectives in a conflict. For example, ambiguities in the internal authorization process may obscure signals concerning a state's preferences in international affairs, resulting in bargaining failures, crisis escalation, and war.[108]

Brooks identifies two variables that determine the pattern of civil–military relations: (1) the intensity of preference divergence between political and military leaders with regard to corporate, professional, and security issues; and (2) the balance of power between political and military leaders (political dominance, shared power, and military dominance). These two variables interact, generating "logics" that affect four institutional features of strategic assessment.[109]

The first of these four institutional processes is the routine for sharing information between political and military leaders concerning military capabilities and plans. Is it compartmentalized or does it facilitate fluid exchange of information between the two parties?

The second is strategic coordination. Do structures permit assessment of alternative political–military strategies? Do they promote rigorous debate about costs and risks? Do they help coordinate military activity with political and diplomatic objectives and constraints?

The third is the military's structural competence. Is the military able to monitor its own internal activities and procedures for evaluating the militaries of other states? Is it capable of self-critical analysis and net assessment?

The fourth is the authorization process. What is the mechanism for approving and vetoing political–military strategy? Does it promote a clearly defined and coherent decision-making process or is it characterized by contested and ambiguous procedures?[110]

Brooks then hypothesizes how the various configurations of power and preference divergence affect the four components of strategic assessment and therefore the overall quality of strategic assessment as a whole, using case studies to illustrate the relation between various patterns and strategic assessment. She hypothesizes that the combination of political dominance and low preference divergence leads to the "best" strategic assessment. The combination of shared power and high preference divergence leads to the "worst" strategic assessment. Other combinations lead to "poor" or "fair" strategic assessment.[111]

Of course, the quality of a state's strategic assessment is not the only determinant of a state's success or failure in the international arena. The competing strategies of other states and other exogenous factors may well trump even the best strategic assessment. Michael Desch has employed a similar methodology to show that the alleged military advantage of democratic states in international relations is overstated (Figure 1.1).[112]

Stevenson points out that while the president and secretary of defense control the military when it comes to the use of force, including strategy and rules of engagement, Congress controls the military directly regarding force size, equipment, and organization and indirectly regarding doctrine and personnel. It is also the fact that congressional control of the military is strongly influenced by political considerations, or what Samuel Huntington called "structural" or domestic imperatives as opposed to strategic ones. It is

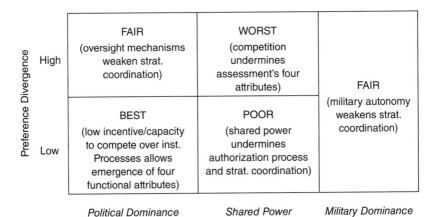

Figure 1.1 **Variation of Strategic Assessment** (*Source*: Risa Brooks, *Shaping Strategy* (Princeton University Press, 2008))

also the fact that when there is disagreement between the legislative and executive branches, the military will side with whichever branch favors the military's view.[113]

Conclusion

Post-9/11 civil–military relations are complex. As mentioned at the beginning of this chapter, the empirical domain of civil–military relations is broad and dynamic, involving political maneuvering, bureaucratic politics, and legislative action. All these processes are part of the civil–military bargain involving the military, the American people, and the civilian leadership of the US government. The environment within which the bargain is constantly being renegotiated is dynamic and fluid. The parties to the bargain must take into account the complex interplay of transnational, international, domestic, historical, and cultural factors.[114]

In many respects, the current state of theorizing about civil–military relations brings to mind the story of the three blind men examining an elephant. Since each can only sense what he is touching (the trunk, a leg, and the tail) and has no concept of the elephant as a whole, each concludes that the beast is something different from what it really is. Despite the lack of an overarching framework for analyzing civil–military relations, the various areas of the field offer many rich "pastures" in which researchers may graze.

Notes

1 Vincent Brooks, Thomas Greenwood, Robert Parker, and Keith Wray, *Two Hands on the Sword: A Study of Political-Military Relations in National Security Policy* (Carlisle, PA: Army War College, 1999).

2 Frank G. Hoffman, "Dereliction of Duty *Redux*? Post-Iraq American Civil-Military Relations," *Orbis*, Spring 2008, pp. 217–235.

3 James Burk, "Theories of Democratic Civil-Military Relations," *Armed Forces and Society*, September 2002, p. 7.

4 Claude Welch, "Civil-Military Relations," in Trevor Dupuy, ed., *International Military and Defense Encyclopedia*, vol. 2 (Washington, DC: Brassey's, 1993), pp. 507–511.

5 Peter Feaver, "The Civil-Military *Problematique*: Huntington, Janowitz, and the Question of Civilian Control," *Armed Forces and Society*, 23, 1996, pp. 149–178.

6   Lawrence Cress, *Citizens in Arms: The Army and Militia in American Society to the War of 1812* (Chapel Hill: University of North Carolina Press, 1982); Rebecca Schiff, *The Military and Domestic Politics: A Concordance Theory of Civil-Military Relations* (London: Routledge, 2009), Chapter 4.

7.   Eliot Cohen, *Supreme Command: Soldiers, Statesmen, and Leadership in Wartime* (New York: Anchor, 2002), p. 247.

8   Samuel Huntington, *The Soldier and the State* (Cambridge: Harvard University Press, 1957).

9   Morris Janowitz, *The Professional Soldier: A Social and Political Portrait* (New York: Free Press, 1960); Cf. James Burk, "Morris Janowitz and the Origins of Sociological Research on Armed Forces and Society," *Armed Forces and Society*, 1993, pp. 167–186; Burk, *The Adaptive Military: Armed Forces in a Turbulent World*, 2nd edition (New York: Transaction, 1998); and Charles Moskos, John Allen Williams, and David R. Segal, *The Postmodern Military: Armed Forces After the Cold War* (New York: Oxford University Press, 2000).

10   Schiff, op. cit., and Schiff, "Civil-Military Relations Reconsidered: A Theory of Concordance," *Armed Forces and Society*, 1995, pp. 7–24.

11   D.L. Bland, "A Unified Theory of Civil-Military Relations," *Armed Forces and Society*, 1999, pp. 7–26.

12   Stepan, *The Military in Politics: Changing Patterns in Brazil* (Princeton: Princeton University Press, 1971), p. 55.

13   Risa Brooks, *Shaping Strategy: The Civil-Military Politics of Strategic Assessment* (Princeton: Princeton University Press, 2008).

14   Ibid., and Jack Snyder, "Civil-Military Relations and the Cult of the Offensive, 1914 and 1984," *International Security*, 1984, pp. 108–146.

15   Dale Herspring, *Rumsfeld's Wars: The Arrogance of Power* (Lawrence: University Press of Kansas, 2008).

16   Thomas Ricks, *Fiasco: The American Military Adventure in Iraq* (New York: Penguin, 2006) and Bing West, *The Strongest Tribe: War, Politics, and the Endgame in Iraq* (New York: Random House, 2008).

17   Brooks, pp. 226–255.

18   Cohen, *Supreme Command*.

19   Don Snider and Miranda Carlton-Carew, *U.S. Civil-Military Relations: In Crisis or Transition?* (Washington, DC: Center for International Strategic Studies, 1995), p. 16.

20   Huntington, pp. 83–85; Michael Desch, *Civilian Control of the Military* (Baltimore: Johns Hopkins University Press, 1999), pp. 4 and 5; Feaver,

op. cit.; Richard Kohn, "The Erosion of Civilian Control of the Military in the United States Today," *Naval War College Review*, Summer 2002, pp. 8–59.

21   Alan Millett, *The American Political System and Civilian Control of the Military: A Historical Perspective* (Columbus: Mershon Center, 1979).

22   Cohen, op. cit.

23   "Militarization" and "militarism" are not quite the same. Michael Sherry defines militarization as "the process by which war and national security [become] consuming anxieties and [provide] the memories, models and metaphors that [shape] broad areas of national life." Michael S. Sherry, *In the Shadow of War: The United States Since the 1930s* (New Haven, CT: Yale University Press, 1995), p. xi. Richard Kohn describes the phenomenon as "the degree to which a society's institutions, policies, behaviors, thought, and values are devoted to military power and shaped by war." Kohn, "The Danger of Militarization in an Endless 'War' on Terrorism," *The Journal of Military History*, January 2009, p. 182. The more elusive term "militarism" describes the dominance of the military over civilian authority, or the prevalence of warlike values in a society. The *Oxford English Dictionary* defines militarism as "the prevalence of military sentiments or ideals among a people; the political condition characterized by the predominance of the military class in government or administration; the tendency to regard military efficiency as the paramount interest of the state." Alfred Vagts defined militarism (pp. 13ff) as "a vast array of customs, interests, prestige, actions, and thought associated with armies and wars and yet transcending true military purposes." Vagts, *A History of Militarism: Civilian and Military*, revised edition (1937; London: Hollis and Carter, 1959), pp. 13ff. Cf. Arthur Ekirch, *Civilian and the Military: A History of the American Anti-Militarist Tradition* (New York: Oxford University Press, 1956).

24   Huntington, op. cit.; Stephanie Guttman, *The Kinder, Gentler, Military: Can America's Gender-Neutral Fighting Force Still Win Wars?* (New York: Scribner's, 2000); J.J. Sheehan, *Where Have All the Soldiers Gone? The Transformation of Modern Europe* (Boston: Houghton Mifflin, 2008).

25   Harold Lasswell, "The Garrison State," *American Journal of Sociology*, January 1941, pp. 455–468, reprinted in Lasswell, *Essays on the Garrison State* (New Brunswick: Transaction Publishers, 1997); Ekirch, op. cit.; Andrew J. Bacevich, *The New American Militarism: How Americans Are Seduced by War* (New York: Oxford University Press, 2005).

26   Huntington, p. 20.

27   Desch, *Civilian Control of the Military*, p. 11.

28 Gordon A. Craig, *The Politics of the Prussian Army, 1640–1945* (Oxford: Oxford University Press, 1955); Hew Strachan, *The Politics of the British Army* (Oxford: Oxford University Press, 1997); and Schiff, op. cit.

29 Demetrios Caraley, *The Politics of Military Unification: A Study of Conflict and the Policy Process* (New York: Columbia University Press, 1965); Gordon W. Keiser, *The US Marine Corps and Defense Unification, 1944–47: The Politics of Survival* (Washington: National Defense University Press, 1982); and Thomas D. Boettcher, *First Call: The Making of the Modern US Military, 1945–1953* (Boston: Little Brown and Company, 1992).

30 Harvey Sapolsky, (1997) "Interservice Competition: The Solution, Not the Problem," *Joint Forces Quarterly,* Spring 1997, pp. 50–53; Mackubin Thomas Owens, "Do We Still Need the Services? The Limits of Jointness," *Armed Forces Journal,* June 2006, pp. 21–25.

31 Samuel Huntington, "National Policy and the Transoceanic Navy," United States Naval Institute *Proceedings,* May 1954, pp. 480–490.

32 Carl Builder, *The Masks of War: American Military Styles in Strategy and Analysis* (Baltimore: Johns Hopkins University Press, 1989).

33 James Locher, *Victory on the Potomac: The Goldwater-Nichols Act Unifies the Pentagon* (College Station: Texas A&M University Press, 2002).

34 Peter Feaver, *Armed Servants* (Cambridge: Harvard University Press, 2003).

35 Lasswell, op. cit.

36 Desch, op. cit.

37 Peter Feaver, *Guarding the Guardians: Civilian Control of Nuclear Weapons in the United States* (Ithaca: Cornell University Press, 1992).

38 Laura Miller and John Allen Williams, "Do Military Policies on Gender and Sexuality Undermine Combat Effectiveness?" in Peter Feaver and Richard Kohn, eds., *Soldiers and Civilians: The Civil-Military Gap and American National Security* (Cambridge: MIT Press, 2001), pp. 361–402; Charles C. Moskos, John Allen Williams, and David R. Segal, eds., *The Postmodern Military: Armed Forces After the Cold War* (New York: Oxford University Press, 2000); and John Allen Williams, "The Military and Society Beyond the Postmodern Era," *Orbis,* Spring 2008, pp. 197–216.

39 Tony Corn, "From War Managers to Soldier Diplomats: The Coming Revolution in Civil Military Relations," *Small Wars Journal,* June 30, 2009, http://smallwarsjournal.com/blog/2009/06/from-war-managers-to-soldier-d/ (accessed March 20, 2010).

40 Eliot A. Cohen, "Twilight of the Citizen Soldier," *Parameters* 2001, 31, pp. 23–28; Eliot Abrams and Andrew J. Bacevich, "A Symposium on

Citizenship and Military Service: A Conference Report on "Citizens and Soldiers: Citizenship, Culture, and Military Service," *Parameters*, 31, 2001, pp. 18–22.

41 Deborah Avant, *The Market for Force: The Consequences of Privatizing Security* (New York: Cambridge University Press, 2005).

42 Carl von Clausewitz, *On War*, Michael Howard and Peter Paret, eds. and trans. (Princeton: Princeton University Press, 1976), p. 141.

43 Desch, *Civilian Control of the Military*, p. 11.

44 Michael I. Handel, *Masters of War: Classical Strategic Thought*, 3rd revised edition (London: Frank Cass, 2001), p. xvii.

45 Feaver, *Armed Servants*; Mackubin Thomas Owens, "Renegotiating the Civil-Military Bargain After 9/11," in Thomas Donnelly and Fred Kagan, eds., *Lessons for a Long War: How America Can Win on New Battlefields* (Washington, DC: American Enterprise Institute, 2010).

46 Schiff, *Domestic Politics and the Military*.

47 Clausewitz, *On War*, p. 87.

48 Ibid., p. 579.

49 Ibid., p. 605.

50 Ibid., p. 607

51 Huntington, *Soldier and the State*, pp. 2 and 3.

52 Ibid., pp. 89–94.

53 Ibid., p. 143.

54 Ibid., p. 156.

55 Ibid., p. 457.

56 Ibid., p. 456.

57 Ibid., p. 464.

58 Ibid., p. 83.

59 Ibid., p. 84.

60 Ibid., pp. 80–83.

61 Samuel Finer, *The Man on Horseback* (Boulder: Westview Press, 1962), pp. 7–10.

62 Ibid., pp. 207ff.

63 Nadia Schadlow and Richard Lacquement, "Winning Wars and Not Just Battles: Expanding the Military Profession to Incorporate Stability Operations," in Suzanne C. Nielsen and Don M. Snider, eds., *American Civil-Military Relations* (Baltimore, MD: Johns Hopkins University Press, 2009), pp. 112–132.

64 Darrel W. Driver, "The Military Mind: A Reassessment of the Ideological Roots of American Military Professionalism," in ibid., pp. 172–193. But cf. Michael Desch, "Hartz, Huntington, and the Liberal Tradition in America: The Clash with Military Realism," in ibid., pp. 133–148.

65 John M. Gates, "The Alleged Isolation of U.S. Army Officers in the Late-19th Century," *Parameters: Journal of the U.S. Army War College*, 10(3), 1980, pp. 32–45 and Mackubin Thomas Owens, "Democracy at Arms: 'The Soldier and the State' is 50 years old, and still relevant," *Weekly Standard*, November 5, 2007, pp. 36–39.

66 Richard Kohn, *Eagle and Sword: The Beginnings of the Military Establishment in America* (New York: Free Press, 1975); Cress, op. cit.; Russell F. Weigley, "The American Military and the Principle of Civilian Control from McClelland to Powell," *Journal of Military History*, October 1993, pp. 27–59.

67 Cohen, *Supreme Command*.

68 Janowitz, *The Professional Soldier*.

69 James Burk, "Theories of Democratic Civil-Military Relations," *Armed Forces and Society*, Fall 2002, p. 10.

70 Ibid., pp. 10 and 11.

71 Ibid., p. 11.

72 Janowitz, *The Professional Soldier*, p. 418.

73 Ibid., pp. 363–367.

74 Ibid., p. 420.

75 Moskos et al., *The Postmodern Military*; Williams, "The Military and Society: Beyond the Postmodern Military"; and Schiff, *The Military and Domestic Politics*.

76 Feaver, *Armed Servants*, p. 7.

77 Desch's theoretical framework can be found in "Soldiers, States, and Structures: The End of the Cold War and Weakening U.S, Civilian Control," *Armed Forces and Society*, 24(3), Spring 1998, pp. 389 and *Civilian Control of the Military*, pp. 11–17.

78 Desch, pp. 17–19.

79 Desch, "Hartz, Huntington, and the Liberal Tradition in America," in Nielsen and Snider, *American Civil-Military Relations*, pp. 91–111.

80 Desch, *Civilian Control of the Military*, p. 19.

81 Krepinevich, *The Army and Vietnam* (Baltimore, MD: Johns Hopkins University Press, 1986).

82 Deborah Avant, *Political Institutions and Military Change: Lessons from Peripheral Wars* (Ithaca, NY: Cornell University Press, 1994), p. 131.

83 Ibid., footnote 2, p. 131.

84 Exceptions include the refusal of the Senate to confirm the promotions of individuals implicated in the Navy's Tailhook affair and congressional insistence on prior experience in "joint"—multiservice—billets before promotion to flag or general rank. No president or secretary of defense relived a general officer for perceived failure during Vietnam,

Lebanon, or Iraq. Typically, general officers who were not successful, e.g., Westmoreland in Vietnam and Casey in Iraq, were "kicked upstairs." In contrast, Secretary of Defense Robert Gates fired two service secretaries and a service chief and forced the retirement of a combatant commander during the Bush administration and fired the top commander in Afghanistan during the first year of the Obama administration and a second a year later.

85   This is the first step in what Eliot Cohen has called the "doctrine of the Cycle." According to this formulation, "Americans in peacetime persuade themselves of their immunity to international violence, discover in time that they are not immune after all, belatedly rush to arms at the last minute, win (typically) in the field through 'enormous and unnecessary sacrifice of life and treasure,' and immediately dissolve the armed forces in a headlong rush." Thomas S. Langston, *Uneasy Balance: Civil-Military Relations in Peacetime America Since 1783* (Baltimore, MD: Johns Hopkins University Press, 2003), p. 15. Cohen's description is in "Making Do With Less, or Coping with Upton's Ghost," US Army War College Paper, April 27, 1995, p. 3, http://www.strategicstudiesinstitute.army.mil/pubs/display.cfm?pubID=286 (accessed February 10, 2010). The quote within the quote is from Emory Upton, *The Military Policy of the United States* (Washington, DC: Government Printing Office, 1904), p. vii.

86   Huntington, *The Soldier and the State*, pp. 155 and 156.

87   Langston, p. 6.

88   Ibid., pp. 28ff.

89   Feaver, *Armed Servant*, p. 27.

90   Ibid., p. 37.

91   Ibid., p. 119.

92   Ibid., p. 178.

93   Huntington, *The Soldier and the State*, pp. 8–10.

94   Feaver, *Armed Servants*, p. 129.

95   Ibid., pp. 180–233.

96   Ibid., pp. 190–210.

97   Ibid., p. 302.

98   Edward S. Corwin et al., *The President: Office and Powers 1787–1984*, 5th revised edition (New York: New York University Press, 1984), p. 201.

99   Charles A. Stevenson, *Warriors and Politicians: US Civil-Military Relations Under Stress* (New York: Routledge, 2006), pp. 207 and 208.

100 Schiff, *Domestic Politics and the Military*, p. 32.

101   Ibid., p. 33.
102   Ibid., p. 33.
103   Ibid., Chapters 5–7.
104   Ibid., Chapter 4.
105   Huntington, 1957, pp. 351 and 353.
106   R.S. Wells "The Theory of Concordance in Civil-Military Relations: A Commentary," *Armed Forces and Society*, 23, 1996, pp. 269–275.
107   Schiff, "Concordance Theory: A Response to Recent Criticisms," *Armed Forces and Society*, 23, 1996, pp. 277–283; Schiff, *The Military and Domestic Politics*, pp. 42 and 43.
108   Brooks, *Shaping Strategy*, p. 10.
109   Ibid., pp. 2–34.
110   Ibid., p. 4.
111   Ibid., pp. 42–54.
112   Michael Desch, *Power and Effectiveness: The Fallacy of Democratic Triumphalism* (Baltimore, MD: Johns Hopkins University Press, 2008).
113   Samuel Huntington, *The Common Defense: Strategic Programs in National Politics* (New York: Columbian University Press, 1961); Charles A. Stevenson, *Warriors and Politicians: US Civil-Military Relations Under Stress* (New York: Routledge, 2006). Cf. Mackubin Thomas Owens, "Strategy and the Strategic Way of Thinking," *Naval War College Review*, Autumn 2007.
114   Peter Feaver and Erika Seeler, "Before and After Huntington: The Methodological Maturing of Civil-Military Studies," in Nielsen and Snider, *American Civil-Military Relations*, pp. 89 and 90.

CHAPTER TWO

Control of the Military and the Military's Influence on American Society

Most of the debate over American civil–military relations since the 1990s has been dominated by concerns about civilian control of the military establishment. Indeed, some observers believe that the focus on civilian control has obscured other equally important elements of civil–military relations.[1]

During this period, the term "crisis" was often bandied about. Some attributed this so-called crisis of civilian control in the 1990s to the fact that President Bill Clinton, who suffered from a lack of credibility in military affairs, was confronted by a popular and activist chairman of the Joint Chiefs of Staff, Gen. Colin Powell, who was taking advantage of expanded powers granted to the chairman by the Goldwater-Nichols Act of 1986.

Others, however, have argued that the "crisis in civilian control" claim was greatly overblown. If the "best indicator of civilian control is who prevails when civilian and military preferences diverge,"[2] it seems clear that civilian control has not eroded. The fact is that even during the Clinton administration, civilian preferences prevailed most of the time, e.g., the involvement of the military in "constabulary" operations (the Balkans and Haiti), substantial force structure cuts, the loss of several weapons systems, and the opening of many military specialties to women, all contrary to the preferences of the military establishment.[3] Other observers concluded that even if Gen. Powell had skewed the civil–military balance against civilian control, that balance had been restored by Powell's successors as Chairman of the Joint Chiefs of Staff.[4]

The issue of civilian control is more complex than some would have it. While the vast majority of US officers accept the principle of civilian control without question, the divided nature of the American government makes the actual exercise of civilian control more difficult. Many observers seem to limit the discussion of civilian control to the executive branch alone, treating Congress as a body outside of the discussion.[5] But while civilian control of the military by the executive branch is important, Congress cannot be ignored. In the past, that body sometimes has chosen to defer to the executive branch when it comes to military affairs, at least with regard to the employment of the military instrument, but it always reserves to itself the option of more forcefully reasserting its authority. Congress exercises its control of the military primarily by means of oversight and the budget process. Congress is always the "force planner" of last resort.[6]

As Charles Stevenson observes, civilian control is both descriptive and prescriptive, both a measurable condition and a norm. "As a principle for resolving disputes, civilian control offers a simple rule: the civilians are supposed to set ends, the military is limited to decisions about means, but the civilians get to draw the line between ends and means."[7]

Three decades ago, Allan Millett established four tests to determine the level of civilian control of the military. First, the armed forces do not dominate the government or impose their unique functional values on civilian institutions. Second, the military has no independent access to resources. Third, military policies regarding recruitment, training, education, promotion, etc., are not inconsistent with basic civil liberties, given some compromises necessary to ensure discipline and combat effectiveness. Finally, the use of military force is not determined by the military establishment itself, but civilian leaders are expected not to disregard the institutional characteristics of the military when those leaders do make the decision.[8]

According to these criteria, the degree of civilian control in the United States remains high. Nonetheless, while the claim that there has been a crisis in civilian control of the military since 9/11 seems overblown, it is also true that there are degrees of military resistance to civilian control, e.g., end runs, "foot-dragging," "slow rolling," and leaks.[9]

Has civilian control eroded in recent years? Where is the line of demarcation between civilians and the military? What accounts for the level of public acrimony that has characterized American civil–military relations both before and after 9/11? How, in practice, has the principle of civilian control played out over the past several years? The remainder of this chapter seeks to answer these and other questions regarding the continuing renegotiation of the civil–military bargain in America.

The Erosion of Civilian Control?

The degree of acrimony visible during the debate over the conception and conduct of the Iraq War and the perception that the uniformed military has actively resisted civilian decisions about the use of military force have contributed to the belief that US civil–military relations are seriously out of balance. But as this chapter illustrates, tension between the civilians and the uniformed military predate 9/11 and the two wars initiated during the presidency of George W. Bush.

The most consistent advocate of the argument that civilian control of the military has weakened in recent years is Richard Kohn,[10] but he has also been joined by scholars such as Peter Feaver, the late Russell Weigley, Michael Desch, and Eliot Cohen.[11] Most of those who hold this position do not fear a coup or the like, but the "repeated efforts on the part of the military to frustrate or evade civilian authority when the opposition seems likely to preclude outcomes the military dislikes." The result, Kohn contends, is that civilian control has diminished to the point "where it could alter the character of American government and undermine national defense."[12]

> My fear, baldly stated, is that in recent years civilian control of the military has weakened in the United States and is threatened today. The issue is not the nightmare of a coup d'état but rather the evidence that the American military has grown in influence to the point of being able to impose its own perspective on many policies and decisions. What I have detected is no conspiracy but repeated efforts on the part of the armed forces to frustrate or evade civilian authority when that opposition seems likely to preclude outcomes the military dislikes.[13]

Kohn continues:

> If one measures civilian control not by the superficial standard of who signs the papers and passes the laws but by the relative influence of the uniformed military and civilian policy makers in the two great areas of concern in military affairs—national security policy, and the use of force to protect the country and project power abroad—then civilian control has deteriorated significantly in the last generation. In theory, civilians have the authority to issue virtually any order and organize the military in any fashion they choose. But in practice, the relationship is far more complex. Both sides frequently disagree among themselves. Further, the military can evade or circumscribe civilian authority by framing the alternatives or tailoring their advice or predicting nasty consequences; by leaking information or appealing to public opinion (through various indirect channels, like lobbying groups or retired generals and admirals); or by approaching friends in the Congress for support. They can even fail to implement decisions, or carry them out in such a way as to stymie their intent. The reality is that civilian control is not a fact but a process,

measured across a spectrum—something situational, dependent on the people, issues, and the political and military forces involved. We are not talking about a coup here, or anything else demonstrably illegal; we are talking about who calls the tune in military affairs in the United States today.[14]

Kohn argues that civilian control of the military in the United States has traditionally rested on four foundations, which, he argues, have eroded: the rule of law and reverence for the Constitution; a small force in peacetime; reliance on the citizen-soldier; and the military's own internalization of military subordination to civilian control. Kohn cites Maj. Gen. John J. Pershing's instructions to First Lieutenant George Patton in 1916, "You must remember that when we enter the army we do so with the full knowledge that our first duty is toward the government, entirely regardless of our own views under any given circumstances. We are at liberty to express our personal views only when called upon to do so or else confidentially to our friends, but always confidentially and with the complete understanding that they are in no sense to govern our actions." Or as Omar Bradley, the first chairman of the Joint Chiefs of Staff, puts it, "Thirty-two years in the peacetime army had taught me to do my job, hold my tongue, and keep my name out of the papers."[15]

While Kohn acknowledges that civil–military tensions are not new, he argues that current conditions are such that the threat of military insubordination is much greater than in past. First, thanks to the Goldwater-Nichols Act of 1986, the military is united in an unprecedented way. In the past, the armed services often were at odds over roles, missions, budgets, and weapons systems, but today they can work together to shape, oppose, evade, or thwart the choices civilians make.

"Second, many of the issues in play today reach far beyond the narrowly military, not only to the wider realm of national security but often to foreign relations more broadly. In certain cases military affairs even affect the character and values of American society itself."

Third, military advice and advocacy is now much more public than it once was and often deals with policies and decisions beyond the military realm. Kohn argues that this expanded role represents a significant encroachment on civilian control of the military.

Fourth, senior officers now lead a large, permanent peacetime military establishment that differs fundamentally from any of its predecessors. On the one hand, Kohn argues, it is increasingly disconnected, even estranged, from civilian society. On the other hand, it has become a recognizable interest group, "larger, more bureaucratically active, more political, more partisan, more purposeful, and more influential than anything similar in American history."[16]

According to Kohn, the erosion of civilian control gives rise to "toxic" civil–military relations, which, he argues, damage national security in at least three ways: by paralyzing national security policy; by obstructing or even sabotaging the ability of the United States to intervene in foreign crises or to exercise international leadership; and by undermining the confidence of the military as an institution in their own uniformed leadership.[17] By all accounts, the Clinton administration tried to avoid conflicts with the military by, for the most part, deferring to the military, not only on such social issues as women in combat and service by open homosexuals, but also on issues related to the use of force in the Balkans, Africa, and Haiti, as well as force structure decisions.

But as Andrew Bacevich argued in 1999, "the dirty little secret of American civil–military relations, by no means unique to [the Clinton] administration, is that the commander-in-chief does not command the military establishment; he cajoles it, negotiates with it, and. As necessary, appeases it."[18] Of course, as a historian, Kohn knows that civil–military tensions in the United States are nothing new. When he characterizes Gen. Powell's actions vis-à-vis President Clinton as "the most open manifestation of defiance and resistance by the American military since the publication of the Newburgh address . . . [N]othing like this had ever occurred in American history"[19] we can only conclude that that he was engaging in hyperbole in order to make a point. But he was also simply wrong.

During the Mexican War, President James Polk, a Democrat had to deal with open resistance to his policies by his two field generals, Zachery Taylor and Winfield Scott, both of whom were Whigs with presidential aspirations.[20] Maj. Gen. George McClellan actively resisted President Lincoln's approach to the conduct of the War of the Rebellion.[21] And of course, there is the case of Truman and Douglas MacArthur.

Kohn softens his original claim by acknowledging that disagreements between the civilians and uniformed military officers are not new. An examination of US civil–military relations since the founding of the Republic illustrates that they "are *messy* and frequently antagonistic; military people *do* on occasion defy civilians; civilian control is situational." But according to Kohn, four factors make current civil–military tensions more problematic.

First, a largely united military is more capable of shaping, opposing, evading, or thwarting civilian choices than in the past when the civilian could frequently play one service off against another. Second, the issues that constitute the heart of the civil–military debate now transcend narrow military questions, affecting broader national security and foreign policy matters. Third, the role of senior military leaders has become much more public than in the past when military advice and advocacy occurred in more of a private setting. Finally, senior officers lead a permanent, professional peacetime military establishment that some have argued is disconnected and even estranged from civilian society.[22]

As is the case with most other students of US civil–military affairs, Kohn narrowly defines civil–military relations in terms of unqualified deference to the executive branch. He treats Congress as a body on the periphery when in fact it has a major role in civil–military relations.[23]

Nonetheless, it is clear that while civilian control in its broadest sense is not at risk in the post-9/11 era, the balance between civilians and the military is once again being renegotiated, calling into question the so-called normal theory of civil–military relations and raising the issue of the limits of dissent on the part of military leaders.

The "Normal" Theory of Civil–Military Relations

Eliot Cohen has called the idea that there is a clear line of demarcation between civilians who determine the goals of the war and the uniformed military who then conduct the actual fighting the "normal" theory of civil–military relations.[24] This is the default position of most presidents since the Vietnam War and is based on the widespread belief that the alleged failure of President Lyndon Johnson and Secretary of Defense Robert McNamara to defer to an autonomous military realm was the cause of US defeat in Vietnam.

The normal theory can be traced to Huntington's *The Solder and the State*. As noted in Chapter 1, Huntington sought a solution to the civil–military *problematique*: how to guarantee civilian control of the military while still ensuring the ability of the uniformed military to provide security? As previously observed, his solution was a mechanism for creating and maintaining a professional, apolitical military establishment, which he called "objective control." Such a professional military would focus on defending the United States but avoid threatening civilian control.[25]

Michael Desch has made a strong case for the normal theory of civil–military relations arguing that the problems the military faced in Iraq were the result of ignoring the line between policy on the one hand and strategy, operations, and tactics on the other hand. He advised Robert Gates, who replaced Donald Rumsfeld as secretary of defense during the last 2 years of the Bush administration,

> to recognize that Rumsfeld's meddling approach contributed in signifi-
> cant measure to the problems in Iraq and elsewhere. The best solution is
> to return to an old division of labor: civilians give due deference to mili-
> tary professional advice in the tactical and operational realms in return
> for complete military subordination in the grand strategic and political
> realms. The success of Gates' tenure in the Pentagon will hinge on his
> reestablishing that proper civil–military balance.[26]

But as Cohen has pointed out, the normal theory of civil–military relations has rarely held.[27] Indeed storied democratic war leaders such as Winston
Churchill and Abraham Lincoln "trespassed" upon the military's turf as
a matter of course, influencing not only strategy and operations but also
tactics. The reason that civilian leaders cannot simply leave the military to
its own devices during war is that war is an iterative process involving the
interplay of active wills. What appears to be the case at the outset of the war
may change as the war continues, modifying the relationship between political goals and military means. The fact remains that wars are not fought for
their own purposes but to achieve policy goals set by the political leadership
of the state.

Like his predecessors since Vietnam, President Bush originally accepted
the normal theory of civil–military relations, and he adhered to its strictures
until he initiated the surge. But while the president may have accepted the
normal theory, Donald Rumsfeld, his first secretary of defense, did not.
Indeed, a major source of the friction between Rumsfeld and the uniformed
military was the secretary's interference in what Desch would call purely
military matters. But although Rumsfeld made some critical mistakes, he
was no more wrong than others when it came to predicting what would tran-
spire. A look at Rumsfeld's actions and those of the uniformed military
during the first years of the war illustrates the dangers of assuming that the
"normal" approach to civil–military relations will always lead to a better
outcome than civilian "meddling."

For instance, while Rumsfeld did not foresee the insurgency and the shift
from conventional to guerilla war, neither did his critics in the uniformed
services. In December 2004, Tom Ricks reported in the *Washington Post* that
while many in the army blamed "Defense Secretary Donald H. Rumsfeld

and other top Pentagon civilians for the unexpectedly difficult occupation of Iraq," one close observer—US Army major Isaiah Wilson III, an official historian of the campaign and later a war planner in Iraq—placed the blame squarely on the army.[28] In an unpublished report, Wilson concluded that senior army commanders had failed to grasp the strategic situation in Iraq and therefore did not plan properly for victory; that army planners suffered from "stunted learning and a reluctance to adapt"; and that army command-ers in 2004 still misunderstood the strategic problem they faced and there-fore were still pursuing a flawed approach.

Critics also charged that Rumsfeld's Pentagon shortchanged the troops in Iraq, in part by failing to provide them with armored "humvees." Yet a review of army budget submissions makes it clear that the army did not immediately ask for the vehicles; the service's priority, as is usually the case with the uniformed services, was to acquire "big ticket" items. It was only after the insurgency began and the threat posed by improvised explosive devices became apparent that the Army began to push for supplemental spending to "up-armor" the utility vehicles.

And while it is true that Rumsfeld downplayed the need to prepare for postconflict stability operations, it is also the case that in doing so he was merely ratifying the preferences of the uniformed military. Only recently has the uniformed military begun to shed the "Weinberger Doctrine," a set of principles long internalized by the US military that emphasize the require-ment for an "exit strategy." But if generals are thinking about an exit strategy they are not thinking about "war termination"—how to convert military success into political success, which is the purpose of post-conflict planning and stability operations. This cultural aversion to conducting stability oper-ations is reflected in the fact that operational planning for Operation Iraqi Freedom took 18 months, while planning for postwar stabilization began half-heartedly only a couple of months before the invasion.[29]

It should also be noted that the most cited example of prescience on the part of the uniformed military—Gen. Eric Shinseki's February 2003 state-ment before Congress suggesting that "several hundred thousand" troops might be necessary in postwar Iraq—was no such thing. As John Garofano has observed, "no extensive analysis has surfaced as supporting Shinseki's figures, which were dragged out of him by Senator Carl Levin only after repeated questioning." Garofano notes that in fact the figures were based on a "straight-line extrapolation from very different environments."[30] The Army's Center for Military History based its figure of 470,000 troops for Iraq on the service's experience in Bosnia and Kosovo, where the primary mission was peacekeeping. This effort to estimate necessary troop strength was inept—critics called it naïve, unrealistic, and "like a war college exercise" rather than serious planning.[31]

Finally, to the extent that Shinseki was correct, it was for the wrong reasons. His focus was on humanitarian concerns rather than on the critical society-building work that the US military had to implement in Iraq.[32] Garofano concludes that the oft-made charge against Rumsfeld—he punished Shinseki for "being right"—is not supported by the evidence. War planning "comes down, as it did in Vietnam, to analysis, getting it right, and providing clear alternatives that address or confront policy goals."[33] This the uniformed military in general and Shinseki in particular failed to do.

As these incidents make clear, adherence to the normal theory of civil–military relations does not necessarily guarantee the best outcome, and President Bush finally abandoned his commitment to the normal theory in pursuit of changing the situation in Iraq. The process began in January 2007, when the president announced the Iraq War surge, changing secretaries of defense and replacing the generals responsible for the actual conduct of operations. To an extent unmatched since Abraham Lincoln issued the Emancipation Proclamation during the Civil War, President Bush assumed responsibility for the strategy and conduct of the war. He continued the process when he nominated David Petraeus as the commander of US Central Command (CENTCOM).

Of course, his critics assailed him for replacing generals who disagreed with his approach with yes-men. But President Bush did nothing more than Abraham Lincoln did when he sacked generals who were not performing to a standard required for Union victory. When it became clear to Lincoln in fall 1862 that Maj. Gen. George B. McClellan did not accept the strategy of striking at the heart of the Confederacy's social system—indeed, that he was undermining it—Lincoln relieved McClellan of his command. While the Emancipation Proclamation made the Civil War Lincoln's war, it was not until early 1864 that he found the general who would take all the steps necessary to win it—Ulysses Grant.[34]

By taking control of the conduct of the war and promoting generals who shared his vision, Lincoln ultimately crushed the rebellion and saved the Union. In January 2007, President Bush replicated Lincoln's approach in Iraq. His elevation of Petraeus to head US CENTCOM indicated that Bush had found his Grant.

Overwhelmingly confirmed by the Senate on July 10, 2008, Gen. Petraeus replaced Admiral William Fallon, who was given to McClellan-like public pronouncements. Just as Lincoln bet that Grant could replicate his earlier successes at Vicksburg and Chattanooga and achieve the final defeat of the Confederacy, Bush bet that Gen. Petraeus would be able to replicate his Iraq success at the theater level, a level that includes operations in Afghanistan as well as Iraq.

Public Acrimony

Civil–military affairs in general and the question of civilian control in particular after 9/11, especially during the war in Iraq, were characterized by unprecedented public acrimony. The clearest example of this public acrimony was the so-called revolt of the generals in 2006, during which six retired Army and Marine generals publicly criticized the Bush administration's conduct of the Iraq War and called for the resignation of Secretary Rumsfeld.[35] Much of the language they used was intemperate, and some was downright contemptuous. For instance, retired Marine Gen. Anthony Zinni, a former commander of US CENTCOM, described the actions of the Bush administration as ranging from "true dereliction, negligence, and irresponsibility" to "lying, incompetence, and corruption."[36] Army Maj. Gen. Paul Eaton called Rumsfeld "incompetent strategically, operationally, and tactically."[37] These public charges by uniformed officers, active or retired, were unprecedented in recent civil–military debates.

While there are no legal restrictions that prevent retired members of the military—even recently retired members—from criticizing public policy or the individuals responsible for it, such public denunciation of civilian authority by soldiers, retired or not, undermines healthy civil–military relations. It is clear that many believed that these retired flag officers were speaking not only on behalf of themselves, but also on behalf of active-duty officers. As Kohn once suggested, retired general and flag officers are comparable in status to the cardinals of the Roman Catholic Church. Whatever they say carries weight.

This public acrimony was fueled in part by the politicization of the Iraq War. Not even Vietnam was politicized to the extent that Iraq has been. Indeed, one must go back to the American Civil War or the Mexican War to find a conflict that stirred comparable partisan rancor. But this animosity actually predates the Iraq War. Its genesis can be traced to Rumsfeld's approach to defense "transformation," his plan to revise the US force structure based on the purported revolutionary impact of emerging technologies, particularly information technologies.[38] The US Army was often seen as being the bill payer for investment in information technology, and Army personnel resented Rumsfeld accordingly.[39]

The acrimony was also by heightened personal animosity toward Rumsfeld on the part of many serving officers.[40] Regarding the Iraq War, the central charges in the case against him include willfully ignoring military advice and initiating the war with a force that was too small; failing to adapt to new circumstances once things began to go wrong; failing to foresee the insurgency that erupted after Saddam Hussein was defeated; and failing to prepare for postconflict stability operations.

These criticisms by uniformed officers were predicated on two assumptions. The first was (and is) that soldiers have the right to a voice in making *policy* regarding the use of the military instrument, that indeed they have the right to *insist* that their views be adopted. This assumption has been encouraged by a serious misreading of the very important book by H. R. McMaster, *Dereliction of Duty: Lyndon Johnson, Robert McNamara, the Joint Chiefs of Staff, and the Lies That Led to Vietnam.*[41] The subject of *Dereliction of Duty* is the failure of the joint chiefs to challenge Defense Secretary Robert McNamara adequately during the Vietnam War. Many serving officers believe the book effectively makes the case that the Joint Chiefs of Staff should have more openly opposed the Johnson administration's strategy of gradualism, and then resigned rather than carry out the policy.

But the book says no such thing. While McMaster convincingly argues that the chiefs failed to present their views frankly and forcefully to their civilian superiors, including members of Congress, he neither says nor implies that the chiefs should have obstructed President Lyndon Johnson's orders and policies by leaks, public statements, or resignation.

This misreading of *Dereliction of Duty* has dangerously reinforced the increasingly widespread belief among officers that they should be advocates of particular policies rather than simply serving in their traditional advisory role. For instance, according to a survey of officer and civilian attitudes and opinions undertaken by Ole Holsti for the Triangle Institute for Security Studies in 1998–1999, "many officers believe that they have the duty to force their own views on civilian decision makers when the United States is contemplating committing American forces abroad." When "asked whether military leaders should be neutral, advise, advocate, or insist on having their way in the decision" to use military force, 50 percent or more of the up-and-coming active-duty officers answered that leaders should "insist" regarding the following issues: "setting rules of engagement, ensuring that clear political and military goals exist, developing an 'exit strategy'," and "deciding what kinds of military units will be used to accomplish all tasks." In the context of the questionnaire, "insist" definitely implied that officers should try to compel acceptance of the military's recommendations.[42]

This view of the role of military leaders is questionable at best and is at odds with the principles and practice of American civil–military relations. In the American system, the uniformed military does not possess a veto over policy. Indeed, civilians even have the authority to make decisions in what would seem to be the realm of purely military affairs. As noted previously, Eliot Cohen has made it clear that successful wartime presidents such as Abraham Lincoln and Franklin Roosevelt "interfered" extensively with military operations—often driving their generals to distraction.[43]

The second assumption underlying the criticism of Rumsfeld—that the judgment and expertise of soldiers are inherently superior to those of civilians when it comes to military affairs and that in time of war the latter should defer to the former—is also open to question. The historical record reveals that even when it comes to strictly military affairs, soldiers are not necessarily more prescient than civilian policy makers. Abraham Lincoln constantly prodded George McClellan to take the offensive in Virginia in 1862. McClellan just as constantly whined about insufficient forces. Despite the image of civil–military comity during World War II, there were many differences between Franklin Roosevelt and his military advisers. George Marshall, the greatest soldier-statesman since Washington, opposed arms shipments to Great Britain in 1940 and argued for a cross-channel invasion before the United States was ready. History has vindicated Lincoln and Roosevelt.

Similarly, many observers, especially those in the uniformed military, have been inclined to blame the US defeat in Vietnam on the civilians. But the US operational approach in Vietnam was the creature of the uniformed military. The consensus today is that the operational strategy of Gen. William Westmoreland was counterproductive; it did not make sense to emphasize attrition of Peoples' Army of Vietnam (PAVN) forces in a "war of the big battalions"—that is, one involving sweeps through remote jungle areas in an effort to fix and destroy the enemy with superior fire power. By the time Westmoreland's successor could adopt a more fruitful approach, it was too late.[44]

During the planning for Operation Desert Storm in late 1990 and early 1991, Gen. Norman Schwarzkopf, commander of CENTCOM, presented a plan calling for a frontal assault against Iraqi positions in southern Kuwait followed by a drive toward Kuwait City. The problem was that this plan was unlikely to achieve the foremost military objective of the ground war: the destruction of the three divisions of Saddam's Republican Guard. The civilian leadership rejected the early war plan presented by CENTCOM and ordered a return to the drawing board. The revised plan was far more imaginative and effective,[45] a further indication that in wartime, the military does not always know best.

Military "Pushback"

The public acrimony that has characterized so much of post-9/11 civil–military relations is a particular manifestation of the idea that the uniformed military should "push back" against civilian leaders when the former disagree with the policies of the latter. This idea, at odds with the theory, if not always the practice, of the US civil–military tradition, has apparently become more acceptable to uniformed officers, leading some observers to call into question the military's subordination to civilian control.

Consider a March 2005 column by David Ignatius for the *Washington Post* about who would likely succeed US Air Force general Richard B. Myers as chairman of the Joint Chiefs of Staff. Ignatius wrote:

> When you ask military officers who should get the job, the first thing many say is that the military needs someone who can stand up to . . . Rumsfeld . . . The grumbling about his leadership partly [reflects] the military's resistance to change and its reluctance to challenge a brilliant but headstrong civilian leader. But in Iraq, Rumsfeld has pushed the services—especially the Army—near the breaking point.

"The military is right," concluded Ignatius. "The next chairman of the JCS must be someone who can push back." In fact, the military had been engaged in pushback more frequently than most of us realize. Pushback was part and parcel of civil–military relations in the 1990s and then, as now, it is a practice that undermines healthy civil–military relations.[46]

While the public's perception of civil–military relations during the 1990s focused on such social issues as women in combat and open homosexuals in the services, the real pushback was military resistance to civilian foreign and defense policy. This manifested itself (to use Peter Feaver's formulation) in various forms of "shirking": "foot-dragging," "slow rolling," and leaks to the press designed to undercut policy or individual policy makers.[47]

On example of pushback occurred when Gen. Colin Powell, then serving as chairman of the Joint Chiefs of Staff, wrote an op-ed for the *New York Times* warning about the dangers of intervening in Bosnia.[48] Not long afterwards, Powell followed up with an article in *Foreign Affairs* that many criticized as an illegitimate attempt by a senior military officer to preempt the foreign policy agenda of an incoming president.[49] Critics argued that Powell's actions constituted a serious encroachment by the military on civilian turf.[50] It was unprecedented, they maintained, for the highest-ranking officer on active duty to go public with his disagreements with the president over foreign policy and the role of the military.

Another instance of pushback was the uniformed military's active resistance to involvement in constabulary missions during the 1990s. This resistance reflected the post-Vietnam view, dominant within the military during the Clinton administration, that only professional military officers could be trusted to establish principles guiding the use of military force. Taking its bearings from the so-called Weinberger Doctrine, a set of rules for the use of force that had been drafted in the 1980s, the US military did everything it could to avoid what came to be known—incorrectly—as "nontraditional missions": constabulary operations required for "imperial policing," e.g., peacekeeping and humanitarian missions. The uniformed military essentially sought to make *military*, not *political*, considerations paramount in the political–military decision-making process—dictating to civilians not only how its operations would be conducted, but also the circumstances under which the military instrument would be used.

Although the military's resistance to Clinton's foreign policy predated Bosnia,[51] the clearest example of its resistance to a mission occurred when the Army—arguing that its proper focus was on fighting conventional wars—insisted that the plans for US interventions in Bosnia, Kosovo, and elsewhere take into account the military's preference for "overwhelming force." As one contemporary source reported, the military greatly influenced the Dayton Agreement establishing an implementation force to maintain peace in Bosnia-Herzegovina. According to Clinton administration officials, the agreement "was carefully crafted to reflect demands from the military . . . Rather than be ignored . . . the military, as a price for its support, has basically gotten anything it wanted."[52]

The uniformed military not only sought to influence the political decision to employ the military instrument, but also sought a say in the issue of resources for defense and readiness. Here, the target was Congress as well as the president. For instance, during the first years of the Clinton administration, the service chiefs for the most part acquiesced in the reduced defense budgets requested by the president, but in 1998, the chiefs changed their tune, testifying that not enough money had been forthcoming from Congress. Members who had consistently supported higher defense spending were enraged. The issue became so acrimonious that "the Joint Chiefs and US senators engaged in public accusations of dishonest testimony and lack of support."[53]

Civilian Control During the Bush Administration

The very real dangers that arise from dysfunctional civil–military relations can be seen in the run-up to the invasion of Iraq. A major source of civil–military tension during the tenure of Secretary of Defense Donald Rumsfeld was his belief that civilian control had atrophied during the Clinton administration. His efforts to reestablish such civilian control was often complicated by his personal style.

Rumsfeld believed that if the Army did not want to do something—as in the Balkans in the 1990s—it would simply overstate the force requirements. ("The answer is 350,000 soldiers. What's the question?") So when Gen. Eric Shinseki testified in 2003 that a larger force than the one civilian defense officials envisioned was necessary to invade Iraq,[54] Rumsfeld interpreted his claim as just another example of foot-dragging. Rumsfeld's decision not to deploy the First Cavalry Division during the war reflected a similar judgment that the "time-phased force deployment list," which guided the deployment of forces into Iraq, had become, like the "two major theater war" planning metric, little more than a bureaucratic tool that the services used to protect their shares of the defense budget. In fact, the army probably *did* need a bigger force in Iraq, but the mutual mistrust between the secretary and the army led Rumsfeld to make some bad decisions.

Some commentators have argued that relative civil–military harmony has prevailed since Robert Gates replaced Rumsfeld as secretary of defense. On the one hand, civilian control seems to have been reinstitutionalized within the US defense establishment. Not only has Gates fired the secretaries of the army and air force, the chief of staff of the air force, a combatant commanders, and two commanders of US forces in Afghanistan,[55] but he has signed a National Defense Strategy document over the objections of the Joint Chiefs of Staff.[56]

But there is evidence that the uniformed military continued to undermine civilian control after Rumsfeld's departure. For instance, according to Bob Woodward, the uniformed military not only opposed the Bush administration's Iraq War surge, *insisting* that its advice be followed, but it subsequently worked to undermine the president once the decision had been made. In one respect, the actions taken by military opponents of the surge—the aforementioned foot-dragging, slow rolling, and selective leaking—are all too characteristic of US civil–military relations during the last decade and a half. But the picture Woodward draws is far more troubling. Even after the surge policy had been laid down, many senior US military leaders—the chairman of the Joint Chiefs of Staff, Admiral Mike Mullen; the rest of the joint chiefs; and Gen. John Abazaid's successor as commander of CENTCOM, Admiral William Fallon— actively worked against the implementation of the president's policy.[57]

If Woodward's account is true, it means that not since Gen. George McClellan actively attempted to sabotage the war policy of Abraham Lincoln

CONTROL OF THE MILITARY   59

in 1862 has the leadership of the United States military so blatantly attempted to undermine a president in the pursuit of his constitutional authority. It should be obvious that such active opposition to a president's policy poses a threat to healthy and balanced civil–military relations, to America's ability to achieve military goals and hence to America itself.

Continuing Civil–Military Tensions in the Obama Administration

Writing before the 2008 election, Richard Kohn predicted that "the new administration, like its predecessors, will wonder to what extent it can exercise civilian 'control.' If the historical pattern holds, the administration will do something clumsy or overreact, provoking even more distrust simply in the process of establishing its own authority."[58] As recent events have illustrated, he was right on the money.

Obama sought to avoid a fight with the military. First Lady Michelle Obama's first official visit outside Washington, DC, was to Fort Bragg, NC. The president retained two holdovers from the Bush administration: Secretary of Defense Gate, and Adm. Michael Mullen, who was nominated for a second term as chairman of the Joint Chiefs of Staff. He appeared to do this in order to show respect for the senior military leadership and to ensure continuity during difficult wartime conditions.

President Obama also insulated himself from criticism with regard to military affairs by seeking out former high-ranking leaders for posts in his administration, including retired Marine Corps general James Jones (as national security adviser), retired Army general Eric Shinseki (as secretary of veterans' affairs), and retired Navy admiral Dennis Blair (as director of national intelligence). In Kohn's words, selecting these individuals for his administration, the president "arranged it so that he is free to ignore the advice of his uniformed chiefs and field commanders because he will have cover of General Jones by his side and other senior military in his administration." At the same time, President Obama was demonstrating that he had been reaching out to the military and that he wanted to have the benefit of military judgment.

Nonetheless, President Obama, perhaps inadvertently, sowed the seeds of the current civil–military discord with his campaign rhetoric, which used Afghanistan as a club to beat the Republicans in general and the party's presidential candidate, John McCain, in particular, over the head about Iraq. In Obama's formulation, Afghanistan became the "good war" and "the central front on terror" from which we had been distracted by our misadventure in Iraq. Yet once he was elected and confronted with the political difficulty of this stance, he backpedaled.

In keeping with his promise to reinvigorate the effort in Afghanistan, President Obama announced in March 2010 a "comprehensive new strategy ... to reverse the Taliban's gains and promote a more capable and accountable Afghan government," pledging to properly resource this "war of necessity."[59] The new operational strategy called for a counterinsurgency approach (like that of the surge in Iraq) and focused on the security of the population; it rejected the "counterterrorism" approach (which NATO had followed during the Bush years) that used Special Operations Forces and air strikes launched from unmanned aircraft to hunt down and kill al Qaeda terrorists. President Obama even replaced the US commander in Afghanistan, Gen. David McKiernan, with Gen. Stanley McChrystal, who had been Gen. Petraeus's right-hand man in Iraq when a counterinsurgency strategy was successfully implemented.

But when McChrystal indicated in a confidential study completed in August that more troops would be needed to pursue the president's strategy, President Obama did nothing. Admiral Michael Mullen, chairman of the joint chiefs, told Congress that more troops would be needed, and experts suggested that the number of additional soldiers and Marines necessary to execute the new strategy was thirty to forty thousand. But this was apparently a truth Obama did not want to hear. In contrast to George Bush in 2007, who pursued what he thought was the right approach in Iraq despite the unpopularity of his decision, President Obama apparently began to rethink his hard line in Afghanistan out of concern that his base did not support any troop increase.

The perception that the president's actions regarding Afghanistan were motivated by political factors rather than strategic ones—a perception that undermined healthy civil–military relations—was reinforced by several clumsy missteps by the administration. These included the naked attempt by retired Marine Gen. James Jones, the national security adviser, to intimidate military commanders in Afghanistan into reducing their troop requests to a politically acceptable level and a White House directive to the Pentagon not to forward a request for more troops.[60] The most serious mistake, reported in the *Wall Street Journal*, was that the White House ordered Gen. McChrystal not to testify before Congress.[61] This move furthered the perception that the administration was trying to muzzle the military.

News reports indicated that officers on Gen. McChrystal's staff and elsewhere were frustrated by the president's failure to make a decision about how to proceed in Afghanistan and about perceived attempts to muzzle the general by cutting off his legitimate access to Congress. They wondered why, after having declared the conflict there a "war of necessity," the president had not provided the necessary means to fight it properly. They wondered why, having selected McChrystal to turn things around in Afghanistan, President Obama had not supported him the way that George Bush supported Petraeus in Iraq.[62]

It is easy to see the truth of Kohn's prediction that a clumsy step by the administration would sow distrust on the part of the soldiers, thereby increasing civil–military tensions, but the steps taken by some in the military made the situation worse. First someone leaked Gen. McChrystal's strategic assessment to Bob Woodward of the *Washington Post*. Then an article published by McClatchy quoted anonymous officers to the effect that McChrystal would resign if the president did not give him what he needed to implement the announced strategy.[63] Such actions on the part of the uniformed military are symptoms of a continuing civil–military relations problem: they reflect the widespread belief among military officers that they should be *advocates* of particular policies rather than simply serving in their traditional *advisory* role.

This civil–military clash was a harbinger of things to come. In late June of 2010, it was reported that Gen. Stanley McChrystal, the top US military commander in Afghanistan, and members of his staff had criticized top Obama administration officials.[64] A story published in *Rolling Stone* quoted officers on McChrystal's staff making disparaging remarks about the vice president, the national security adviser, and the president himself.[65] Gen. McChrystal was summoned to Washington, DC, where he offered his resignation, which the president accepted.[66]

It seems clear that Gen. McChrystal had no choice but to offer his resignation in the wake of the *Rolling Stone* story, and the president had no choice, but to accept it. If nothing else, Gen. McChrystal had created a command climate that did not discourage disrespectful speech on the part of the military for civilian authorities. Some saw this as a more sinister development. For instance, Andrew Bacevich saw this episode as an illustration of the fact that

Long wars are antithetical to democracy. Protracted conflict introduces toxins that inexorably corrode the values of popular government. Not least among those values is a code of military conduct that honors the principle of civilian control while keeping the officer corps free from the taint of politics.

The real problem, wrote Bacevich, is that in the past, "circumstances such as these have bred praetorianism" leading soldiers to become

> enamored with their moral superiority and impatient with the failings of those they are charged to defend. The smug disdain for high-ranking civilians casually expressed by McChrystal and his chief lieutenants—along with the conviction that "Team America," as these officers style themselves, was bravely holding out against a sea of stupidity and corruption—suggests that the officer corps of the United States is not immune to this affliction.[67]

The fear of praetorianism aside, events during both Bush and Obama administrations suggest that the real civil–military danger facing the Republic is not the existence of a threat to civilian control of the military, but the lack of *trust* between civilians and the military. This has been a problem on both sides in both the Bush and Obama administrations. Regarding the latter, news reports indicate that President Obama's civilian aides have been deeply suspicious of the military, accusing them of intentionally "boxing the president in" through a series of coordinated leaks to the media during the Afghanistan policy review.[68] For its part, many officers have seen the Obama administration setting up the military to take the blame should the American enterprise in Afghanistan fail.[69]

As we will see in a later chapter, patterns of civil–military relations have an impact on military effectiveness. Success in war requires healthy civil–military relations and these depend on trust. The good news is that the two new generals put in place in the aftermath of the McChrystal affair—Marine Gen. James Mattis as commander, US CENTCOM, and Gen. David Petraeus as the commander of the effort in Afghanistan proper—both understand the importance of professionalism and trust in fostering healthy civil–military relations.

Military Dissent

The flip side of civilian control is military subordination. Is it the military's responsibility to "salute and obey" even when officers disagree with the policy chosen by civilian authorities? What is the nature of military advice? Should military leaders insist that their advice be heeded? What courses of action are available to military leaders who believe the civilian authorities are making bad decisions?

An extreme view of military dissent appeared in the journal *Joint Forces Quarterly (JFQ)*. The author of the essay argues that "there are circumstances under which a military officer is not only justified but also obligated to disobey a legal order." The essay takes on a special salience because *JFQ* is an official journal published by the National Defense University under the aegis if the chairman of the Joint Chiefs of Staff.[70]

The *JFQ* essay notwithstanding, American military culture traditionally has been deferential to civilian authority. Such deference can be traced to George Washington and the very foundation of the US military establishment. *The Armed Forces Officer*, an official publication that lays out the moral–ethical aspects of officership, lays out the question of military deference to civilian authority in very stark terms:

> Having rendered their candid expert judgment, professionals are bound by oath to execute legal civilian decisions as effectively as possible—even those with which they fundamentally disagree—or they must request relief from their duties, or leave the service entirely, either by resignation or retirement.[71]

Some prominent commentators take issue with this choice, arguing that there is no tradition of resignation in the United States and even more forcefully, that "to threaten resignation—taking disagreements public—directly assaults civilian control of the military."[72] Such an act "amounts to marshalling an officer's military knowledge, expertise, and experience—as well as the profession's standing with the public and reputation for disinterested patriotism—to undercut some undertaking or concept that the officer opposes."[73] According to Richard Kohn, the military's job is "to advise and then execute lawful orders . . . If officers at various levels measure policies, decisions, orders, and operations against personal moral and ethical systems, and act thereon, the good order and discipline of the military would collapse."[74]

But others suggest that the choices laid out in *The Armed Forces Officer* are too narrow. They contend that in terms of Albert Hirschman's classic study of responses to decline in firms, organizations, and states, *The Armed Forces Officer* offers officers only the choices of "loyalty" and "exit." But Hirschman argues that under certain circumstances, the institutionalization of greater "voice," i.e., dissent, can help stem massive exit.[75]

For instance, Leonard Wong and Douglas Lovelace write that there are alternatives "beyond blind obedience, resignation or retirement."[76]

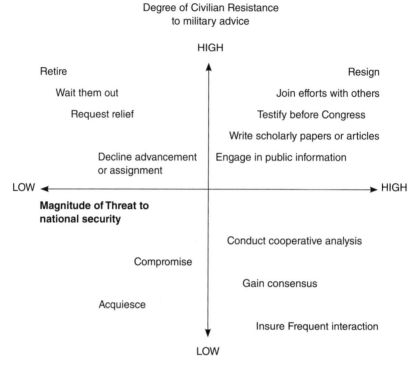

Figure 2.1 **Options for Widening the Policy Debate** (*Credit*: Orbis)

They propose a range of actions available to senior military leaders to give them Hirschman's "voice" when they are confronted with decisions by civilian leaders that military officers believe are flawed. The vertical axis of their framework represents the degree of civilian resistance to military advice; the horizontal axis represents the seriousness of the threat to national security that the policy embodies (Figure 2.1).

When both the degree of civilian resistance to military advice and the magnitude of the treat are low (lower left hand quadrant), the options for the military are acquiescence or compromise. When resistance to military advice is low but the threat is high (lower right hand quadrant), options involve frequent interaction between the uniformed military and the civilians, working to achieve consensus and conducting cooperative analysis.

When the degree of civilian resistance to military advice is high and the magnitude of the threat is low (upper left hand quadrant), the options for military officers include declining advancement or assignment, requesting relief, waiting the civilians out, or retiring. When both civilian resistance to military advice and the level of the threat are high (upper right hand quadrant), the authors suggest options ranging from a public information campaign, writing articles, testifying before Congress, joining efforts with others, to resignation.[77]

Don Snider accepts the idea of broadening the choices available to uniformed officers when faced with what they believe to be flawed policy decisions by civilians but questions whether the two variables employed by Wong and Lovelace—civilian resistance to military advice and the magnitude of the threat to national security—alone provide adequate guidance for a strategic leader of the American military profession who is considering dissent.[78] For Snider, the imperatives of military professionalism and the "trust" relationship between the military profession and other entities within American society and government also must play a role.

Snider suggests three trust relationships, which must be rated along a continuum ranging from "fully trusted"—the ideal—to "not trustworthy." The three relationships are (1) that between the military profession and the American people; (2) that between the military profession and the peoples' elected representatives, both in the executive and legislative branches; and (3) that between the senior leaders of the military profession and their subordinate leaders (Figure 2.2).[79]

Following Huntington, Snider identifies three responsibilities of military leaders. The first is the "representative function," the professional requirement "to represent the claims of military security within the state machinery," i.e., to "express their expert point of view on any matter touching the creation, maintenance, use, or contemplated use of the armed forces."

The second responsibility is to exercise the "advisory function." This is the professional imperative "to analyze and to report on the implications of alternative courses of action from the military point of view," i.e., to provide

	Trust with the American People	Trust with Civilian Leaders	Trust with Junior Leaders
Gravity of Issue			
Relevance to Expertise			
Degree of Sacrifice			
Timing of Dissent			
Authenticity as a Leader			

Figure 2.2 (*Credit*: Orbis)

"candid professional military advice to elected and appointed civilian leaders, regardless of whether the advice was solicited or regardless of whether the advice is likely to be welcomed." Such advice does not include policy advocacy, which both Huntington and Snider consider to be beyond the legitimate role of military officers.

The third responsibility is to exercise the "executive function." This requires the professional military "to implement state decisions with respect to state security even if it is a decision which runs violently counter to his military judgment."[80] Snider quotes Huntington at length:

> The military profession exists to serve the state. To render the highest possible service the entire profession and the military force which it leads must be constituted as an effective instrument of state policy. Since political direction comes from the top, this means that the profession has to be organized into a hierarchy of obedience. For the profession to perform its function, each level within it must be able to command the instantaneous and loyal obedience of subordinate levels. Without these relationships, military professionalism is impossible. Consequently, loyalty and obedience are the highest military virtues.[81]

Having laid out the three trust relationships and the three responsibilities of professional military leaders, Snider addresses how the "other" in each trust relationship involving the military profession—the American, people, civilian leaders, and junior leaders within the military profession itself—perceives and understands acts of dissent on the part of the military profession's senior leaders. Such a moral analysis, he argues, must address at least five considerations.

The first is the gravity of the issue to the nation and therefore to the clients of the military profession.

The second is the relevance of the strategic leader's expertise with regard to the issue that might impel dissent. Does the issue at hand fall squarely within the scope of the dissenter's expertise as a military professional?

The third consideration is the degree of sacrifice on the part of the dissenter. Is the dissent motivated solely by a disinterested desire to serve the nation, even in the face of personal sacrifice, or does it involve a self-serving subtext, such as the advancement of the dissenter's own professional or political ambitions?

The fourth consideration is the timing of the act of dissent. Is it timed to undercut the actions or policy from which the officer wishes to dissent?

Finally, is the act of dissent congruent with the prior, long-term character and beliefs of the dissenter? Does the dissent strike those who know the dissenter as being uncharacteristic or atypical?[82] Snider goes on to argue that a complete assessment on the part of the dissenter would require that he analyzes the five considerations in the light of the three trust relationships.

Of course, in practice, argues Snider, some factors are more salient than others. Like Wong and Lovelace, he believes that the gravity of the issue with regard to national security is most important. "Logically, the higher the stakes, the greater the temptation and justification will be for dissenters to speak out."[83] This is the case because the only reason to have a military is to ensure national security. That is what the military profession is all about. Of course, to engage in dissent, no matter the stakes, seems to be in conflict with the inviolate principle of the subordination of the military to civilian authority. The interpretation of acts of dissent is complicated, argues Snider, by the deeply polarized nature of American politics today and the perception on the part of some that the military as an institution has become too identified with the Republican Party.[84]

But Snider points out that recent research suggest that the identification of the US military with a conservative agenda and the Republican Party is overstated and that therefore public dissent may represent "a positive development, suggesting that [what Huntington called] the military mind is not . . . monolithically partisan."[85] It also seems to be the case that acts of dissent can help to create informed public discourse on matters of national security. Risa Brooks notes several ways that the military can provide expert information and its policy preferences without violating necessary limits on military participation in political activities: access to civilians within the executive branch; informal communications with Congress and congressional staffs; as well as interaction with journalists, business leaders, and other public figures.[86] However, Snider cautions that "when dissent begins to shade over into political activity, or comes to be regarded as such, the dissenters incur the risk of being seen as little more than uniformed lobbyists advocating a cause in (sic) behalf of their uniformed interest group—to the extreme detriment of both."[87]

The moral calculus of dissent also requires that we consider the relevance of the expertise and knowledge of the dissenter. Why should we listen to the dissenter? "If the issue does not fit within the compass of the profession's expertise, or only marginally so, one would expect observers to dismiss dissenters as free-lancers operating without standing, much as an Oscar-winning Hollywood actor who sets up shop as an authority on national defense."[88]

Part of the problem with this criterion is that the meaning of professional military expertise has changed since Huntington's time. Following Harold Lasswell, Huntington referred to the expertise of the professional military officer as the "management of violence." But today, that description seems far too narrow. The fact is that today's military officer is really a "national security professional," whose expertise extends to the interconnected intellectual space of everything from strategic theory, strategic thinking, and strategy formation to diplomacy, nation-building, and homeland defense.[89] Thus, in practice, it is sometimes difficult to differentiate between what military and civilian national security professionals do.[90] And as historical examples cited earlier in this chapter illustrate, even when it comes to purely military affairs, the professional military officer is not necessarily more correct than the civilians.

The sacrifice incurred by the dissenter and the timing of the dissent must be judged according to the standard of common sense. "For the true professional, a right understanding of one's loyalties always places loyalty to self dead last. Thus, absent personal sacrifice, such dissent quickly leads to the suspicion of and the search for ulterior motives . . ."[91]

The same applies to the timing of the dissent. "If something is worthy of an act of dissent, then it is worthy. Thus, as soon as that is discerned and decided by the strategic leader, the act should follow immediately." If there is a substantial delay, the other partners in the trust relationship, especially the subordinate leaders within the profession, may suspect a lack of moral agency on the part of the dissenter as well as the impact of ulterior motives on the act.

Finally, it is critical that the strategic leader contemplating dissent is an authentic leader of competence and moral integrity who has previously displayed a steadfastness of character. Subordinates, especially those who judge leaders to be cynical or lacking in integrity, are unlikely to construe an act of dissent by such an individual as disinterested.

Gen. George Marshall offers a compelling example of the limits of dissent: military leaders must inform civil leaders if they have reservations about a proposed policy—but they must put doubts aside once the policy is decided on. As Secretary Gates explained in an address at the US Military Academy,

The Germans [in mid-1940] had just overrun France and the battle of Britain was about to begin. FDR believed that rushing arms and equipment to Britain, including half of America's bomber production, should be the top priority in order to save our ally. Marshall believed that rearming

America should come first. Roosevelt overruled Marshall and others, and came down on what most historians believe is the correct decision—to do what was necessary to keep England alive.

The significant thing is what did *not* happen next. There was a powerful domestic constituency for Marshall's position among a whole host of newspapers and congressmen and lobbies, and yet Marshall did not exploit and use them. There were no overtures to friendly congressional committee chairmen, no leaks to sympathetic reporters, no ghostwritten editorials in newspapers, no coalition-building with advocacy groups. Marshall and his colleagues made the policy work and kept England alive.[92]

The Marshall case illustrates that uniformed officers have an obligation to stand up to civilian leaders if they think a policy is flawed. They must convey their concerns to civilian policy makers forcefully and truthfully. If they believe the door is closed to them at the Pentagon or the White House, they also have access to Congress. But once a policy decision is made, soldiers are obligated to carry it out to the best of their ability, whether their advice is heeded or not.

So using Snider's calculus of dissent, how should we judge those who publicly criticized Rumsfeld during the revolt of the generals? In terms of gravity of the issue and expertise, they had the authority and, indeed, a responsibility to speak out. The proper venue, however, was Congress rather than the press.

However, the retired officers suffered no sacrifice by going public after they had left active service. And their case was not helped by the timing of their dissent, which was broadly interpreted as an effort to undercut the Bush administration's policies in Iraq and to undermine Rumsfeld.

Reasonable people can disagree concerning the relative importance given to each of Snider's criteria. However, critics of the dissenters stress the fact that none of them went public when they might have suffered personal and professional costs, or when their dissent would not have been seen as "piling on" at a time when public opinion had turned against the war.

In principle, US military officers accept the principle of civilian control and recognize the limits of dissent. But as the previous discussion illustrates, the actual practice of military subordination is complicated by a number of factors. The first of these is organizational and institutional: the separation of powers related to military affairs between the executive and legislative branches. But even more important is the tension between the loyalty and obedience of the military professional on the one hand and his military judgment and moral beliefs on the other hand. The civil–military tensions visible both before and since 9/11 are illustrative of these complications.

The Military's Influence in America

A corollary of civilian control of the military instrument is the question of the military's influence on American society. Does the military have too much impact on American society beyond the military's own proper sphere?

This is not a new question, of course.[93] During the period following the American Revolution, many Americans were concerned about the establishment of the Society of the Cincinnati, a hereditary organization created by veterans of the War of Independence, including prominent individuals such as Washington himself. Mercy Otis Warren argued that the Society was an affront to the principles of a young republic. As she wrote, the officers of the American army who assumed the name CINCINNATUS might have been expected to imitate the

> Humble and disinterested virtues of the ancient Roman; [to] have retired satisfied with their own efforts to save their country, and the competent rewards it was ready to bestow, instead of ostentatiously assuming hereditary distinctions, the *insignia* of nobility. But the eagle and the ribbon dangled at the button-hole of every youth who had for three years borne an office in the army, and taught him to look down with proud contempt on the patriot grown grey in the service of his country.[94]

Of course, the military was directly involved in supporting Reconstruction governments throughout the South after the Civil War. But the Army also built roads, established forts, and protected settlers during the western expansion. The fact that the Military Academy at West Point was primarily an engineering school meant that much of the infrastructure of the expanding republic was built by graduates of that institution.

Union veterans were instrumental in establishing the Grand Army of the Republic (GAR) after the War of Rebellion, an organization that helped extend the influence of veterans throughout the land. A prominent member of the GAR, John A. Logan, helped to institute Memorial Day in 1867, and other Union generals established the American Rifle Association—later renamed the National Rifle Association (NRA)—in 1871. Presidents of the NRA included Ulysses Grant, Phil Sheridan, and Ambrose Burnside.

Military leaders were also instrumental in spreading military ideas throughout American society. For example, Spanish–American War veteran and former President Theodore Roosevelt joined with Maj. Gen. Leonard Wood, his colleague as a member of the "Rough Riders" in Cuba and Army chief of staff until 1914, to convince the American citizenry of the need to prepare for possible involvement in the Great War raging in Europe. The "Preparedness Movement" sought to demonstrate that a country unprepared for war was doomed to suffer the fate of Belgium. Roosevelt wrote two books on the subject, *America and the World War* (1915) and *Fear God and Take Your Own Part* (1916).

Both Roosevelt and Wood supported universal conscription and the latter was instrumental in establishing the Plattsburg Movement, a voluntary nonenlistment summer program designed to train potential officers. During the summers of 1915 and 1916, the Plattsburg camps drilled some 20,000 men, primarily from business and the professions, in military fundamentals. The Plattsburg camps became superfluous after the United States began to mobilize, but they served as the model for the citizens' military training camps authorized by the National Defense Act of 1920 as a compromise that rejected universal military training.

It is likely that the apogee of military influence in the United States occurred during the period extending from the beginning of World War II until the Vietnam War. Of course, during this time, the United States maintained a large standing army maintained with the draft. In 1961, 3 days before stepping down from the presidency, Dwight D. Eisenhower warned his countrymen of the dangers of a "military-industrial complex."

Until the latest of our world conflicts, the United States had no armaments industry. American makers of plowshares could, with time and as required, make swords as well. But now we can no longer risk emergency improvisation of national defense; we have been compelled to create a permanent armaments industry of vast proportions. Added to this, three and a half million men and women are directly engaged in the defense establishment. We annually spend on military security more than the net income of all United States corporations.

This conjunction of an immense military establishment and a large arms industry is new in the American experience. The total influence—economic, political, even spiritual—is felt in every city, every State house, every office of the Federal government. We recognize the imperative need for this development. Yet we must not fail to comprehend its grave implications. Our toil, resources and livelihood are all involved; so is the very structure of our society.

In the councils of government, we must guard against the acquisition of unwarranted influence, whether sought or unsought, by the military-industrial complex. The potential for the disastrous rise of misplaced power exists and will persist.[95]

The military is much smaller than when Eisenhower delivered his farewell speech, but it still exerts a powerful influence. Some think that its influence is too great.

James Burk has provided a useful way of thinking about the military's influence in America. His framework is based on the concept of "institutional presence," i.e., "the social significance of an institution in society."[96] According to Burk, there are two dimensions of institutional presence, material and moral. The first concerns the degree to which social contact with the institution is likely, i.e., the degree to which the institution must be taken into account as an actor in society. The second concerns the degree to which an institution is integrated into the normative order, in other words, how the institution in question relates to the understanding of what constitutes a good society.[97]

In the context of these two dimensions of social presence, Burk offers a typology of institutions based on the character of their presence in society. When an institution ranks high in both dimensions, it can be described as *central* to society. When an institution is morally integrated but not materially salient, it can be described as *peripheral*. Burk calls institutions that are high in terms of material salience but low in moral integrations *predatory*. If an institution is neither materially salient nor morally integrated, it is *alienated*. [98]

According to Burk's framework, we can describe the US military as a central institution in American society. It has been peripheral at times, viz., the period between the War of 1812 until World War I, with the obvious exceptions of the Mexican and Civil Wars and again between the World Wars, but probably never alienated. The biggest concern has been that the military would become predatory, an institution that society considers illegitimate, that claims a disproportionate share of society's resources, or that comes to dominate society in terms of influence. Some consider Eisenhower's farewell address a warning about such an outcome, and certainly numerous writers addressed this issue during the Cold War.[99]

Since 9/11, some have expressed similar concerns. For example, Richard Kohn expressed concern that an "endless war on terror" will lead to a militarized America. He observes that the United States has been militarized in government, economy, society, and culture since the 1930s, but he warns that "a Global War on Terrorism that may last a generation or more promises to continue and even intensify militarization. Such a war even poses the possibility of militarism—the domination of war values and frameworks in American thinking, public policy, institutions, and society to the point of dominating rather than influencing or simply shaping American foreign relations and domestic life."[100]

Andrew Bacevich goes further, arguing that a "new American militarism" has already taken hold.[101] This condition has manifested itself in a number of ways. The first is the tendency to value military power for its own sake, indeed to see it as the truest measure of national greatness. The second is an increased propensity to use force, leading to the normalization of war. The third is the emergence of a new "aesthetic" of war in which the old vision of war as barbarism, brutality, ugliness, and sheer waste has been replaced by one of high-tech, surgical, frictionless, postmodern, and "virtual" war, in other words, war as spectacle, to be conducted at a safe distance. The fourth is the boost in the status of military institutions and a romanticized view of soldiers, creating a society in which the biggest sin is failure to "support the troops."

Unlike many other books critical of US defense and military policy since 9/11, Bacevich does not lay the blame for a militaristic approach to the world at the feet of the administration of George W. Bush.

> . . . well before September 11, 2001, and before the younger Bush's ascent to the presidency, a militaristic predisposition was already in place both in official circles and among Americans more generally. In this regard, 9/11 deserves to be seen as an event that gave added impetus to already existing tendencies rather than as a turning point. For his part, President Bush himself ought to be seen as a player reciting his lines rather than as a playwright drafting an entirely new script.[102]

Bacevich contends that these factors have changed the basis of American civil–military relations by undermining the ancient American tradition of the citizen-soldier and destroying the link between citizenship and military service. An ironic effect of treating military service as a matter of individual choice rather than a requirement of citizenship, he argues, has been the emergence of a cultural gap between American society and military professionals.

Bacevich recommends a number of steps that he argues would restore a semblance of balance and good sense to the way Americans think about military power. These include revitalizing the concept of separation of powers; viewing force as a last resort; enhancing US strategic self-sufficiency; organizing US military forces for national *defense* rather than the broader concept of national *security* by, for instance, shedding unnecessary overseas obligations; developing a gauge for determining the appropriate level of US defense spending; enhancing non-military instruments of statecraft; reviving the concept of the citizen-soldier; reexamining the role of the National Guard; and reconciling the military profession to American society.[103]

Whether Americans are willing to embrace these principles is open to question. But they are certainly part of the discussion and pertinent to the renegotiation of the civil–military bargain after 9/11.

One element of the debate concerns the alleged militarization of US foreign policy. Many observers believe that the role of the military in shaping and conducting US foreign policy is far too great. Critics of a militarized foreign policy point to the vast influence wielded by US combatant commanders, whose power in a given region far exceeds that of any diplomat. Even when regional combatant commands attempt to downplay the military's role, as they do especially in Latin America—Southern Command (SOUTHCOM)—and Africa (AFRICOM)—the perception on the part of the locals is still that the military is in charge.

Combatant commands were created by the Goldwater-Nichols Department of Defense Reorganization Act of 1986. Goldwater-Nichols was the culmination of a defense unification process that began before the end of World War II but that accelerated during the early 1980s. Congress was roused to action by the confluence of three factors: perceived military failures (or at most, marginal successes) stretching from the Vietnam War to the Iran hostage rescue, the Beirut bombing, and Grenada; public criticism of the existing defense structure by high-ranking officials; and critiques by respected defense analysts and think tanks. Both houses of Congress began a process of investigations and hearings expected to culminate in legislation calling for substantial changes in the Department of Defense.[104]

In passing Goldwater-Nichols, Congress sought to address two central concerns: (1) the excessive power and influence of the separate services; and (2) the mismatch between the authority of the combatant commanders and their responsibilities. On the one hand, congressional reformers believed that the influence of the four services was out of proportion to their legally assigned and limited formal responsibilities, making it difficult, if not impossible, to integrate the separate capabilities of service components into effective units capable of the joint operations called for in modern war. On the other hand, while a major goal of the Department of Defense Reorganization Act of 1958 had been to create truly unified combatant commands, "singly led and prepared to fight as one, regardless of service," this provision was more honored in the breach than in the observance.

In 1970, a Blue Ribbon Defense Panel established by President Richard Nixon found that "'unification' of either command or the forces is more cosmetic than substantive."[105] Goldwater-Nichols rectified this problem by specifying in detail the command authority of the combatant commanders and by placing the bulk of US armed forces under the commanders' authority.

But while it is possible to argue that the quality of military operations has improved since the passage of Goldwater-Nichols, the Act in effect established regional proconsuls with vast *statutory* powers that exceed those of military officers in the past. As one observer has put it, "The real power in the military today is in the field leading one of America's five [now six] geographic commands."[106]

Of course, American soldiers have previously served as military governors of counties that the United States had occupied after defeating them in war. American officers served in such a capacity in Mexico after the end of hostilities and the signing of the peace treaty that provided for US annexation of New Mexico and California. While the Democrats, under James Polk, defended these unprecedented governments as necessary, Whigs expressed apprehension at the prospect of "American Pompeys roaming the West," not subject to congressional control.[107] American soldiers also served as military governors in Cuba and the Philippines after the Spanish American War and in Japan after World War II.

But these previous military governors lacked statutory power. The combatant commanders created by Goldwater-Nichols possess it. And this power permits them to overshadow the diplomats that have traditionally been responsible for American foreign policy. In addition, they possess advantages that the Washington, DC-based bureaucracies lack. The combatant commanders "are forward deployed, have more flexibility than DC-based institutions, and have robust travel budgets to frequent countries throughout each commander's [Area of Responsibility or AOR]. Having one commander for an entire region allows combatant commanders to develop foreign policy with all his countries of responsibility in mind."[108]

While efficiency has its advantages, some observers of American civil–military relations wonder it is really a good thing for senior military officer to possess such power over the creation and implementation of US foreign policy: to speak as a single voice for the United States that "provides clear, unambiguous policy to an entire region."[109]

The power of the combatant commander and his influence on US foreign policy can undercut the ability of the president to convey a coherent foreign policy. This occurred in the case of Admiral William J. "Fox" Fallon, commander of US CENTCOM, a regional combatant command that includes Iraq and Iran—who stepped down from his post on March 11, 2008. He offered as his reason the public "misperception" that he had disagreed with the Bush administration over policy in the Middle East, especially with regard to Iran. In a letter to Secretary of Defense Robert Gates, Fallon wrote that "the current embarrassing situation and public perception of differences between my views and administration policy and the distraction this causes from the mission make this the right thing to do."[110]

The proximate cause of Fallon's departure was an article by Thomas Barnett in the April 2008 issue of *Esquire*. Entitled "The Man Between War and Peace," the piece began: "As head of U.S. Central Command, Admiral William 'Fox' Fallon is in charge of American military strategy for the most troubled parts of the world. Now, as the White House has been escalating the war of words with Iran, and seeming ever more determined to strike militarily before the end of this presidency, the admiral has urged restraint and diplomacy. Who will prevail, the president or the admiral?"[111]

Barnett portrayed Fallon as "brazenly challenging" President Bush on Iran, pushing back "against what he saw as an ill-advised action." Certainly, reasonable people can disagree over the wisdom of the Bush administration's Iran policy; what is troubling is the extent to which a combatant commander took it on himself to develop and disseminate policy independently of the president. In doing so, Fallon placed himself in opposition to conventions governing American civil–military relations in place since the time of the American Revolution.

Claims to the contrary notwithstanding, the differences between Fallon and the administration were real, not the result of any "misperception." It is well established that Fallon worked to undermine the surge in Iraq by pushing for faster troop reductions than the commander on the ground in Iraq, Gen. David Petraeus, thought prudent.[112] He attempted to banish the phrase "the Long War" because, according to Barnett, it "signaled a long haul that Fallon simply finds unacceptable."

Fallon also undercut the cornerstone of the Bush administration's Iran policy, which held that all options, including the use of military force, had to be kept open in order to pressure Iran to forgo its nuclear ambitions.

Bush's policy made diplomatic sense. As Frederick the Great once observed, diplomacy without force is like music without instruments. But in November of 2008, Fallon told Al Jazeera TV, "This constant drumbeat of conflict . . . is not helpful and not useful. I expect that there will be no war, and that is what we ought to be working for. We ought to try to do our utmost to create different conditions."[113] And before a trip to Egypt during the same month, Fallon told the *Financial Times* that a military strike against Iran was not "in the offing. Another war is just not where we want to go."[114]

It is thus undeniable that as commander of US CENTCOM, Fallon exceeded his authority.[115] Fallon's public pronouncements were in stark contrast to statements by other high-ranking military officers who—whatever their views of going to war with Iran while the US military was heavily engaged in Iraq and Afghanistan—did not attempt, even indirectly, to constrain American foreign policy to the extent that Fallon did. Indeed, had Fallon not stepped down, the president would have been perfectly justified in firing him, as Abraham Lincoln fired Maj. Gen. George B. McClellan, as Franklin Roosevelt fired Rear Admiral James O. Richardson, and as Harry Truman fired Gen. Douglas MacArthur.[116]

Critics of the power of combatant commanders in general and Fallon in particular argue that the problem was not that Fallon was merely "pushing back" within the administration against a policy he did not like. The problem was that a uniformed officer was actively working to undermine that policy after the decision had been made—that he was speaking out against the policy publicly while being charged with executing it. The playing field is not level for commanders speaking in public. They have a responsibility to support the missions they have been given, not to publicly evaluate the wisdom of the policy; among other things, such a public evaluation undermines the confidence of their subordinates as they go into battle.

Most American military commanders have understood this. For instance, according to Dana Priest's book *The Mission*, the Clinton White House wanted US pilots in the no-fly zone to provoke the Iraqis into attacking American planes.[117] The head of CENTCOM at the time, Gen. Anthony Zinni, believed that this could lead to war with Iraq and insisted that the White House issue him a direct order to undertake such an action. Faced with leaving a paper trail, the White House changed its mind.

Unfortunately, the power of a theater combatant commander, which exceeds that of just about every civilian in government except the president and secretary of defense, makes it tempting for him go beyond implementing policy to presuming to make it. Those who presume to do so, especially in public, pose a danger to civil–military relations and to republican government.

A second defense reorganization measure with significant implications for military influence on US security policy was the establishment of US Special Operations Command. Galled by the failure of Operation Eagle Claw, the attempt to rescue US hostages at the American embassy in Tehran, reformers in Congress agitated for changes that would improve the performance of US Special Operations Forces and raise their status within the department. Congress sought, among other goals, to provide close civilian oversight for special operations and low-intensity conflict activities; to ensure that genuine expertise and a diversity of views were available to the president and secretary of defense regarding special operations requirements and low-intensity threats; to improve interagency planning and coordination for special operations and low-intensity conflict; and to bolster special operations capabilities in such areas as joint doctrine and training, intelligence support, command and control, budgetary authority, personnel management, and mission planning.[118]

Despite substantial resistance on the part of the Pentagon, both the House and Senate passed reform bills for Special Operations Forces in 1986. The reconciled bill amended the Goldwater-Nichols Act by establishing a unified Special Operations Command for the Special Operations Forces of all services, headed by a four-star general or admiral, an assistant secretary of defense for special operations and low-intensity conflict, a coordinating board for low-intensity conflict within the National Security Council, and a new major force program, that is, a separate budgetary category for Special Operations Forces. The final bill, which became known as the Nunn-Cohen Amendment to the 1987 Defense Authorization Act, was signed into law in October 1986.[119]

The establishment of the command has done much to improve special operations, which in the 1970s and 1980s were characterized by a low state of readiness, ad hoc command and control, and lack of focus. US Special Operations Forces are now second to none in quality. Several years ago, Special Operations Command was designated a supported command in the war on terrorism.

What makes the Special Operations Command problematic for civil–military relations, however, is the classified nature of much of what these forces do. Specifically, there is a problem of oversight. The United States has always had clandestine operators—for example, much of what the CIA does is classified—but these longstanding intelligence functions are subject to scrutiny by special congressional committees. Congress currently lacks the same sort of oversight regarding "direct action" by Special Operations Forces. As a result, there is no genuine civilian control of the command.

Conclusion

The cornerstone of US civil–military relations is simple and straightforward: the uniformed military is expected to provide its best advice to civil authorities, who alone are responsible for policy. Despite the concerns expressed by some observers, civilian control of the military has remained strong since 9/11. In cases of disagreements between civilian policy makers and the uniformed military, for the most part the former have prevailed.

Much of the concern about civilian control ignores the fact that Congress has a role to play in civil–military relations. Military officers have an obligation to answer the questions of that body truthfully and completely. To treat military interaction with Congress as an "end run" around the executive branch misses the point. The legislative branch has budget and oversight authority over the military. Congress's use of these powers is discretionary, but students of American civil–military relations sometimes act as if they do not exist.

As Charles Stevenson reminds us, the American founders "created a dual system of civilian control—direct control from the President within the Executive Branch but also control by the Legislative Branch by means of law and money."[120] This dual system is inefficient, but it has permitted the United States to avoid many of the pitfalls that have plagued other countries.

While civilian control has prevailed, military subordination since 9/11 has been uneven. The attempts by certain military officers to undercut the "surge" in Iraq after President Bush authorized it and Admiral Fallon's public differences with President Bush over Iran are both troubling indicators of military insubordination. Many commentators believed that the uniformed military was too deferential to Donald Rumsfeld when he was secretary of defense.

As noted above, there have been increasing attempts to create a "calculus of dissent" that provides more options than "blind obedience" or resignation. Don Snider and others have tried to make such a calculus of dissent an explicit component of the military's professional ethic.

The military's influence on American society does not seem to have increased since 9/11. One expects increased military influence during wartime, e.g., World War II, but for the most part, this seems not to have occurred in this instance. Of course, when it comes to the influence of the military, the fact is that the size, budget, available manpower, and attitude of the American defense establishment enable the military to take on challenges that are not within the capacity of other government agencies.

In the end, it must always be remembered that war has always been the great destroyer of free government. It seems always to have been the case that the necessities, accidents, and passions of war undermine liberty. The forces that contributed to the collapse of free government in Germany, Russia, China, and Japan in the twentieth century are the same ones that destroyed the possibility of free government among the ancient Greeks, as catalogued by Thucydides in his history of the Peloponnesian war.

The United States, in contrast, has remained free while fighting numerous wars, both major and minor, both declared and undeclared, both hot and cold, during the Republic's 200 plus years. This unprecedented ability of the United States to wage war while still preserving liberty is the legacy of the American Founders, who created institutions that have enabled the United States to minimize the inevitable tension between the necessities of war and the requirements of free government.

Notes

1   Mackubin Thomas Owens, "Civil-Military Relations and the Strategy Deficit," FPRI E-Note, February 2010; Frank Hoffman, "Dereliction of Duty Redux? Post-Iraq American Civil-Military Relations," *Orbis*, Spring 2008.

2   Michael Desch, *Civilian Control of the Military: The Changing Security Environment* (Baltimore: The Johns Hopkins University Press, 1999), p. 4.

3   Mackubin Thomas Owens, "Civilian Control: A National Crisis?" *Joint Forces Quarterly*, No. 66, Autumn/Winter 1994/95, pp. 82 and 83. Cf. Richard D. Hooker, Jr. "Soldiers of the State: Reconsidering American Civil-Military Relations," *Parameters*, 23(4), Winter 2003–2004, pp. 4–17.

4   Lyle J. Goldstein, "General John Shalikashvili and the Civil-Military Relations of Peacekeeping," *Armed Forces and Society*, 3(26), Spring 2000, pp. 387–411.

5   Two who don't are Charles A. Stevenson, *Warriors and Politicians: US Civil-Military Relations Under Stress* (New York and London: Routledge, 2006); and Dale R. Herspring, *The Pentagon and the Presidency: Civil-Military Relations from FDR to George W. Bush* (Lawrence: University Press of Kansas, 2005).

6   Mackubin Thomas Owens, "Strategy and the Logic of Force Planning," in Strategy, Security, and Forces Faculty, eds., *Strategy and Force Planning*, Fourth Edition (Newport: Naval War College Press, 2004). Cf. Owens, "Strategy and the Strategic Way of Thinking," *Naval War College Review*, Autumn 2007. See also Risa Brooks, "Militaries and Political Activity in Democracies," in Suzanne C. Nielsen and Don M. Snider, eds., *American Civil-Military Relations: The Soldier and the State in a New Era* (Baltimore,

MD: Johns Hopkins University Press, 2009), especially pp. 223 and 224. For an example of how the military seeks to influence Congress, see Stephen Scroggs, *Army Relations with Congress* (Westport, CT: Praeger, 2000).

7   Stevenson, *Warriors and Politicians*, p. 195. Cf. Desch, *Civilian Control of the Military*, and Kenneth W. Kemp and Charles Hudlin, "Civilian Supremacy Over the Military: Its Nature and Limits," *Armed Forces and Society*, 19(1), Fall 1992, p. 8.

8   Allan R. Millett, *The American Political System and Civilian Control of the Military: A Historical Perspective*, Mershon Center Position Papers in the Policy Sciences, No. 4, April 1979, p. 3.

9   Peter Feaver, *Armed Servants: Agency, Oversight, and Civil-Military Relations* (Cambridge: Harvard University Press, 2003), p. 68.

10   His most complete treatment of the issue is "The Erosion of Civilian Control of the Military in the United States Today," *Naval War College Review*, Summer 2002. But see also Richard Kohn, "Out of Control: The Crisis in Civil-Military Relation," *The National Interest*, No. 35, Spring 1994; Richard Kohn, "The Forgotten Fundamentals of Civilian Control of the Military in Democratic Government," John M. Olin Institute for Strategic Studies, Project on US Post-Cold War Civil-Military Relations, Working Paper 13, Harvard University, June 1997; and Richard Kohn, "Coming Soon: A Crisis in Civil-Military Relations," *World Affairs*, Winter 2008, http://www.worldaffairsjournal.org/2008%20-%20Winter/ full-civil-military.html.

11   Feaver, *Armed Servants*; Desch, *Civilian Control of the Military*; Russell Weigley, "The American Military and the Principle of Civilian Control from McClellan to Powell," *Journal of Military History*, October 1993; and Eliot Cohen, *Supreme Command: Soldiers, Statesmen, and Leadership in War* (New York: Free Press, 2002).

12   Kohn, "The Erosion of Civilian Control," p. 9.

13   Ibid., p. 9. Cf. Kohn, "Civil-Military Relations: Civilian Control," in John Whiteclay Chambers II, ed., *The Oxford Companion to American Military History* (New York: Oxford University Press, 1999), pp. 122–125.

14   Kohn, "The Erosion of Civilian Control," pp. 15 and 16.

15   Ibid., p. 23.

16   Ibid., pp. 21 and 22.

17   Ibid., p. 12.

18   Andrew Bacevich, "Discord Still: Clinton and the Military," *The Washington Post*, 3 January 1999, p. C1.

19   Kohn, "The Erosion of Civilian Control," p. 10.

20   John C. Pinheiro, *Manifest Ambition: James K. Polk and Civil-Military Relations During the Mexican War* (Westport, CT: Praeger, 2007).

21   Mackubin Thomas Owens, *Abraham Lincoln: Leadership and Democratic Statesmanship in Wartime* (Philadelphia: Foreign Policy Research Institute, 2009), pp. 30–33.

22   Kohn, "The Erosion of Civilian Control," pp. 20–22.

23   Stevenson, op. cit.

24   Cohen, *Supreme Command*, p. 4.

25   Chapter 1, supra.

26   Michael Desch, "Bush and the Generals," *Foreign Affairs*, May/June 2007, http://www.foreignaffairs.org/20070501faessay86309/michael-c-desch/bush-and-the-generals.html. For replies to Desch, see Richard B. Myers and Richard H. Kohn; Mackubin Thomas Owens; and Lawrence Korb, "Salute and Disobey?" *Foreign Affairs*, September/October 2007, pp. 147–156, http://www.foreignaffairs.org/20070901faresponse86511/richard-b-myers-richard-h-kohn-mackubin-thomas-owens-lawrence-j-korb-michael-c-desch/salute-and-disobey.html.

27   Cohen, *Supreme Command*, pp. 1–15.

28   Thomas E. Ricks, "Army Historian Cites Lack of Postwar Plan: Major Calls Effort in Iraq 'Mediocre,'" *Washington Post*, December 25, 2004, p. A01, http://www.washingtonpost.com/wp-dyn/articles/A24891–2004 Dec24.html. Passages from Wilson's report quoted here are taken from the *Washington Post* article by Ricks.

29   On Rumsfeld and the plans for the Iraq War, see Michael Gordon and Bernard Trainor, *Cobra II: The Inside Story of the Invasion and Occupation of Iraq* (New York: Pantheon, 2006) and Thomas Ricks, *Fiasco: The American Military Adventure in Iraq* (New York: Penguin, 2006).

30   John Garofano, "Effective Advice in Decisions for War: Beyond Objective Control," *Orbis*, 52(2), Spring 2008, p. 253.

31   Ricks, *Fiasco*, pp. 79 and 80.

32   Ibid., p. 97.

33   Garofano, "Effective Advice," p. 254.

34   Owens, *Abraham Lincoln*, pp. 25–30.

35   See Greg Newbold, "Why Iraq Was a Mistake," *Time*, April 17, 2006 and David S. Cloud and Eric Schmitt, "More Retired Generals Call for Rumsfeld Resignation," *New York Times*, April 14, 2006, p. A1. For a concise but useful summary of the episode, see David Margolick, "The Night of the Generals," *Vanity Fair*, March 13, 2007, www.vanityfair.com/politics/features/2007/04/iraqgenerals200704?printable=true&c.

36 The remarks were made during an interview on *60 Minutes*, May 21, 2004, http://www.cbsnews.com/stories/2004/05/21/60minutes/main 618896.shtml.

37 Quoted in Paul Eaton, "A Top-Down Review for the Pentagon," *New York Times*, March 19, 2006, http://www.nytimes.com/2006/03/19/opinion/ 19eaton.html?_r=1.

38 Matthew Moten, "A Broken Dialogues: Rumsfeld, Shinseki, and Civil-Military Tensions," in Nielsen and Snider, *American Civil-Military Relations*, pp. 42–71.

39 Brooks, *Shaping Strategy: The Civil-Military Politics of Strategic Assessment* (Princeton: Princeton University Press, 2008), pp. 227–235; Mackubin Thomas Owens, "Reshaping Tilted Against the Army," *Washington Times*, November 24, 2002. For a critique of the ideas underpinning "transformation," see Owens, "Technology, the RMA, and Future War," *Strategic Review*, 26(2), Spring 1998, pp. 63–70.

40 Academics have not been immune to such animosity. See, for instance, Dale Herspring, *Rumsfeld's Wars: The Arrogance of Power* (Lawrence, KA: University Press of Kansas, 2008). For a contrary assessment, see Robert Kaplan, "What Rumsfeld Got Right: How Donald Rumsfeld Remade the U.S. Military for a More Uncertain World," *Atlantic Monthly*, July/August 2008, http://www.theatlantic.com/doc/200807/rumsfeld.

41 H. R. McMaster, *Dereliction of Duty: Lyndon Johnson, Robert McNamara, the Joint Chiefs of Staff, and the Lies That Led to Vietnam* (New York: Harper Collins, 1997).

42 Ole Holsti, "Of Chasms and Convergences: Attitudes and Beliefs of Civilians and Military Elites at the Start of a New Millennium," in Peter D. Feaver and Richard H. Kohn, eds., *Soldiers and Civilians: The Civil-Military Gap and American National Security* (Cambridge, MA: MIT Press, 2001), pp. 84 and 489 and tables 1.27 and 1.28.

43 Cohen, *Supreme Command*.

44 See Lewis Sorley, *A Better War: The Unexamined Victories and Final Tragedy of America's Last Years in Vietnam* (New York: HBJ/Harvest Books, 2000).

45 See Michael Gordon and Bernard Trainor, *The Generals' War: The Inside Story of the Conflict in the Gulf* (Boston: Little Brown and Company, 1995).

46 David Ignatius, "Rumsfeld and the Generals," *Washington Post*, March 30, 2005, p. A15, http://www.washingtonpost.com/wp-dyn/articles/ A11309–2005Mar29.html.

47 See Peter Feaver, *Armed Servants*, supra, note 9.

48   Colin Powell, "Why Generals Get Nervous," *New York Times*, October 8, 1992.

49   Colin Powell, "U.S. Forces: Challenges Ahead," *Foreign Affairs*, Winter 1992/93, pp. 32–42.

50   See, for example, Kohn, "Out of Control: The Crisis in Civil-Military Relations," pp. 3–17 and Weigley, "The American Military and the Principle of Civilian Control from McClellan to Powell," pp. 28–30.

51   See, for example, Richard A. Serrano and Art Pine, "Many in Military Angry Over Clinton's Policies," *Los Angeles Times*, October 19, 1993, p. 1.

52   Warren Strobel, "This Time Clinton is Set to Heed Advice from Military," *Washington Times*, December 1, 1995, p. 1.

53   Kohn, "Erosion of Civilian Control," no. 5, p. 21. Cf. Eric Schmitt, "Joint Chiefs Accuse Congress of Weakening U.S. Defense," *New York Times*, September 30, 1998, p. 1 and Elaine Grossman, "Congressional Aide Finds Spending on 'Core Readiness' in Decline," *Inside the Pentagon*, June 28, 2001, p. 1.

54   See Michael Gordon and Bernard Trainor, *Cobra II*, p. 117.

55   Thom Shanker, "2 Leaders Ousted from Air Force in Atomic Errors," *New York Times*, June 6, 2008, http://www.nytimes.com/2008/06/06/washington/06military.html?_r=1&adxnnl=1&ref=todayspaper&adxnnlx=1212735795–6qfVDvbLA5+MI1/c0v7/bg&oref=slogin.

56   "Gates Approves New Defense Strategy Over Objections of Service Chiefs," *The Insider from Inside Defense*, June 12, 2008, http://insidedefense.com/secure/insider_display.asp?f=defense_2002.ask&docid=6122008_june12d.

57   See Bob Woodward, *The War Within: A Secret White House History, 2006-2008* (New York: Simon and Schuster, 2008), pp. 340, 342, 343, 348, and 349.

58   Richard Kohn, "Coming Soon: A Crisis in Civil-Military Relations," *World Affairs*, Winter 2008, http://www.worldaffairsjournal.org/2008%20-%20Winter/full-civil-military.html.

59   President Barack Obama, "Remarks on a Strategy for Afghanistan and Pakistan," March 27, 2009, http://www.cfr.org/publication/18952#.

60   Bob Woodward, "Key in Afghanistan: Economy, not Military," *Washington Post*, July 1, 2009, http://www.washingtonpost.com/wp-dyn/content/article/2009/06/30/AR2009063002811_pf.html.

61   "Obama and the General: The White House Finds a Four-Star Scapegoat for its Afghan Jitters," *Wall Street Journal*, October 7, 2009, http://online.wsj.com/article/SB10001424052970204488304574428961222276106.html.

62   See Nancy A. Youssef, "Military Growing Impatient with Obama on Afghanistan," McClatchy Washington Bureau, September 18, 2009, http://www.mcclatchydc.com/227/v-print/story/75702.html.

63   See Bob Woodward, "McChrystal: More Forces or 'Mission Failure,' " *Washington Post*, September 21, 2009, http://www.washingtonpost.com/wp-dyn/content/article/2009/09/20/AR2009092002920.html? referrer=emailarticle and Youssef, "Military Growing Impatient."

64   Helen Cooper, Thom Shanker, and Dexter Filkins, "McChrystal's Fate in Limbo as He Prepares to Meet Obama," *New York Times*, June 22, 2010, http://www.nytimes.com/2010/06/23/world/asia/23mcchrystal.html?_r=1.

65   Michael Hastings, "The Runaway General," *Rolling Stone*, June 22, 2010, http://www.rollingstone.com/politics/news/17390/119236.

66   Scott Wilson and Michael D. Shear, "Gen. McChrystal is Dismissed as Top US Commander in Afghanistan," *Washington Post*, June 24, 2010, http://www.washingtonpost.com/wp-dyn/content/article/2010/06/23/AR2010062300689.html.

67   Andrew Bacevich, "Endless War, A Recipe for Four Star Arrogance," *Washington Post*, June 27, 2010, p. B1.

68   Evan Thomas, "McChrystal's War," *Newsweek*, October 5, 2009.

69   See, for example, Bob Woodward, *Obama's Wars*, (New York: Simon and Schuster, 2010) and Mackubin Owens, "The War on Terror and the Revolt of the Generals," *Wall Street Journal*, October 1, 2010, p. A19.

70   Lt. Col. Andrew R. Milburn, USMC, "Breaking Ranks: Dissent and the Military Professional," *Joint Forces Quarterly*, 4th Quarter, 2010, p. 101. Cf. David Wood, "Military Officers Chafe for Bigger Role in Policy Decisions," PoliticsDaily.com,, October 4, 2010.

71   Department of Defense, *The Armed Forces Officer* (Washington, DC: Department of Defense, 2006).

72   Richard B. Myers and Richard H. Kohn, "Salute and Disobey?" *Foreign Affairs*, September/October 2007.

73   Kohn, "The Erosion of Civilian Control of the Military," p. 32.

74   Kohn, "Building Trust: Civil-Military Behaviors for Effective National Security," in Nielsen and Snider, *American Civil-Military Relations*, p. 282.

75   Albert O. Hirschman, *Exit, Voice, Loyalty: Responses to Decline in Firms, Organizations, and States* (Cambridge: Harvard University Press, 1970).

76   Leonard Wong and Douglas Lovelace, "Knowing When to Salute," *Orbis*, 52(2), Spring 2008, p. 284.

77   Ibid., pp. 284–287.

78   Don Snider, "Dissent and Strategic Leadership of the Military Profession," *Orbis*, 52(2), Spring 2008, pp. 256–277.

79   Ibid., p. 266.

80   Ibid., pp. 267 and 268. Cf. Huntington, *The Soldier and the State*, p. 72.

81   Snider, "Dissent and Strategic Leadership," p. 268. Huntington, *The Soldier and the State*, p. 73.

82   Snider, "Dissent and Strategic Leadership," p. 269.

83   Ibid., p. 269.

84   Andrew Bacevich and Richard Kohn, "Grand Army of the Republicans: Has the U.S. Military Become a Partisan Force?" *New Republic*, December 8, 1997, pp. 22–25.

85   Snider, "Dissent and Strategic Leadership," p. 270. The research to which Snider points is found in Darrell W. Driver, "The Military Mind: A Reassessment of the Ideological Roots of American Professionalism," in Nielsen and Snider, pp. 172–193. But for a contrary view suggesting that military dissent during the Iraq War was precisely the response of the military's "conservative realism" to policies motivated by the traditional liberalism of American politics, in this case under the guise of "neocon-servatism," see Michael Desch, "Hartz, Huntington, and the Liberal tradition in America: The Clash with Military Realism," in Nielsen and Snider, pp. 91–111.

86   Brooks, "Militaries and Political Activity in Democracies," in Nielsen and Snider, pp. 218–224.

87   Snider, "Dissent and Strategic Leadership," p. 271. Cf. Richard Kohn, "Building Trust: Civil-Military Behaviors for Effective National Security," in Nielsen and Snider, pp. 277 and 278.

88   Snider, "Dissent and Strategic Leadership," p. 271.

89   Harry Yarger, *Strategy and the National Security Professional: Strategic Thinking and Strategy Formulation in the 21st Century* (Westport, CT: Praeger, 2008). Cf. George W. Bush, Executive Order 13434 of May 17, 2007, "National Security Professional Development," http://www.fas.org/irp/offdocs/eo/eo-13434.htm.

90   On the difficulty of defining the content and boundaries of the military profession, see Richard Lacquement, "Mapping Army Professional Expertise and Clarifying Jurisdictions of Practice," in Don Snider and Gayle Watkins, eds., *The Future of the Army Profession*, 2nd edition (New York: McGraw-Hill, 2005). On the negative consequences of defining the military profession too narrowly, see Lacquement and Nadia Schadlow, "Winning Wars, Not Just Battles: Expanding the Military Profession to Incorporate Stability Operations," in Nielsen and Snider, pp. 112–132.

91   Snider, "Dissent and Strategic Leadership," p. 274.

92   Secretary of Defense Robert M. Gates, "Evening Lecture at the U.S. Military Academy at West Point," April 21, 2008, http://www. defenselink.mil/speeches/speech.aspx?speechid=1233.

93   For an excellent overview of this topic, see James Burk, "The Military's Presence in American Society, 1950–2000," in Peter D. Feaver and Richard H. Kohn, eds., *Soldiers and Civilians: The Civil-Military Gap and American National Security* (Cambridge, MA: MIT Press, 2001), pp. 247–274.

94   Mercy Otis Warren, *History of the Rise, Progress and Termination of the American Revolution*, vol. 2 (Indianapolis: Liberty Fund, 1988. Reprint: Originally published in three volumes, 1805), p. 618.

95   Public Papers of the Presidents, Dwight D. Eisenhower, 1960, pp. 1035–1040, http://coursesa.matrix.msu.edu/~hst306/documents/indust.html.

96   Burk, "The Military's Presence in American Society," p. 249.

97   Ibid., pp. 249 and 250.

98   Ibid., pp. 250 and 251.

99   C. Wright Mills, *The Power Elite* (New York: Oxford University Press, 1957); Walter Millis, *Arms and Men: America's Military History and Military Policy from the Revolution to the Present* (New York: 1956); Arthur A. Ekirch, Jr., *The Civilian and the Military A History of the American Antimilitarist Tradition* (New York: Oxford University Press, 1956); Harold Lasswell, "The Garrison State Hypothesis Today," in Samuel Huntington, ed., *Changing Patterns of Military Politics* (New York; Free Press, 1962).

100   Richard Kohn, "The Danger of Militarization in an Endless 'War' on Terrorism," *Journal of Military History*, January 2009.

101   On the distinction between "militarization" and "militarism," see Chapter 1, note 23.

102   Andrew Bacevich, *The New American Militarism: How Americans are Seduced by War* (New York: Oxford University Press, 2005), pp. 4 and 5.

103   Ibid., pp. 208–224.

104   For a comprehensive—if partisan—examination of the process that culminated in the passage of Goldwater-Nichols, see James R. Locher III, *Victory on the Potomac: The Goldwater-Nichols Act Unifies the Pentagon* (College Station: Texas A&M Press, 2003).

105   Blue Ribbon Defense Panel, *Report to the President and the Secretary of Defense on the Department of Defense* (Washington, DC: Department of Defense, 1970), p. 50.

106   Derek S. Reveron and Michael D. Gavin, "America's Viceroys," in Reveron, ed., *America's Viceroys: The Military and US Foreign Policy*

(New York: Palgrave Macmillan, 2004), p. 1. Cf. Dana Priest, "The Proconsuls: Patrolling the World," *Washington Post*, September 28–30, 2000.

107   See John C. Pinheiro, *Manifest Ambition: James K. Polk and Civil-Military Relations During the Mexican War*, p. 106. Chapter 5 of this book examines in particular Philip Kearney's military governorship of what would become New Mexico Territory and John C. Fremont's similar role in California.

108   Reveron and Gavin, p. 3.

109   Ibid.

110   Quoted in Tim Reid, "Admiral William Fallon quits over Iran policy," *Times* Online, March 12, 2008, http://www.timesonline.co.uk/tol/news/world/us_and_americas/article3534102.ece.

111   Thomas P.M. Barnett, "The Man Between War and Peace," *Esquire*, April 23, 2008, http://www.esquire.com/features/fox-fallon. Subsequent quotations of Barnett are from this article.

112   Woodward, *The War Within*, supra, note 57.

113   Cited in ibid.

114   "Fallon: Iran Strike 'Strategic Mistake,' " Press TV, November 12, 2007, http://www.presstv.ir/detail.aspx?id=30790.

115   For a sympathetic portrait of Fallon, see Elaine Sciolino, "Push for New Direction Leads to Sudden Dead End for a 40-Year Naval Career," *New York Times*, May 31, 2008, p. 7.

116   The firing of Richardson as commander of the U.S. Pacific Fleet makes clear that even a private disagreement can cause a commander in chief to lose confidence in his subordinates. When President Roosevelt decided to move the U.S. Pacific Fleet from California to Pearl Harbor during the summer of 1940 in an effort to deter Japanese expansionism, Richardson objected, arguing that the move was provocative and could precipitate a war with Japan. The president fired him and replaced him with Rear Admiral Husband E. Kimmel. As Admiral Harold Stark, the chief of naval operations, wrote to Kimmel after the affair, "This, of course, is White House prerogative and responsibility, and believe me, it is used these days." Cited in Eric Larrabee, *Commander in Chief: Franklin Delano Roosevelt, His Lieutenants, and Their War* (New York: Harper and Row, 1987), p. 48. To his credit, Richardson kept his objections to FDR's decision private and went quietly into retirement.

117   Dana Priest, *The Mission: Waging War and Keeping Peace with America's Military* (New York: Norton, 2003).

118 Bryan Brown, "U.S. Special Operations Command; Meeting the Challenges of the 21st Century," *Joint Forces Quarterly* 40, 1st Quarter 2006, p. 39.

119 Public Law 99–661, 99th Congress, 2nd Session (November 14, 1986).

120 Stevenson, p. xii.

CHAPTER THREE

The Role of the Military and
Military Effectiveness

This chapter addresses two more of the fundamental questions of civil–military relations. First, what is the purpose of the US military? On what security problems should it focus its doctrine and budgets and how do such decisions affect civil–military relations? Second, what pattern of civil–military relations maximizes the effectiveness of the military instrument? The two questions are treated together because judgments concerning military effectiveness depend a great deal on what the military is expected to do.

In a book he wrote shortly after *The Soldier and the State*, Samuel Huntington observed that decisions concerning military issues take place in two realms, external and internal.

> The most distinctive, the most fascinating, and the most troubling aspect of military policy is its Janus-like quality. Indeed, military policy not only faces in two directions, it exists in two worlds. One is international politics, the world of the balance of power, wars and alliances, the subtle and brutal uses of forces and diplomacy. The principle currency of this world is actual and potential military strength, battalions, weapons, and warships. The other world is domestic politics, the world of interest groups, political parties, social classes, with their conflicting interests and goals. The currency here is the resources of society: men, money, material. Any major decision in military policy influences and is influenced by both worlds. A decision made in terms of one currency is always payable in the other. The rate of exchange, however, is usually in doubt.[1]

These two worlds give rise to what Huntington calls the *functional* imperative of the military—effectiveness in war making and deterrence—and the *societal* imperative—how well the professional military conforms to American liberal principles, especially having to do with the maintenance of civilian control.

Four years earlier he had written: "Previously the primary question was: what pattern of civil–military relations is most compatible with American liberal democratic values? Now this has been superseded by the more important issue: what pattern of civil–military relations will best maintain the security of the American nation."[2] This is the question of military effectiveness.

Despite Huntington's admonitions, the primary focus of those who have examined civil–military relations since the 1990s has been on the issue of civilian control of the military, which frequently obscures the question of military effectiveness. As noted in Chapter 2, civilian control is important, especially in a liberal society such as the United States, but it is only one part of the civil–military *problematique*. Military effectiveness is also important because failure on the battlefield threatens the very existence of the polity the military is sworn to defend. Of course, being effective depends a great deal on what the military is expected to do. Unfortunately, the often myopic focus on civilian control has obscured the impact of civil–military relations on the effectiveness of the military instrument.

In the introduction to a classic study of the effectiveness of various militaries from World War I through World War II, Allan Millett, Williamson Murray, and Ken Watman defined military effectiveness as "the process by which armed forces convert resources into fighting power. A fully effective military is one that derives maximum combat power from the resources physically and politically available. . . . Combat power is the ability to destroy the enemy while limiting the damage he can inflict in return."[3]

The authors argue that there are four different levels of military effectiveness: the *political*, the level of national policy and national objectives; the *strategic*, the level of applying the military instrument in pursuit of national goals; the *operational*, the level of campaigns—the integration of *operations* including movements and combat—necessary to achieve strategic goals within a theater of operation; and the *tactical*, the level of conducting battles as parts of a campaign. "Each category overlaps others, but each is characterized by different actions, procedures and goals." It is doubtful, they contend, that any military organization can be completely effective at all four levels simultaneously. And effectiveness at the tactical and operational levels may be offset by failures at the political and strategic levels. For instance, it is generally agreed that the German military was superior to its opponents at the tactical and operational levels during both of the World Wars, but that these advantages were undermined by serious shortcomings in strategy making and political failures.

This means, ironically, that military effectiveness is not always synonymous with "victory." Victory is an outcome, "not what a military organization does in battle. Victory is not a characteristic of an organization but rather a result of organizational activity. Judgments on effectiveness should retain some sense of proportional cost and organizational process."[4] Of course, military effectiveness may be the *necessary*, but not *sufficient*, cause of victory.

Millett, Murray, and Watman provide a number of criteria that identify the characteristics of military organizations at each level of effectiveness. At the *political* level, military organizations are effective when they can assure themselves a regular share of the national budget sufficient to meet their major needs; when they have access to the industrial and technological resources necessary to produce the equipment they need; and when they have access to manpower sufficient in quantity and quality.

At the *strategic* level, military organizations are effective to the extent that the achievement of the organization's strategic objectives secure the political goals of the state; to the extent that the risks associated with the desired strategic objectives are consistent with the stakes involved and the consequences of failure; to the extent that military leaders are able to influence political leaders concerning militarily logical national goals; to the extent that strategic goals and courses of action are consistent with force size and structure, as well as with the national industrial and technical base; to the extent that strategic objectives are integrated with those of allies; and to the extent that strategic plans and objectives match the strength of the military organization against the critical weaknesses of the enemy.

At the *operational* level, military organizations are effective to the extent that they possess a professional ethos that allows them to deal with operational problems realistically; to the extent that their operational methods are integrated so as to maximize strengths and minimize weaknesses; to the extent that they are "mobile and flexible," both intellectually (capable of adapting in the face of Clausewitz's "fog of uncertainty") and physically, at the operational level; to the extent to which their operational concepts and doctrines are consistent with available technology; to the extent that supporting activities are integrated with operational concepts and doctrine; to the extent that their operational concepts and doctrines are consistent with strategic objectives; and to the extent to which their operational concepts and doctrine pit their strengths against the adversary's weaknesses.

At the *tactical* level, military organizations are effective to the extent that their tactical approaches are consistent with their strategic objectives and operational capabilities; to the extent to which their tactical systems integrated all arms; to the extent to which their tactical conceptions emphasize surprise and rapid exploitation of opportunities; to the extent to which their tactical systems are consistent with their approaches to morale, unit cohesion, officer-NCO–enlisted relations, and training; and to the extent that their tactical systems are consistent with support capabilities.[5]

Although Millett, Murray, and Watman were addressing military effectiveness in the context of large-scale conventional warfare, their criteria would seem to be applicable across the entire "spectrum of conflict." However, this should not be interpreted to mean that there are universal standards with regard to the effectiveness of the military instrument since the effectiveness of the means (the military) can be judged only in relation to the ends those means are intended to serve. In other words, the effectiveness of a military organization is dependent on what it is expected to do.

For instance, no one doubts the excellence of the US military in the conduct of conventional operations. Indeed, the consensus seems to be that conventionally, the American military is the best in the world and will continue to be for the foreseeable future. But much of the post-9/11 civil–military debate has centered on the ability of the US military to conduct operations that are part of "small wars:" "irregular warfare," counterinsurgency (COIN), counter-terrorism, and stability operations. In response to the terrorist threat, natural disasters, and border security issues, some have also called for an increased military role in domestic affairs.

Military Effectiveness in the Context of Military Roles: The Constraints of Service Culture and Civil–Military Relations

With the end of the Cold War, each of the services struggled to redefine its respective "strategic concepts," which according to Samuel Huntington constitute "the fundamental element of a military service," the basic "statement of [its] role . . . or purpose in implementing national policy."[6] A clear strategic concept is critical to the ability of a service to organize and employ the resources that Congress allocates to it.

A service's strategic concept also largely determines that service's organizational culture. Some years ago, the late Carl Builder of Rand wrote a book called *The Masks of War*, in which he demonstrated the importance of the organizational cultures of the various military services in creating differing "personalities," identities, and behaviors. His point was that each service possesses a preferred way of fighting and that "the unique service identities . . . are likely to persist for a very long time."[7]

The organizational culture of a service in turn exerts a strong influence on civil–military relations, frequently constraining what civilian leaders can do and often constituting an obstacle to change and innovation. Despite the passage of the Goldwater-Nichols Department of Defense Reorganization

Act of 1986, which revised and simplified the military command structure, service cultures persist, with implications for civil–military relations. At issue here is the question broached at the outset of this chapter: what impact does a given pattern of civil–military relations have on the effectiveness of the military instrument? And who decides whether the military instrument is effective, the civilian policymakers or the military itself? What is the role of the military professional in providing judgments concerning military effectiveness?

An illuminating illustration of this phenomenon at work has been the recent attempt to institutionalize counterinsurgency doctrine within the US Army, a difficult task, given the Army's preference for fighting large-scale conventional war, despite the fact that throughout most of its existence, the conflicts in which it engaged were actually irregular wars. Most of this constabulary work was domestic, the Indian Wars representing the most important case. But the US Army also successfully executed constabulary operations in the Philippines after the Spanish–American War, which involved both nation building and counterinsurgency.[8]

As Morris Janowitz observed, such conflicts were "essentially . . . punitive action[s] . . . to bring people who lived outside the rules of law and order within the orbit of civilization . . . . There was little concern with the philosophy of organized violence to achieve a specific political settlement or a new balance of power. Military action was designed to facilitate total incorporation, or merely to 'punish' the lawless."[9]

Notwithstanding this history, the US Army's strategic concept and the resulting organizational culture have emphasized "big wars" over irregular warfare and constabulary missions. This preference owes much to the influence of Emory Upton, an innovative officer with an outstanding Civil War record.[10] An 1861 graduate of West Point, he was a brevet brigadier general by the end of the war and later became a protégé of William Tecumseh Sherman. When Sherman became general in chief of the army, he sent Upton around the world as a military observer.

Upton believed the constabulary focus was outdated. He was especially impressed by Prussian military policy, Prussia's ability to conduct war against the armies of other military powers, and its emphasis on professionalism. Certainly Prussia's overwhelming successes against Denmark, Austria, and France in the Wars of German Unification (1864–1871) made the Prussian army the new exemplar of military excellence in Europe.

Upon his return to the United States, Upton proposed a number of radical reforms, including abandoning the citizen-soldier model and relying instead on a professional soldiery, reducing civilian "interference" in military

affairs, and deemphasizing the constabulary operations that had characterized the Army's role during most of the nineteenth century—with the exception of the Mexican War and the Civil War—in favor of preparing for a
potential conflict with a foreign enemy.[11] Given the tenor of the time, all his
proposals were rejected. In ill health, Upton resigned from the Army and
in 1881, he committed suicide.

But the triumph of Progressivism, a political program that valued scien-
tific expertise and professionalism, the end of the army's constabulary duties
on the western frontier, and the problems associated with mobilizing for and
fighting the Spanish–American War made Upton's proposed reforms more
attractive, especially within the Army's officer corps. In 1904, Secretary of
War Elihu Root published Upton's *Military Policy of the United States*. While
many of Upton's more radical proposals remained unacceptable to republican America, the idea of reorienting the Army away from constabulary
duties toward defeat of other states' conventional forces caught on.

While the Army returned to constabulary duties after World War I,
Upton's spirit now permeated the professional Army culture. World War II
vindicated Upton's vision, and his view continued to govern US Army thinking throughout the Cold War. In Vietnam, especially under the command of
General William Westmoreland, it remained dominant and problematic.

Westmoreland's operational strategy emphasized the attrition of the
forces of the Peoples' Army of Vietnam (PAVN): it relied on multibattalion,
and sometimes even multidivision, sweeps to find and destroy the enemy
with superior fire power. Westmoreland emphasized the destruction of
enemy forces instead of seeking to control key areas in order to protect
the South Vietnamese population. Unfortunately, such search-and-destroy
operations were generally unsuccessful—the enemy could usually avoid
battle unless it was advantageous for him to accept it—and they were costly
to both the American soldiers who conducted them and the Vietnamese
civilians in the area. In addition, General Westmoreland ignored the insurgency and pushed the South Vietnamese aside.

When General Creighton Abrams replaced General Westmoreland as
overall US commander in Vietnam shortly after the Tet Offensive, he adopted
a new approach—one similar to that of the Marines—that came close to
winning the war. He emphasized protection of the South Vietnamese population by controlling key areas rather than the destruction of enemy forces
per se. He then concentrated on attacking the enemy's prepositioned supplies,
which disrupted North Vietnamese offensive timetables and bought more
time for Vietnamization, the plan under which the South Vietnamese would
assume a greater role as the Americans began to withdraw. Finally, rather

than ignoring the insurgency and pushing the South Vietnamese aside, as General Westmoreland had done, General Abrams followed a policy of "one war," integrating all aspects of the struggle against the Communists.[12]

But despite an improved security situation from 1969 to 1974, Congress ended support for South Vietnam, Saigon fell, and the Army, badly hurt by the war, concluded that it should avoid such "irregular" conflicts in the future. In the 1970s, the Army discarded the doctrine for small wars and counterinsurgency it had developed in Vietnam, choosing once again to focus on big wars.

It did so with a vengeance. Beginning in the late 1970s, the Army embraced the idea of the "operational level of war" as its central organizing concept. As Hew Strachan has observed, "the operational level of war appeals to armies: it functions in a politics-free zone and it puts primacy on professional skills."[13]

As an essay published by the US Army War College's Strategic Studies Institute puts it, the operational level of war has become an "alien" that "devoured" strategy.

> Rather than meeting its original purpose of contributing to the attainment of campaign objectives laid down by strategy, operational art—practiced as a "level of war"—assumed responsibility for campaign planning. This reduced political leadership to the role of "strategic sponsors," quite specifically widening the gap between politics and warfare. The result has been a well-demonstrated ability to win battles that have not always contributed to strategic success, producing "a way of battle rather than a way of war."
>
> The political leadership of a country cannot simply set objectives for a war, provide the requisite materiel, then stand back and await victory. Nor should the nation or its military be seduced by this prospect. Politicians should be involved in the minute-to-minute conduct of war; as Clausewitz reminds us, political considerations are "influential in the planning of war, of the campaign, and often even of the battle."[14]

And herein lies the problem for civil–military relations: the focus on the operational level of war creates a disjunction between operational excellence in combat on the one hand and *policy*, which determines the reasons for which a particular war is to be fought, on the other. It explains why, in the words of Colin Gray, there is "All too often . . . a black hole where American strategy ought to reside."[15]

But the reason civilian leaders cannot simply leave the military to its own devices during war is that war is an iterative process involving the interplay of active wills. What appears to be the case at the outset of the war may change as the war continues, modifying the relationship between political goals and military means. The fact remains that wars are not fought for their own purposes but to achieve policy goals set by the political leadership of the state.

The US military's focus on the nonpolitical operational level of war means that all too often the conduct of a war disconnected from the goals of the war. Among other things, the American concept of operational art and the operational level of war have perverted the original purpose of operational art—facilitating the dialog between tactics and strategy—while creating an independent layer of command that has usurped the role of strategy and thereby undermined the role of the civilian leadership in campaign planning.[16]

But Iraq and Afghanistan prove that we do not always get to fight the wars we want—and that the service branches must be able to function beyond the preferences dictated by their respective cultures. While the Army must continue to plan to fight conventional wars, it must also—given the likelihood that future adversaries will seek to avoid our conventional advantage—be able to fight irregular wars. General Petraeus's success in Iraq indicates that the Army has begun the necessary transformation. The question, of course, is whether the service will internalize these lessons, something Emory Upton's Army has resisted in the past.

Nonetheless, this is an important step. As Williamson Murray has observed, officers who are only prepared to fight wars in the operational framework of conventional military forces might very well offer faulty advice to the civilian leadership at the outset of war and then fail to adapt to the actual conditions arising from the conflict that they have been asked to fight. This seems to have been the case with Gen. Westmoreland in Vietnam, Gen. Abazaid and Gen. Casey in Iraq, and Gen. McKiernan in Afghanistan.[17]

There are indications that Secretary Gates has attempted to address the problem. Significantly, he has attempted to institutionalize a small-wars/counterinsurgency mind-set by placing the army's promotion policy in the hands of General Petraeus and those who share his view.[18] Of course, the budgets of the services—what they recognize as priorities—will also provide evidence concerning the degree to which they have adapted to new circumstances.

But even as the Army has begun to focus more of its attention on small wars, this shift has generated a heated debate concerning the shape of that service, the outcome of which may very well have important implications for civil–military relations.[19] On the one hand, the "crusaders"—advocates of the "Long War"—argue that Iraq and Afghanistan are characteristic of the protracted and ambiguous wars America will fight in the future. Accordingly, they say, the Army should be developing a force designed to fight the Long War on terrorism, primarily by preparing for "small wars" and insurgencies.[20]

On the other hand, the "traditionalists" or "conservatives" concede that although irregular warfare will occur more frequently in the future than interstate war, such conflicts do not threaten US strategic interests in the way large-scale conflicts do. They fear that the focus of the Long War school on small wars and insurgencies will transform the Army into a constabulary force, whose enhanced capability for conducting stability operations and nation building would be purchased at a high cost: the ability to conduct large-scale conventional war.[21]

The primary implication of this debate for American civil–military relations lies in the suggestion by some observers who claim that the goal of the traditionalists is to shape Army force structure in such a way that limits the ability of the executive branch to commit military forces to wars such as Iraq and Afghanistan.[22] This possibility raises a critical question: to what extent should military decisions constrain policy and strategy questions that lie within the purview of civilian authorities? In other words, can military doctrine and force structure be left strictly to the military?

The United States has made force structure choices in the past that have hamstrung the country's ability to respond to a broad range of threats and contingencies. A case in point illustrating the danger of choosing one military planning strategy to the exclusion of the other is the Eisenhower administration's "New Look" defense policy of the 1950s. The New Look, which made long-range nuclear air power the centerpiece of force structure, resulted in severe strategic inflexibility: the United States lacked the ability to respond to threats at the lower end of the spectrum of conflict. As a result, adversaries developed asymmetric responses to America's dominant nuclear capability—"peoples' wars" and "wars of national liberation." The deficiencies in the New Look strategy led to its replacement in the 1960s by the strategy of "flexible response," which required a capability to address threats from nuclear war to conventional war and insurgencies, such as the one in Vietnam.

The shortcomings of the New Look strategy can be laid at the feet of an elected president; the resulting strategic inflexibility was his responsibility. But when a military service makes force structure decisions that constrain the national leadership, this becomes an issue of civil–military relations. This is what some argue that the Army did after Vietnam.

Badly bruised by that conflict, the US Army concluded that it should avoid irregular conflict in the future and focus on "real" wars: large-scale conventional combat. Thus, in the 1970s, the Army discarded the doctrine for small wars and counterinsurgency that it had reluctantly developed for Vietnam. Class time devoted to counterinsurgency at the US Army Command and General Staff College at Fort Leavenworth was reduced substantially. Later, the Army's focus on real wars led its leadership to resist committing Army units to "military operations other than war" during the post–Cold War era.

More significantly, Gen. Creighton Abrams, Army chief of staff from 1972 to 1974, made a far-reaching force structure change during his tenure.[23] On the one hand, his plan to "round out" every active-duty division with one National Guard brigade (of three brigades per division) allowed the Army to field 16 divisions rather than 13½. On the other hand, such a move had the practical effect of seriously limiting the ability of the president to commit the Army to a conflict; to do so, it would require the civilian authorities to mobilize the National Guard and reserves, something that President Lyndon Johnson did not do during the Vietnam War. In addition to using National Guard brigades to round out active-duty Army divisions, shifting of most of the Army's combat service support function to the reserve component meant that even the smallest commitment of Army units during a contingency would require a call-up of reserves.

Did Abrams take this step purposely to limit the ability of future presidents to commit the Army to war? Future chairman of the Joint Chiefs of Staff (JCS) during the Reagan administration, Gen. John Vessey, thought so. He reported that he heard Abrams say on many occasions that "they're not taking us to war again without calling up the reserves." Abrams' biographer records Vessey's responses to his queries on the topic:

> Was part of the thinking in integrating the reserves so deeply into the active force structure that we were making it very difficult, if not impossible for the president to deploy any significant force without calling up the reserves? "That's it, with malice aforethought," said Vessey, "the whole exercise . . . part and parcel of [Abram's restructuring plan] was that you couldn't go to war without calling up the reserves."[24]

This view is supported by another Army historian who quotes Abrams as insisting that the "Army should not go to war without the involvement and tacit approval of the American people."[25]

Former secretary of defense James Schlesinger was more circumspect but agreed in principle: "There is no question but that Abrams was deliberately integrating reserve and active forces in that manner," Schlesinger observed. Asked by Abrams' biographer, if Abrams' actions constituted a "forcing function" that limited the executive's freedom of action, Schlesinger replied, "that would not really be like [Abrams]," he said. "He had the view that the military must defer to civilians, even to an extraordinary degree. I speculate that the military sought to fix the incentives so that the civilians would act appropriately."[26]

Some observers disagree that the goal of the so-called Abrams Doctrine was to create "an extra-constitutional tripwire on the presidential use of military power." They argue that the primary purpose of Abrams' force structure plan for the Army was to find an affordable way to provide 16 divisions, the minimum number of divisions that Army planners believed was necessary in the event of a war with the Warsaw Pact. Without the round-out concept, a 16-division Army was simply not fiscally possible. These writers contend that the Abrams Doctrine flowed logically from the Total Force concept established by President Richard Nixon's secretary of defense, Melvin Laird, and that there was no intent to limit the ability of the president to commit forces to a conflict.[27]

As is the case with most interpretations of historical events, there is contentious debate concerning Abrams' motives in integrating active and reserve forces. But the civil–military implications are clear. Constraints on executive power may very well be a good and necessary thing, but it is not up to the Army—or any other uniformed military service—to decide on what these constraints should be. If, in the current debate, the traditionalists are indeed seeking to constrain the executive by deemphasizing the capabilities necessary for waging small wars in order to limit the use of US military power, they are wrong to do so.

By law, the services are responsible for organizing, training, and equipping their units and for developing doctrine, i.e., determining how to fight. But the services owe civilian leaders an instrument that is capable of advancing US interests against threats that may occur across the entire spectrum of conflict. Healthy civil–military relations make such an instrument possible.

The Use of the Military in Domestic Affairs

The issue of COIN vs. a conventional war focus is not the only debate over the use of the military after 9/11. Terrorist attacks and Hurricane Katrina, along with the subsequent failure of local, state, and federal agencies to react in a timely manner, have led some to call for an expansion of the military's role in domestic affairs, including law enforcement. "The question raised by the Katrina fiasco," Daniel Henninger wrote in the *Wall Street Journal*, "is whether the threat from madmen and nature is now sufficiently huge in its potential horror and unacceptable loss that we should modify existing jurisdictional authority to give the Pentagon functional first-responder status."[28]

In the wake of Katrina, President Bush agreed. In a national address in September of 2005, President Bush asked Congress to consider a larger role for US armed forces in responding to natural disasters. "Clearly, in the case of a terrorist attack, that would be the case, but is there a natural disaster—of a certain size—that would then enable the Defense Department to become the lead agency in coordinating and leading the response effort. That's going to be a very important consideration for Congress to think about." He continued: "It is now clear that a challenge on this scale requires greater federal authority and a broader role for the armed forces—the institution of our government most capable of massive logistical operations on a moment's notice."[29]

Some in Congress took the same tack. Even before the president's speech, Republican Sen. John Warner, then- chairman of the Senate Armed Services Committee, wrote a letter to then-Defense Secretary Rumsfeld saying that his committee would be looking into "the entire legal framework governing a President's power to use the regular armed forces to restore public order in . . . a large-scale, protracted emergency." He asked the secretary of defense to take the issue under consideration. In response, Secretary Rumsfeld informed Sen. Warner that the Pentagon was reviewing pertinent laws, including the 1878 Posse Comitatus Act, to determine whether revisions that would give the military a greater role during major domestic disasters are needed.[30]

On the one hand, the call for increasing the military's role in domestic affairs is understandable. It is capable of responding to a massive disaster in ways that local, state, and other federal agencies most often can't. But those who demand a greater domestic role for the military must consider the impact of such a step on healthy civil–military relations in the United States. In addition, they must also take account of the fear, traditionally expressed by officers, that involving the military in domestic tasks will undermine the war-fighting capabilities of their units and cause their "fighting spirit" to decline.

Nearly two decades ago, an Air Force staff judge advocate officer painted a disturbing picture of future civil–military relations if the military became involved in domestic affairs. Charles Dunlap described his article,

"The Origins of the Military Coup of 2012" published in the professional journal of the US Army, as a "darkly imagined excursion into the future."[31] The article takes the form of a letter from an officer awaiting execution for opposing the military coup that has taken place in the United States. The letter argues that the coup was the result of trends identifiable as early as 1992, including the massive diversion of military forces to civilian uses.

Dunlap's doomed officer opines that in the 1990s, Americans became disillusioned with the apparent inability of elected government to solve the nation's dilemmas. "We were looking for someone or something that could produce workable answers. The one institution of government in which the people retained faith was the military." Buoyed by the military's obvious competence in the First Gulf War, the public increasingly turned to it for solutions to the country's problems. Americans called for an acceleration of trends begun in the 1980s: tasking the military with a variety of new, nontraditional missions and vastly escalating its commitment to formerly ancillary duties.

> Though not obvious at the time, the cumulative effect of these new responsibilities was to incorporate the military into the political process to an unprecedented degree. These additional assignments also had the perverse effect of diverting focus and resources from the military's central mission of combat training and warfighting.

What Dunlap describes in this article is the "salami slice" method of overthrowing democratic government: instead of a coup d'état that seizes the salami of government all at once, power is taken one slice at a time. The military is asked to do more and more in the domestic arena, and it concludes that it might as well run the government as a whole. This coup is the result of an accretion of power by the military. But in the end, the result is the same: a military good at maintaining itself in power, but unable to defeat a foreign enemy.

Critics of greater involvement by the military in domestic affairs contend that all of these tensions will be exacerbated if the statutes and regulations are changed to permit increased military participation in domestic affairs. Even if we do not reach the point described by Dunlap, it almost is given that the military will be politicized to a dangerous extent. Indeed, the main reason that Congress passed the Posse Comitatus Act in 1878 was concern that the Army was becoming too involved in politics.

The undeniable fact is that most commentators do not understand the Posse Comitatus Act. It does not constitute a bar to the use of the military in domestic affairs. It does, however, make sure that such use is authorized only by the highest constitutional authority: Congress and the president.

Contrary to what many Americans believe, the Constitution itself does not prohibit the use of the military in domestic affairs. Indeed, the US military has intervened in domestic affairs some 167 times since the founding of the Republic. In the Anglo-American tradition, the first line of defense in enforcing the law was the *posse comitatus*, literally "the power of the county," understood to be the people at large who constituted the constabulary of the shire. When order was threatened, the "shire-reeve" or sheriff would raise the "hue and cry" and all citizens who heard it were bound to render assistance in apprehending a criminal or maintaining order. Thus, the sheriff in the American west would "raise a posse" to capture a lawbreaker.

If the *posse comitatus* was not able to maintain order, the force of first resort was the militia of the various states, the precursor of today's National Guard. In 1792, Congress passed two laws that permitted implementation of Congress's constitutional power "to provide for calling forth the militia to execute the laws of the union, suppress insurrections and repel invasions," the Militia Act and the "Calling Forth" Act, which gave the president limited authority to employ the militia in the event of domestic emergencies. In 1807, at the behest of President Thomas Jefferson, who was troubled by his inability to use the regular Army as well as the militia to deal with the Burr Conspiracy of 1806–07, Congress also declared the Army to be an enforcer of federal laws, not only as a separate force, but as a part of the *posse comitatus*.[32]

Accordingly, troops were often used in the antebellum period to enforce the fugitive slave laws and suppress domestic violence. The Fugitive Slave Act of 1850 permitted federal marshals to call on the *posse comitatus* to aid in returning a slave to his owner, and in 1854, Franklin Pierce's Attorney General, Caleb Cushing, issued an opinion that included the Army in the *posse comitatus*, writing that

A marshal of the United States, when opposed in the execution of his duty, by unlawful combinations, has authority to summon the entire able-bodied force of his precinct, as a posse comitatus. The authority comprehends not only bystanders and other citizens generally, but any and all organized armed forces, whether militia of the states, or officers, soldiers, sailors, and marines of the United States.

Thus, in April 1851, federal marshals in Boston arrested Thomas Sims, a 17-year-old slave who had escaped from Georgia. He was held in a courthouse guarded by police and soldiers for 9 days while his case was argued before a federal commissioner. When the commissioner found for Sims's owner, 300 armed deputies and soldiers took him from the courthouse before dawn and marched him to the Boston Navy yard where another 250 soldiers waited to place him aboard a ship that would carry him back into bondage.[33]

In May of 1854, a deputy marshal arrested Anthony Burns, an escaped Virginia slave, also in Boston. While a federal commissioner decided Burns's fate, abolitionists tried to rescue him. President Franklin Pierce sent federal troops to Boston to keep the peace, admonishing the district attorney to "incur any expense to insure the execution of the law."[34] Troops were also used to suppress domestic violence between pro- and antislavery factions in "Bloody Kansas." Soldiers and Marines participated in the capture of John Brown at Harpers Ferry in 1859.

After the Civil War, the US Army was involved in supporting the Reconstruction governments in the southern states, and it was the Army's role in preventing the intimidation of black voters and Republicans at southern polling places that led to the passage of the Posse Comitatus Act. In the election of 1876, President Ulysses S. Grant deployed Army units as a *posse comitatus* in support of federal marshals maintaining order at the polls. In that election, Rutherford B. Hayes defeated Samuel Tilden with the disputed electoral votes of South Carolina, Louisiana, and Florida. Southerners claimed that the Army had been misused to "rig" the election.

While the Posse Comitatus Act is usually portrayed as the triumph of the Democratic Party in ending Reconstruction, the Army welcomed the legislation. The use of soldiers as a posse removed them from their own chain of command and placed them in the uncomfortable position of taking orders from local authorities who had an interest in the disputes that provoked the unrest in the first place. As a result, many officers came to believe that the involvement of the Army in domestic policing was corrupting the institution.

And this is the crux of the issue. The Posse Comitatus Act (Section 1385, Title 18 U.S.C.) prohibits the use of the military to aid civil authorities in enforcing the law or suppressing civil disturbances *except in cases and under circumstances expressly authorized by the Constitution or Act of Congress*. As the foremost authority on the use of the military in domestic affairs has written:

> All that [the Posse Comitatus Act] really did *was to repeal a doctrine whose only substantial foundation was an opinion by an attorney general [Caleb Cushing], and one that had never been tested in the courts. The president's*

power to use both regulars and militia remained undisturbed by the Posse Comitatus Act . . . . But the Posse Comitatus Act did mean that troops could not be used on any lesser authority than that of the president and he must issue a "cease and desist" proclamation before he did so. Commanders in the field would no longer have any discretion but must wait for orders from Washington (italics added).[35]

Those who seek to expand the military's role in domestic affairs need to ask themselves if they really want to return to the days when "lesser authority" than the president could use the military for domestic purposes. The issue here is not the Posse Comitatus Act but the quality of American civil–military relations and a healthy military establishment.

Patterns of Civil–Military Relations and the Making of Strategy

Richard Kohn has called into question the effectiveness of the American military in the conduct of operations other than those associated with large-scale conventional war. "Nearly twenty years after the end of the Cold War, the American military, financed by more money than the entire rest of the world spends on its armed forces, failed to defeat insurgencies or fully suppress sectarian civil wars in two crucial countries, each with less than a tenth of the US population, after overthrowing those nations' governments in a matter of weeks."[36]

He attributes this lack of effectiveness to a decline in the military's professional competence with regard to strategic planning. "In effect, in the most important area of professional expertise—the connecting of war to policy, of operations to achieving the objectives of the nation—the American military has been found wanting. The excellence of the American military in operations, logistics, tactics, weaponry, and battle has been manifest for a generation or more. Not so with strategy."[37]

This phenomenon manifests itself, he argues, in the recent failure to adapt to a changing security environment in which the challenges to global stability are "less from massed armies than from terrorism; economic and particularly financial instability; failed states; resource scarcity (particularly oil and potable water); pandemic disease; climate change; and international crime in the form of piracy, smuggling, narcotics trafficking, and other forms of organized lawlessness. He observes that this decline in strategic competence has occurred during a time in which the US military exercises enormous influence in the making of foreign and national security policies.

The view that its leadership has failed to prepare the US military for the sorts of conflicts it faces today is not limited to critics outside of the military establishment. In a blistering critique of US Army leadership in the April 2007 issue of *Armed Forces Journal*, an active-duty US Army lieutenant colonel, Paul Yingling, wrote:

> For the second time in a generation, the United States faces the prospect of defeat at the hands of an insurgency. In April 1975, the U.S. fled the Republic of Vietnam, abandoning our allies to their fate at the hands of North Vietnamese communists. In 2007, Iraq's grave and deteriorating condition offers diminishing hope for an American victory and portends risk of an even wider and more destructive regional war.
>
> These debacles are not attributable to individual failures, but rather to a crisis in an entire institution: America's general officer corps. America's generals have repeated the mistakes of Vietnam in Iraq. First, throughout the 1990s our generals failed to envision the conditions of future combat and prepare their forces accordingly. Second, America's generals failed to estimate correctly both the means and the ways necessary to achieve the aims of policy prior to beginning the war in Iraq. Finally, America's generals did not provide Congress and the public with an accurate assessment of the conflict in Iraq.[38]

A centerpiece of the renegotiation of the civil–military bargain since 9/11 has been the question of what the American public believes its military should be doing, how well it is doing what it is supposed to do, and what pattern of civil–military relations will best ensure that the military establishment can succeed.

Patterns of Civil–Military Relations and Military Effectiveness

As noted in Chapter 1, Samuel Huntington proposed one solution to ensure military effectiveness while avoiding a military threat to the United States. His solution was a mechanism for creating and maintaining a professional, apolitical military establishment, which would focus on defending the United States but avoid threatening civilian control.[39] Huntington called this mechanism "objective control" of the military. Eliot Cohen has called this Huntingtonian pattern the "normal" theory of civil–military relations.[40]

For Huntington, the key to both civilian control and military effectiveness was "professionalism." This is especially true in the case of military effectiveness. Interpreting Clausewitz, Huntington writes that "the fact that war has its own grammar requires that the military professionals be permitted to develop their expertise at this grammar without extraneous influence . . . The inherent quality of a military body can only be evaluated in terms of independent military standards."[41] Elsewhere he writes that "the particular skill of the military officer is universal in the sense that its essence is not affected by changes in time or location."[42]

But as Suzanne Nielsen and others have shown, Huntington's claim that professionalism is an adequate indicator of effectiveness is problematic. First, the claim that there is a set of independent military standards valid for any time and place seems counterintuitive. The characteristics of an effective military force depend on many factors that differ from case to case. Ultimately, the effectiveness of the military instrument can be evaluated only in relation to the political ends that the military means are meant to serve.[43]

Second, the historical record illustrates that Huntington's claim that the pattern of civil–military relations that produces the most effective military is the one that impinges the least on an autonomous military realm is false. For instance, as noted in Chapter 2, Eliot Cohen has provided a number of historical cases illustrating that civilian leaders in liberal democracies at war have often contributed to victory by trespassing on the military's "turf."[44] And Chapter 2 also demonstrated that the mistakes in Iraq, usually attributed to the civilian leadership of the Bush administration, could just as easily be ascribed to the uniformed military.

The historical record suggests that military organizations tend to stagnate during peacetime without civilian involvement, often failing to adapt to changing situations. The result is that they are ill-suited to meet the requirements established by the policy and grand strategy of the state when called upon to do so.[45] Resistance to change is often a function of organizational culture.

Donald Rumsfeld and Strategic Assessment for the Iraq War

Part of ensuring military effectiveness is good strategic assessment. The quality of strategic assessment is strongly influenced by the pattern of civil–military relations that prevails in the state. As discussed in Chapter 1, Risa Brooks has argued that the quality of strategic assessment is affected by the interaction of two variables: the intensity of civilian and military preferences; and the balance of civil–military power.

This interaction affects four sets of institutional processes that constitute the element of strategic assessment. As noted in Chapter 1, the first is the routine for information sharing. The second is strategic coordination regarding the assessment of strategic alternatives, risk and cost, and the integration of political and military policies and strategies. The third is the military's structural competence in conducting sound net assessment. The fourth is the authorization process for approving or vetoing political-military actions.[46]

Brooks' model can effectively be applied to civil–military relations after 9/11. For instance, it is clear that one of the major shortcomings of US strategic assessment during the Iraq War was the failure to plan adequately for the postconflict phase. Explanations for that failure frequently focus on the abrasive style of Secretary of Defense Rumsfeld[47] or the "tunnel vision" of the Bush administration and its failure to abandon flawed assumptions about the postwar environment in Iraq or to entertain alternative views.[48]

In contrast, Brooks argues that the real problem was a pattern of civil–military relations that predated the Iraq War, exacerbated by Rumsfeld's attempt to "transform" the US military in the face of strenuous opposition, especially from the Army.

In terms of the civil–military balance of power after 9/11, the civilian side was dominant. The military lacked a leader with the stature of Colin Powell. No one on the military side of the civil–military divide possessed the standing to challenge civilian leadership, especially a domineering secretary of defense such as Rumsfeld.

At the same time, the intensity of preference divergence was high. It did not begin that way because the military believed that George Bush would be more supportive of its preferences than Al Gore. After all, Americans in general and the officer corps in particular had perceived the Democratic Party as "soft" on national security since Vietnam. In Brooks' model, the combination of political dominance and high preference divergence results in only "fair" strategic assessment, primarily because oversight mechanisms weaken strategic coordination.[49]

The source of the preference divergence was how to "reform" the military, a high priority for President Bush. Indeed, military transformation was a cornerstone of his 2000 presidential campaign. While the Army was most affected, the other services were also unhappy with the prospect of losing programs that they truly believed were required by their respective strategic concepts.

The Navy believed its aircraft carriers might be on the chopping block. The Air Force was concerned lest it lose its next-generation fighter aircraft, the F-22. But the disagreements were most profound between Rumsfeld, who took his marching orders on transformation from the president's policy directives, and the Army. This dispute between the secretary and the

Army would have a negative impact on civil–military relations in general and strategic assessment in particular during the Iraq War.

In many respects, Rumsfeld simply reflected the conventional wisdom among defense analysts in the 1990s and early 2000s, who held that the three components of a transformed US military would comprise the following: (1) intelligence, surveillance, and reconnaissance (ISR) technologies; (2) advanced command, control, communications, and computer (C4) systems; and (3) precision strike munitions.[50] Since a transformed military would substitute information, speed, and flexibility of action for mass on the battlefield, many believed that large formations of ground troops were at best obsolescent and at worst obsolete.

Accordingly, because C4ISR and long-range precision strike would enable future operations, the programs that provided these capabilities became known as "high demand/low density" (HD/LD), which meant that there were not enough of these systems available to meet user demand in multiple theaters. The conventional wisdom held that HD/LD programs should be funded and that the bill-payer should be forces and systems perceived to be "low demand/high density", such as the conventional heavy formations of the US Army. Unfortunately, as the war in Iraq was to demonstrate, "Rumsfeld's view of transformation was 'profoundly self-referential,' concerned with what we could do, not what the enemy could."[51]

Despite being perceived, along with the Marine Corps, as the least technological of the services, the Army had, in fact, adopted many aspects of the "revolution in military affairs". Accordingly, the Army was not opposed to transformation. On the contrary, Gen. Eric Shinseki, the Chief of Staff of the Army, laid out a plan designed to shift the service away from its Cold War orientation toward the creation of a more strategically mobile, expeditionary force.

William Cohen, Bill Clinton's secretary of defense, had selected Gen. Shinseki as Army chief of staff, and when the latter assumed his post in 1999, Secretary Cohen charged him with the task of modernizing the service in order to make it more rapidly deployable to trouble spots around the globe. The task was not easy because although Cohen had given Shinseki his marching orders, he had not committed any additional resources to help achieve transformation. Nonetheless, Shinseki was able to rearrange some internal Army priorities and to convince Congress to add some funds to the service budget for transformation.[52] Nonetheless, Shinseki's vision of transforming the Army did not match that of Rumsfeld.

Rumsfeld's vision, centering on high-tech systems, a network-centric view of war, information age intelligence, and ballistic missile defense, became manifest during the 2001 Quadrennial Defense Review process.

As Rumsfeld made clear in congressional testimony in June 2001, the role of the Army would play a limited role in this vision.[53]

Shinseki resisted Rumsfeld's plan to cut up to four divisions. Although the service prevailed (it lost two divisions), the exercise convinced Rumsfeld that the Army was hidebound, resistant to change, and conservative in its approach to war.[54] It was also the case, as observed in Chapter 2, that Rumsfeld believed civilian control of the military had atrophied during the Clinton administration. Rumsfeld interpreted Shinseki's resistance to his transformation approach as a vindication of his view.[55]

After the attacks of 9/11, President Bush ordered an offensive in that country in retaliation against al Qaeda and the Taliban. Rumsfeld rejected the plan proposed by US Central Command (CENTCOM) calling for a large joint force that would have taken months to assemble and deploy. Many believed that Rumsfeld's vision of transformation had been validated when a light force of US Special Operations Forces (SOF) and airpower in concert with allied Afghan fighters quickly defeated the Taliban. More than ever, it appeared that light forces, precision weapons, and a concept of warfighting called "effects-based operations" had displaced ponderous, heavy land formations as the force of choice in the future.

Accordingly, any program that did not fit Rumsfeld's vision was expendable. One that did not was the Army's Crusader artillery program. Shinseki himself had been critical of earlier versions of the Crusader; in order to avoid the risk that the program would be cancelled, he had directed that its weight be drastically reduced in order to make it more deployable. This was done and the weight dropped from 100 tons to 40.

Unfortunately, for the secretary of defense, the chief of staff of the Army, and US civil–military relations in general, the Crusader episode further poisoned relations between Rumsfeld and the Army. This would have implications for the Iraq War. Although the civil–military power balance was clearly dominated by Rumsfeld, he faced a disaffected military at odds with his views and priorities.

In applying Brooks' framework for strategic assessment to the Iraq case, the one process that was clearly defined and unambiguous was that for authorization. This was largely because Rumsfeld himself retained decision-making authority, setting the agenda and approving or disapproving military policy and action. Indeed, he reclaimed prerogatives that had typically been delegated to the military, including—most controversially— approving the pace and design of force deployments to Kuwait and Iraq. Although his decisions can be criticized, the fact is that they were well within his authority and had the advantage of imposing a clearly defined process of authorization, ensuring that clear decisions could be made.

Information sharing was also not necessarily problematic because Rumsfeld was able to monitor and oversee the military. The issue was not poor information sharing, but the selective nature of the information he received or filtered. The authorization and information sharing processes undermined the comprehensiveness of debate and made it likely that alternative perspectives were not brought to bear.[56]

Thus, Rumsfeld relied primarily on military officers who shared his views—the chairman and vice chairman of the JCS and the commander of CENTCOM—and marginalized others who did not, including the service chiefs who also comprised the corporate body of the JCS.[57] Although not in the chain of command, which since Goldwater-Nichols runs from the combatant commanders to the secretary of defense to the president, the service chiefs/JCS could have played an important consultative role.

Rumsfeld also worked to replace those who disagreed with him with individuals who did. This included interviewing two- and three-star officers instead of just those with four stars. Contrary to popular opinion, Rumsfeld never "fired" Shinseki, who completed two full two-year terms as chief of staff of the Army. However, 14 months before Shinseki's second term as chief of staff was up, "leaks" indicated that Rumsfeld intended to appoint the Army vice-chief of staff, Gen. John Keane, to succeed Shinseki. Although Keane did not in fact replace him, the leak essentially marginalized Shinseki.

The individual who did replace Shinseki, Gen. Peter Schoomaker, was a special operator whose views were more in line with those of Rumsfeld than other generals with conventional backgrounds. In addition, Schoomaker was pulled out of retirement to replace Shinseki, signaling to active-duty officers that there were no serving three- or four-star generals acceptable to Rumsfeld.

While appointing individuals with views more in line with those of the leader is a powerful means of effecting change within an organization, Rumsfeld's actions undermined open debate and eliminated consideration of alternative views. In sum, writes Brooks:

> . . . processes for strategic coordination were seriously troubled in the Department of Defense in 2002 and early 2003. With the exception of Tommy Franks and those few individuals with whom Rumsfeld saw eye to eye, the military and civilians were alienated and not fully engaging in the evaluative processes. The oversight methods to which Rumsfeld

resorted in order to protect the corporate interests had compromised the overall quality of strategic assessment at the civil–military apex.[58]

The process of strategic assessment in 2002–2003 had a profound impact on planning for the Iraq War.

On the positive side, it provided an operational approach clearly superior to earlier alternatives offered by both CENTCOM and the Office of the Secretary of Defense (OSD). The contingency plan that formed the basis of the discussion, OPLAN 1003, reflected the approach that had been employed during the 1991 Gulf War. It called for a force of about 330,000 and envisioned a lengthy air operation prior to a ground attack. Rumsfeld, on the contrary, envisioned a "bolt from the blue," a surprise rush to Baghdad with a force of 50,000–75,000 troops. The authorization process was iterative and yielded a compromise for of about 200,000 to enable a simultaneous air-ground campaign integrating SOF. The consensus that Rumsfeld achieved was aided by the fact that he was able to vet it only among individuals who shared his views, avoiding bureaucratic resistance by the services who had their own views about how to fight.

However, the pathological aspects of the strategic assessment far outweighed the positive. First, Rumsfeld was not provided with a range of opinion regarding what might occur during the postconflict phase. Outside views were not solicited and the joint chiefs in particular were not involved in the consultation process. As a number of writers have observed, the JCS had little role in the war-planning process. "The JCS had been pushed to the margins of war planning" and "were kept at arm's length from the planning process."[59]

In addition, the process and its clear indication that "obstruction" would not be tolerated seem to have encouraged self-censorship on the part of the senior military leadership. Given the personal and organizational costs associated with offering alternative view, military leaders did not develop the full logic of those views and the supporting evidence. This had the effect of discouraging open debate. In the words of retired Marine Lt. Gen. Paul Van Riper, such an environment means that "you don't get the sort of push back you need to have the dialogue, the understanding, the debate out of which you will synthesize better ideas."[60]

But some of this self-censorship was cultural. In the words of an Army general anonymously quoted in The New York Times Magazine, "'If you pushed back at Rumsfeld, he accepted it.' But, he added, senior military leaders are trained not to push back too hard at civilian authority. So instead they grew silent, disgruntled and demoralized. The Pentagon was veering toward the dysfunctional."[61]

As Brooks observes, a second problem with the war planning for Iraq followed from the first. By excluding from the process those who would have been most concerned with postwar stability, Rumsfeld missed an opportunity to influence those who were not. This included most of the Army leadership, which is responsible for postwar stabilization but is predisposed by its organizational culture to view such tasks as a distraction from its real task: warfighting.

Accordingly, Army culture played a role in this failure as well. As argued above, Army doctrine emphasized the operational level of war and conventional, state-on-state conflict. In addition, that service, like the US military as a whole, had embraced the tenets of the Weinberger Doctrine, with its emphasis on clear objectives, decisive force, and an exit strategy. The Army believed that its doctrine had been vindicated during the first Gulf War.

As we have also seen, the Army did everything in its power to avoid engaging in such operations as those in the Balkans during the Clinton years. In the Army's view, its purpose was warfighting and not peacekeeping or "nation building." In the 1970s, the Army had abandoned the study of counterinsurgency based in part on the belief that such doctrine had led to its involvement in Vietnam. Thus, it was culturally averse to focusing on such tasks as postconflict stability operations. Accordingly, Franks "was inclined to think of nation-consolidating efforts as an afterthought."[62]

Had the civilians in OSD consulted with a broader circle including those might have stressed the importance of postconflict stability, they might have applied pressure on Franks to plan for that phase. But the "prevailing assumption of the civilians—sustained by the failure to engage those who did have alternative perspectives about the stabilization phase of the war—suggested there would be no postwar security problem, so why push Franks to plan for it?"[63]

Finally, the structural pattern of civil–military relations and the poor consultative environment turned the Iraq War into a bureaucratic battle between Rumsfeld and his generals. Because he had shut off other ways of convincing the military leadership to accept his vision of transformation, Rumsfeld used Iraq as a laboratory to validate his approach. Therefore, he was personally and bureaucratically invested in fighting the war in a particular way in order to "prove" that his vision of transformation was correct.

Part of this vision involved a modification of the Weinberger Doctrine, a principle embraced by the uniformed military. For instance, he did not jettison the requirement for "decisive force" to achieve clear objectives, but he adapted that principle to mean what came to be known as "shock and awe," an application of precision airpower that was less dependent on ground forces.

His vision of how to fight the war also emphasized something that, although not explicitly part of the Weinberger Doctrine, was nonetheless implied—the idea of an "exit strategy." The problem here is, of course, that if strategic planners are thinking about an exit strategy as they are planning for the war, they are not thinking about how to convert military success into political success. This view reinforced the military's own preferences—the military had long internalized the idea of an exit strategy—and contributed in large part to the failure to think about the need for postconflict planning. And of course, the need for postwar planning conflicted with Rumsfeld's desire to use Iraq as a showcase for his view of transformation. As former Secretary of the Army Thomas White put it, "a stability operation [requires] boots on the ground and is very untransformational." Thus, Rumsfeld was disinclined to invest in an analysis of a major postwar stabilization effort because doing so "went against the whole thrust of Rumsfeld's Defense Department, in which the overriding goal was military transformation."[64]

These three procedural problems had a significant negative impact on the US operational plan for Iraq. First, the plan for postwar stability operations was underdeveloped. Second, focusing on major combat operations (MCOs) and treating postwar planning as an afterthought meant that not enough troops were available for stability operations. Third, Rumsfeld cut off the flow of follow-on forces to the theater. These additional troops could have mitigated, at least to some extent, the severe problems that occurred after the close of MCOs.

Thus, while CENTCOM spent 18 months, beginning in November 2001, on the war plan for MCOs, no real postwar plan was developed before February 2003 and not completed until April, a full month after the war began and even then it was only "power point deep."[65] Additionally, the plan that was developed was based on assumptions that conflicted with the MCO portion of the operational plan.

For instance, it was assumed that security could be quickly turned over to the Iraqi army and police. But the war plan called for destroying Iraqi command and control installations to facilitate the destruction of the Iraqi army and the overthrow of Saddam. However, command and control would be necessary for the Iraqis to restore and maintain order after the fall of Saddam. In addition, the disposition of troops necessary to win the war made it difficult to carry out security operations after the end of MCOs.

As Brooks observes, "herein lie the root of the problem with the planning activities: the combat plan and its relationship to postwar stabilization had not been conceptualized."[66]

The failure to adequately plan for postwar stability operations had an obvious impact on force levels. As noted earlier, the number of troops assembled at the beginning of MCOs was a compromise, but it was based on assumptions that ignored the postwar situation. Even though it was the case, as argued in Chapter 2, that Shinseki's assessment of the troop level was based on a flawed model, at least he was, unlike Rumsfeld and Franks, thinking about the postwar phase. Again, Rumsfeld assumed that after Saddam was toppled, anti-Saddam Iraqis would be able to quickly assume governing powers, permitting US forces to rapidly disengage. Under such a scenario, no increase in the force level was necessary.

The same reasoning applied to Rumsfeld's decision to cut off the flow of forces into Iraq after the end of MCOs. Although these forces presumably could have helped with postconflict stabilization, the additional forces would have undercut Rumsfeld's vision of transformation. Brooks attributes his decision to the dysfunctional civil–military strategic assessment process that prevailed at the time. "In the absence of constructive dialogue with the service chiefs, and especially the army, Rumsfeld sought to prove the merits of his fighting philosophy by showing—not just telling—the generals that one did not need a large, heavily armored force to prevail in Iraq. Allowing the reinforcements would have diluted the lesson . . . ."[67]

As predicted by Brooks' model, the poor strategic assessment that emerged from the dysfunctional pattern of civil–military relations prevailing in 2002–2003 had a negative impact in the theater of operations as well as harmful international implications. First, it contributed to failure because of deficient net assessment of military capabilities and available resources. Second, it made it difficult to anticipate political constraints governing the use of force in an interstate dispute. Third, it compromised the ability of US planners to integrate political goals and military strategy, contributing to a long and costly war. Finally, it led to a failure to recognize the differences between some Sunni insurgents and al Qaeda and to drive a wedge between them as was done in 2007 with the surge.

In essence, the failure to plan for the postwar environment created a power vacuum in Iraq following the fall of Baghdad, which sent signals to both Iraqi citizens and potential insurgents. Widespread disorder and looting created a strong sense of uncertainty and insecurity among the Iraqi population. In addition, the limited number of US forces required the Americans to establish priorities concerning what facilities to protect, and the choices led many Iraqis to question the motives of the United States. For example, US forces provided security for the Oil Ministry but not the National Museum of Iraq. Such choices did little to win Iraqi "hearts and minds." All these factors helped fuel the insurgency.

The combination of the absence of a fully developed plan for postwar stabilization and too few troops meant that the United States was unable to arrest the nascent insurgency, even as its existence was only dimly realized at first. As an intelligence officer observed, "first we did not have enough troops to conduct combat patrols in sufficient numbers to gain solid intelligence and paint a good picture of the enemy on the ground. Secondly, we needed more troops to act on the intelligence we generated. The insurgents took advantage of our limited numbers."[68]

While Brooks is correct to point to the dysfunctional pattern of civil–military relations stemming from Rumsfeld's focus on transforming the military as a cause of poor strategic assessment in 2002–2003, the preferences of the uniformed services contributed to the problems. As the insurgency metastasized, the US military had three alternatives: continue offensive operations along the lines of those in al Anbar Province after Fallujah; adopt a counterinsurgency approach; or emphasize the training of Iraqi troops in order to transition to Iraqi control of military operations. Gen. John Abizaid, commander of the US CENTCOM, and Gen. George Casey, commander of Multi-National Forces-Iraq (MNF-I), supported by Rumsfeld and Chairman of the Joint Chiefs, Gen. Richard Myers, chose the third.

But while transitioning to Iraqi control was a logical option for the long run, it did little to solve the proximate problem of the insurgency and the sectarian violence that it had generated. Based on the belief by many senior commanders, especially Abizaid, that US troops were an "antibody" to Iraqi culture, the Americans consolidated their forces on large "forward-operating bases" (FOBs), maintaining a presence only by means of motorized patrols that were particularly vulnerable to attacks by IEDs. This approach—sometimes called "commuter counterinsurgency"—ceded territory and population alike to the insurgents. Critics of this approach, such as then-Colonel H.R. McMaster, who commanded the 3rd Armored Cavalry Regiment during a successful 2005 counterinsurgency operation in Tel Afar, a city in northern Iraq, believed this approach was a mistake, arguing that security of the population is the fundamental basis of any successful counterinsurgency strategy.

The withdrawal of US forces to FOBs also contributed to a "kick-in-the-door" mentality among American troops when they did interact with Iraqis. This undermined US attempts to pacify the country and was completely at odds with an effective counterinsurgency approach. It was not until the appointment of Gen. David Petraeus as the commander of MNF-I in January 2007 and the implementation of a new counterinsurgency doctrine in conjunction with a troop "surge" that the situation in Iraq began to turn around.[69]

Robert Gates and Civil–Military Relations

In consonance with Brooks' model, civil–military relations improved when Robert Gates replaced Rumsfeld as secretary of defense. While the balance of power still remained firmly on the civilian side (during his tenure, Gates has fired two service secretaries and a service chief, encouraged the resignation of a combatant commander over a policy disagreement, declined to nominate the chairman and vice-chairman of the JCS for second terms, and overseen the replacement of two US commanders in Afghanistan), the intensity of preference differences between civilian and military leaders declined to a considerable degree. As Kori Schake has observed:

> Secretary Gates has returned the Defense Department to a well-managed large business. He has had a clear priority—the war in Iraq—that is both well understood within the Department and supported by its "board of directors," the Congress. He has focused on the strategic, allowing subordinates to implement his decisions, a welcome reprieve from the second-guessing to which his predecessor, Secretary Donald Rumsfeld, subjected every lieutenant colonel in the planning process. He respects the expertise of the military while insisting on his prerogative to set the Department's course . . . . Where Secretary Gates is not expert, he has sought outside counsel, forming the Schlesinger Commission on nuclear security and the Punaro Commission on reserve affairs, and using the Defense Policy Board to greater effect.[70]

This is not to say that there are no disagreements between the uniformed military and civilians. It is simply that those differences became less pronounced after Gates replaced Rumsfeld.

But the shift from civilian dominance/high preference divergence (Rumsfeld) to civilian dominance/low preference divergence (Gates) suggests that quality of strategic assessment has improved. In Brooks' model, the former pattern results in "fair" strategic assessment and the latter produces the "best" strategic assessment.

If the main source of high preference divergence during the Rumsfeld era was the former secretary's emphasis on transformation, even as the wars in

Iraq and Afghanistan were raging, Gates has made it clear that his focus is on winning the current unconventional wars rather than on transforming the military for future conventional ones. As he wrote in Foreign Affairs,

> All told, the 2008 National Defense Strategy concludes that although U.S. predominance in conventional warfare is not unchallenged, it is sustainable for the medium term given current trends. It is true that the United States would be hard-pressed to fight a major conventional ground war elsewhere on short notice, but as I have asked before, where on earth would we do that? U.S. air and sea forces have ample untapped striking power should the need arise to deter or punish aggression—whether on the Korean Peninsula, in the Persian Gulf, or across the Taiwan Strait. So although current strategy knowingly assumes some additional risk in this area, that risk is a prudent and manageable one.

Gates focuses on what have been called "hybrid" threats.

> When thinking about the range of threats, it is common to divide the "high end" from the "low end," the conventional from the irregular, armored divisions on one side, guerrillas toting AK-47s on the other. In reality, as the political scientist Colin Gray has noted, the categories of warfare are blurring and no longer fit into neat, tidy boxes. One can expect to see more tools and tactics of destruction—from the sophisticated to the simple—being employed simultaneously in hybrid and more complex forms of warfare.
>
> Russia's relatively crude—although brutally effective—conventional offensive in Georgia was augmented with a sophisticated cyberattack and a well-coordinated propaganda campaign. The United States saw a different combination of tools during the invasion of Iraq, when Saddam Hussein dispatched his swarming Fedayeen paramilitary fighters along with the T-72 tanks of the Republican Guard.
>
> Conversely, militias, insurgent groups, other nonstate actors, and developing-world militaries are increasingly acquiring more technology, lethality, and sophistication—as illustrated by the losses and propaganda victory that Hezbollah was able to inflict on Israel in 2006. Hezbollah's restocked arsenal of rockets and missiles now dwarfs the inventory of many nation-states. Furthermore, Chinese and Russian arms sales are putting advanced capabilities, both offensive and defensive, in the hands of more countries and groups. As the defense scholar Frank Hoffman has noted, these hybrid scenarios combine "the lethality of state conflict with

the fanatical and protracted fervor of irregular warfare," what another defense scholar, Michael Evans, has described as "wars . . . in which Microsoft coexists with machetes and stealth technology is met by suicide bombers."

Just as one can expect a blended high-low mix of adversaries and types of conflict, so, too, should the United States seek a better balance in the portfolio of capabilities it has—the types of units fielded, the weapons bought, the training done.[71]

This shift in focus is a marked departure from Rumsfeld's vision of transformation and accounts for less divergence between the preferences of OSD and the services, a major source of dysfunctional civil–military relations during the Rumsfeld years.

In addition, Gates has reversed the marginalization of the JCS that prevailed during much of Rumsfeld's tenure. This reversal has been effected by both personnel changes and the interaction between the secretary and the chiefs. In June 2007, Gates declined to renominate Marine General Peter Pace—considered too passive by many observers—as chairman of the JCS. He did so in order to avoid a "backward-looking and contentious instead of forward-looking" congressional confirmation hearing, i.e., one focused on Iraq.[72] The man he did nominate to replace Pace, Admiral Mike Mullen, has been much more of an activist chairman.

In terms of process, Gates usually meets with Joint Chiefs once a week in "the tank." "Rumsfeld seldom visited the tank; when he wanted to see the chiefs, he called them into his office."[73] The improved working relationship between Gates and the JCS was not achieved at the cost of rapport with the combatant commanders. He has maintained an excellent relationship with Gen. David Petraeus, the former commander of CENTCOM (now the senior officer in Afghanistan), the primary theater of war, as well as the former top commanders in Iraq and Afghanistan, Gen. Ray Odierno and Gen. Stanley McChrystal, respectively.

One of the most significant changes between Gates' Pentagon and Rumsfeld's is the former's approach to military advice. Unlike Rumsfeld, Gates has stressed the need for military officers to provide candid advice to the civilian policy makers. As he said in April 2008 during a lecture to the Corps of Cadets at the US Military Academy,

we will still need men and women in uniform to call things as they see them and tell their subordinates and superiors alike what they need to hear, not what they want to hear . . . . More broadly, if as an officer one does not tell blunt truths or create an environment where candor is encouraged, then they have done themselves and the institution a disservice.

The time will come when a leader in today's military must stand alone and make a difficult, unpopular decision, or challenge the opinion of superiors and tell them you can't get the job done with the time and resources available . . . These are the moments when your entire career is a risk.

He argued that when it comes to handling "disagreements with superiors and in particular with civilians vested with control of the armed forces under our Constitution," the duties of an officer are "to provide blunt and candid advice always, to keep disagreements private, and to implement faithfully decisions that go against you."[74]

Only a month earlier, Gates had accepted the resignation of Admiral William J. "Fox" Fallon, the commander of CENTCOM, over perceived public differences concerning Bush administration war policies, especially regarding Iran. He noted in his lecture that:

In my time as Secretary of Defense, I have changed several important decisions because of general officers disagreeing with me and persuading me of a better course of action. For example, at one point I had decided to shake up a particular command by appointing a commander from a different service than had ever held the post. A senior service chief persuaded me to change my mind.[75]

His actions suggest that the advice Gates gave to the Corps of Cadets did not constitute merely empty words.

Conclusion

The chief failure of the American defense establishment since 9/11 has been the inability to generate a strategy that links campaigns and operations within a theater of war to policy. As cited in previously, Colin Gray once wrote that "All too often, there is a black hole where American strategy ought to reside."

This failure to generate strategy can be attributed to the confluence of three factors. The first of these is the continued dominance of the "normal" theory of civil–military relations, the belief that there is a clear line of demarcation between civilians who determine the goals of the war and the uniformed military who then conduct the actual fighting.

The second factor, strongly reinforced by the normal theory of civil–military relations, is the influence of the uniformed services' organizational cultures. As noted above, the organizational culture of a service in turn exerts a strong influence on civil–military relations, frequently constraining what civilian leaders can do and often constituting an obstacle to change and innovation. In the case of the Army's tardiness in shifting to a counterinsurgency approach in Iraq, much of that service's problem could be traced to its embrace of the "operational level of war," which manifests itself as a preference for fighting large-scale conventional war—despite the fact that throughout most of its existence, the conflicts in which the US Army engaged were actually irregular wars.

As Hew Strachan observes in a citation above, "the operational level of war appeals to armies: it functions in a politics-free zone and it puts primacy on professional skills." This generates a disjunction between operational excellence in combat on the one hand, and *policy*, which determines the reasons for which a particular war is to be fought, on the other, which is precisely the problem for civil–military relations when it comes to military effectiveness. The combination of the dominant position of the normal theory of civil–military relations in the United States and the US military's focus on the nonpolitical operational level of war means that all too often the conduct of a war disconnected from the goals of the war.

Also, as noted above, the third factor contributing to the perseverance of the American strategic black hole is one that was, ironically, intended to improve US strategic planning: the Goldwater-Nichols Department of Defense Reorganization Act of 1986. The JCS are responsible for integrating theater strategy and national policy. But if they are marginalized, as they were during much of the time during the Bush administration, such integration does not occur.

The result of such a disjunction between the military and political realms is that war plans may not be integrated with national policy and that strategy, despite lip service to its importance, in practice becomes an orphan. And in the absence of strategy, other factors rush to fill the void, resulting in strategic drift.

Rectifying this situation requires that the parties to the civil–military bargain, in this case, the uniformed military and the civilian policy makers, adjust the way they do business. On the one hand, the military must recover its voice in strategy making while realizing that politics permeates the conduct of war and that civilians have a say, not only concerning the goals of the war but also how it is conducted. On the other hand, civilians must understand that to implement effective policy and strategy requires the proper military instrument. They must also insist that soldiers present their views frankly and forcefully throughout the strategy-making process. To his credit, Secretary Gates seems to understand this requirement better than his predecessor.

Notes

1   Samuel Huntington, *The Common Defense: Strategic Programs in National Politics* (New York: Columbia University Press, 1961), p. 1.

2   Samuel Huntington, *The Soldier and the State: The Theory and Politics of Civil-Military Relations* (Cambridge, MA: Belknap Press of Harvard University Press, 1957), pp. 2 and 3.

3   Allan Millett, Williamson Murray, and Kenneth Watman, "The Effectiveness of Military Organizations," in Millett and Murray, eds., *Military Effectiveness*, vol. 1 (Boston: Allen and Unwin, 1988), p. 2.

4   Ibid., p. 3.

5   Ibid., pp. 4–26.

6   Samuel P. Huntington, "National Policy and the Transoceanic Navy," US Naval Institute *Proceedings*, May 1954, p. 483.

7   Carl H. Builder, *The Masks of War: American Military Styles in Strategy and Analysis* (Baltimore: Johns Hopkins University Press, 1989), p. 39.

8   For example, see Brian MacAllister Linn, *The Philippine War, 1899–1902* (Lawrence, KA: University Press of Kansas, 2000); Max Boot, *Savage Wars of Peace: Small Wars and the Rise of American Power* (New York: Basic Books, 2002); John Gates, "Indians and Insurrectos: The U.S. Army's Experience with Insurgency," *Parameters*, March 1983, pp. 59–68.

9   Morris Janowitz, *The Professional Soldier: A Social and Political Portrait* (New York: Free Press, 1971), pp. 260 and 261.

10   See Stephen Ambrose, *Upton and the Army* (Baton Rouge: Louisiana State University Press, 1964).

11   See Emory Upton, *The Military Policy of the United States* (Washington, DC: Government Printing Office, 1904).

12   For an excellent account of this argument, see Lewis Sorley, *A Better War: The Unexamined Victories and Final Tragedy of America's Last Years in Vietnam* (New York: Harcourt Brace, 1999).

13   Hew Strachan, "Making Strategy: Civil-Military Relations After Iraq," *Survival*, Autumn 2006, p. 60.

14   Brigadier Justin Kelly and Dr. Michael James Brennan, *Alien: How Operational Art Devoured Strategy* (Carlisle, PA: US Army War College, Strategic Studies Institute, 2009), p. viii.

15   Colin Gray, *Another Bloody Century: Future Warfare* (London: Orion, 2005), p. 111.

16 Kelly and Brennan, *Alien*, p. 63.

17 Williamson Murray, "Professionalism and Professional Military Education" in Suzanne Nielsen and Don Snider, eds., *American Civil-Military Relations: The Soldier and the State in a New Era* (Baltimore: Johns Hopkins University Press, 2009), p. 134.

18 See Ann Scott Tyson, "Army's Next Crop of Generals Forged in Counterinsurgency," *Washington Post*, May 15, 2008, p. A4 and Tyson, "Petraeus Helping to Pick New Generals," *Washington Post*, November 17, 2007, p. A1.

19 Andrew J. Bacevich, "The Petraeus Doctrine," *The Atlantic Monthly*, October 2008, http://www.theatlantic.com/doc/200810/petraeus-doc-trine; Michael Horowitz, "The Future of War and American Strategy," *Orbis*, Spring 2009, pp. 300–318.

20 John Nagl, "Let's Win the War We're In," *Joint Forces Quarterly*, no. 52, 2009, pp. 20–26; Bruce Floersheim, "Forging the Future of American Security Total Force Strategy," *Orbis*, Summer 2009, pp. 471–488. Cf. Thomas Ricks, "The COINdinistas," *Foreign Policy*, December 2009, p. 63.

21 Gian Gentile, "Let's Build and Army to Win *All* Wars," *Joint Forces Quarterly*, no. 52, 2009, pp. 27–33; Gentile, "The Imperative for an American General Purpose Army that Can Fight," *Orbis*, Summer 2009, pp. 457–470.

22 Bacevich, "The Petraeus Doctrine."

23 Lewis Sorley, *Thunderbolt: From the Battle of the Bulge to Vietnam and Beyond: General Creighton Abrams and the Army of His Times* (New York: Simon and Schuster, 1992), pp. 361–366.

24 Ibid., p. 364.

25 Robert H. Scales, *Certain Victory* (Washington, DC: Brassey's, 1993), p. 18.

26 Ibid., p. 364.

27 James Jay Carafano, "The Army Reserves and the Abrams Doctrine: Unfulfilled Promise, Uncertain Future," The Heritage Foundation, Washington, DC, Heritage Lecture 869, April 18, 2005. Cf. John R. Brinkerhoff and David W. Grissmer, "The Reserve Forces in an All-Volunteer Environment," in William Bowman, Roger Little, and G. Thomas Sicilia, eds., *The All-Volunteer Force After a Decade: Retrospect and Prospect* (Washington, DC: Brassey's, 1985).

28 Dan Henninger, "Who Calls the Cavalry? The Pentagon Was Prepared for Hurricane Katrina," *Wall Street Journal*, September 9, 2005.

29 Bill Sammon, "Bush Offers Pentagon As 'Lead Agency' In Disasters," *Washington Times*, September 26, 2005, p. 1.

30   Mark Sappenfield, "Disaster Relief? Call in the Marines: Bush Suggests Lifting the Ban on Using the Military Domestically," *The Christian Science Monitor*, September 19, 2005, http://www.csmonitor.com/2005/0919/p01s01-usmi.html; Megan Scully, "Pentagon Begins Review of Law on Military's Domestic Role," *Government Executive*, September 27, 2005.

31   Charles Dunlap, "The Origins of the Military Coup of 2012," *Parameters*, Winter 1992/93.

32   The most complete history of the use of the US military in a domestic role prior to passage of the Posse Comitatus Act of 1878 is available in Robert W. Coakley, *The Role of Federal Military Forces in Domestic Disorders, 1789–1878* (Washington, DC: United States Army Center of Military History, 1988).

33   James McPherson, *Battle Cry of Freedom: The Civil War Era* (New York: Oxford University Press, 1988), p. 83.

34   Ibid., pp. 119 and 120.

35   Coakley, p. 344.

36   Richard Kohn, "Tarnished Brass: Is the US Military Profession in Decline?" *World Affairs*, Spring 2009, p. 73.

37   Ibid., p. 76.

38   Lieutenant Colonel Paul Yingling, "A Failure in Generalship," *Armed Force Journal*, May 2007, http://www.armedforcesjournal.com/2007/05/2635198.

39   Huntington, *The Soldier and the State*.

40   Cohen, *Supreme Command*, p. 4.

41   Huntington, *The Soldier and the State*, p. 57.

42   Ibid., p. 13.

43   Suzanne Nielsen, "Civil-Military Relations Theory and Military Effectiveness," *Public Administration and Management*, 10(2), 2005, p. 64.

44   Cohen, *Supreme Command*, pp. 1–15.

45   Barry Posen, *The Sources of Military Doctrine* (Ithaca, NY: Cornell University Press, 1984); Jack Snyder, *The Ideology of the Offensive: Military Decision Making and the Disasters of 1914* (Ithaca, NY: Cornell University Press, 1984); Deborah Avant, *Political Institutions and Change: Lesson from Peripheral Wars* (Ithaca, NY: Cornell University Press, 1994).

46   Risa Brooks, *Shaping Strategy: The Civil-Military Politics of Strategic Assessment* (Princeton: Princeton University Press, 2008), pp. 34–42.

47   Dale Herspring, *Rumsfeld's Wars: The Arrogance of Power* (Lawrence, KA: University Press of Kansas, 2008).

48 Thomas Ricks, *Fiasco: The American Adventure in Iraq, 2003–2005* (New York: Penguin, 2007); Michael Gordon and Bernard Trainor, *Cobra II: The Inside Story of the Invasion and Occupation of Iraq* (New York: Pantheon, 2006); Bing West, *The Strongest Tribe: War, Politics, and the Endgame in Iraq* (New York: Random House, 2008); Bob Woodward, *Bush at War* (New York: Simon and Schuster, 2002).

49 Brooks, *Shaping Strategy*, p. 7.

50 See, for example, William Owens, "System-of-Systems: US' Emerging Dominant Battlefield Awareness Promises to Dissipate 'Fog of War'," *Armed Forces Journal International*, January 1996, p. 47; Thomas Duffy, "Owens Says Technology May Lift 'Fog of War': Breakthroughs Could Give Forces Total Command of Future Battlefield," *Inside the Navy*, January 23, 1995, p. 5; David Alberts, "The Future of Command and Control with DBK [Dominant Battlespace Knowledge]," in Stuart E. Johnson and Martin C. Libiki, eds., *Dominant Battlespace Knowledge* (Washington, DC: National Defense University Press, 1995), p. 93; James R. Blaker, "The American RMA Force: An Alternative to the QDR," *Strategic Review*, XXV(3), Summer 1997; William A. Owens, speech before the Navy RMA Roundtable, Center for Naval Analyses, May 5, 1997; Arnold Beichman, "Revolution in the warfare trenches," *Washington Times*, January 31, 1996, p. 17; Andrew Krepinevich, "Transforming the American Military," Center for Strategic and Budgetary Assessments (CSBA) Backgrounder, September 1997; Mike Vickers, "The Future of Land Forces," CSBA Highlight, April 21, 1999; Andrew Krepinevich, "W(h)ither the Army?" CSBA Highlight, January 18, 2000; and Steven Kosiak, Andrew Krepinevich, and Michael Vickers, "Strategy for a Long Peace," CSBA Report, January 30, 2001.

51 Thomas Donnelly, quoted in Robert Kaplan, "What Rumsfeld Got Right," *The Atlantic Monthly*, July/August 2008. For critical treatments of the theories underlying Rumsfeld's vision of transformation, see for example, Williamson Murray, "Clausewitz Out, Computer In," *The National Interest*, Summer 1997; Mackubin Thomas Owens, "Technology, The RMA, and Future War," *Strategic Review*, Spring 1998; H. R. McMaster, "Crack in the Foundation: Defense Transformation and the Underlying Assumption of Dominant Knowledge in Future War," US Army War College Strategic Studies Institute, April 2007; and McMaster, "Learning from Contemporary Conflicts to Prepare for Future War," *Orbis*, Fall 2008.

52 Peter Boyer, "A Different War," *The New Yorker*, July 1, 2002, pp. 60–62.

53   Rumsfeld, Testimony Before the Senate Armed Services Committee (SASC) on the Defense Strategy Review, June 21, 2001.

54   Boyer, pp. 63–65; Ricks, *Fiasco*, pp. 68–70.

55   Dave Moniz and John Diamond, "Rumsfeld is Perched at the 'Pinnacle of Power'," *USA Today*, May 1, 2003, p. 10; Seth Stern, "Pentagon Iconoclast," *Christian Science Monitor*, April 29, 2003, p. 1. For an excellent assessment of the dysfunctional relationship between Rumsfeld and Shinseki, see Matthew Moten, "A Broken Dialogue: Rumsfeld, Shinseki, and Civil-Military Tension," in Nielsen and Snider, *American Civil-Military Relations*, pp. 42–71.

56   Brooks, *Shaping Strategy*, p. 236.

57   Gordon and Trainor, *Cobra II*, p. 140; Stevenson, *Warriors and Politicians*, p. 186; Herspring, *Rumsfeld's War*, p. 396.

58   Brooks, *Shaping Strategy*, p. 239.

59   Gordon and Trainor, *Cobra II*, p. 140; Stevenson, *Warriors and Politicians*, pp. 185–190; Herspring, *Rumsfeld's War*, p. 399.

60   Brooks, *Shaping Strategy*, p. 241.

61   Fred Kaplan, "The Professional," *The New York Times Magazine*, February 10, 2008, p. 41.

62   Gordon and Trainor, *Cobra II*, p. 139.

63   Brooks, *Shaping Strategy*, p. 242.

64   Packer, p. 117.

65   Ricks, *Fiasco*, pp. 79, 80, 109, and 110; George Packer, *The Assassins' Gate: America in Iraq* (New York: Farrar, Straus, and Giroux, 2005), p. 119; Gordon and Trainor, *Cobra II*, p. 145.

66   Brooks, *Shaping Strategy*, p. 245.

67   Ibid., p. 251.

68   Michael Gordon, "The Strategy to Secure Iraq Did Not Foresee a Second War," *New York Times*, October 19, 2004.

69   On Abazaid's belief that US troops were anti-bodies to the Iraqi people, see West, *The Strongest Tribe*, and Ricks, *The Gamble: General David Petraeus and the American Adventure in Iraq, 2006–2008* (New York: Penguin, 2009). On McMaster and Tel Afar, see Mackubin Thomas Owens, "Counterinsurgency from the Bottom Up: Col. H.R. McMaster and the 3rd Armored Cavalry Regiment in Tel Afar, Spring-Fall 2005," US Naval War College Faculty Paper, July 2009.

70   Kori Schake, "Choices for the Quadrennial Defense Review," *Orbis*, Summer 2009, p. 440.

71   Robert Gates, "A Balanced Strategy: Reprogramming the Pentagon for a New Age," *Foreign Affairs*, January/February 2009, http://www.ciaonet.

org/journals/fa/v88i1/03.html. On hybrid threats, see Frank Hoffman, "Complex Irregular Warfare: The Next Revolution in Military Affairs," *Orbis*, Summer 2006; Hoffman, "Lessons from Lebanon: Hezbollah and Hybrid Warfare," Foreign Policy Research Institute E-note, August 24, 2006, http://www.fpri.org/enotes/20060824.military.hoffman.hezbollahhybridwars.html; Hoffman, "Hybrid Threats: Reconceptualizing the Evolving Character of Modern Conflict," Strategic Forum, no. 240, April 2009; Mackubin Thomas Owens, "Reflections on Future War," *Naval War College Review*, Summer 2008.

72 Maj. Gen. Thomas L. Wilkerson, US Marine Corps (ret.), "Sprinting Through the Tape," US Naval Institute *Proceedings*, July 2008.

73 Kaplan, p. 41.

74 Robert Gates, Evening Lecture at West Point, April 21, 2008, published as Robert M. Gates, "Reflections on Leadership," *Parameters*, Summer 2008, pp. 9 and 11–13.

75 Ibid, p. 10.

CHAPTER FOUR

Who Serves?

Those who study security issues place a great deal of emphasis on the policy and strategy decisions of a state. History seems to illustrate that a coherent and effective strategy is the necessary, if not sufficient, cause of success in the international arena. But to be successful in the end, a strategy must be *implemented*: strategy in the abstract is little more than poetry. Strategy requires the right tool—among other things a military force that can execute the strategy. Accordingly, one of the most important undertakings of a state is to recruit, retain, train, and properly employ its soldiers. The effectiveness of a country's military, the topic of chapter 2, depends a great deal on the quality of the force that a country is able to provide.

With regard to the question of who serves in the US military, the civil–military bargain has been renegotiated a number of times throughout American history. Most Americans believe that the backbone of US defense has been the "citizen-soldier," for whom "military service is either an obligation imposed by the state or the result of mobilization for some pressing cause."[1] While the citizen-soldier rallies to the colors during a time of war, he maintains his essentially civilian outlook. When the emergency is over, he returns home in the tradition of Cincinnatus. In recent popular culture, the Steven Spielberg film, *Saving Private Ryan*, best captures the American concept of the citizen-soldier.

Today's force is different. Although today's active-duty service member is a citizen-soldier in the legal sense, he or she is not one in the traditional sense described above. Members of the reserve component and National Guard are a different matter, of course. As might be expected, the idea of the citizen-soldier resonates strongly in the American mind.

The question of who serves, unlike the other fundamental questions of civil–military relations, is usually examined through the lens of sociology. As observed in Chapter 1, the sociological lens of civil–military relations examine such broad question as military culture vs. liberal society; the role of individuals and groups, e.g. women, minorities, enlisted servicemen and service women within the military, and the relationships among them; the effectiveness of individual service members in combat; small-unit cohesion; the relationship between military service and citizenship (to include the civic republican tradition); the nature of military service (occupation, profession, etc.); and the relationship between militaries and the societies from which they stem.

The relationship between American society and the US military changed with the end of the Cold War and has changed again as the United States has embarked on a war against global jihadism since 9/11. The nexus of two wars in Iraq and Afghanistan, the explosion of communications, both electronic and otherwise, and the unprecedented reliance of the military services on the reserve component arguably have made the military more visible to the American public than it was in the era of the draft and Vietnam.

Today's military force is quite diverse, with racial and ethnic minorities and women playing an unprecedented role. The reserves and National Guard, once called upon only in the most extreme emergencies, now are central to the national effort in two ongoing wars and other tasks. They are no longer "weekend warriors".

What are the civil–military relations implications of these changes? First, the idea of a civil–military "gap" that took hold in the 1990s was probably overstated then and is less salient now. Second, the military as an institution enjoys a favorable image among the American public. This is a source of concern to some who note that it is somewhat unseemly for democratic people to hold arguably the least democratic institution in America in much higher regard than the most democratic—the US Congress. But this high regard may reflect two phenomena that arise from the fact that the military burden of the nation is borne by only a few: first, what Charles Moskos has called "patriotism lite"—public support for the troops as a substitute for any broader sacrifice in time of war[2] and second, a "romanticized view of soldiers" and a "nostalgia for military ideals."[3]

Third, the concept of the citizen-soldier—with the exception of the reserve component and National Guard—has been supplanted by what some have called the "postmodern military," which tends to dissolve absolutes such as the idea that military effectiveness—Huntington's "functional imperative"—requires a unique military culture or ethos. The issue of military culture underpins the debate over women in combat and military service by open homosexuals. The discussion that follows is an attempt to illustrate how the civil–military bargain regarding who serves is being renegotiated.

The Citizen-Soldier

The idea of the citizen-soldier is deeply embedded in the political thought of republicanism that helped shape the American Founding. Its oldest manifestation of this idea was the militia, which as a staple of republican thought can be traced to Machiavelli, who wrote in *The Prince* "that without having its own arms, no principate is secure; on the contrary, it is wholly obligated to fortune, not having that virtue which with faith defends it in adversity. . . . One's own arms are those which are composed either of subjects or citizens or your own dependents; all others are either mercenaries or auxiliaries."[4]

Machiavelli's idea about the necessity of citizen-soldiers as the bulwark of state safety was echoed in James Harrington's *Commonwealth of Oceana* (1656), written in opposition to Cromwell's Protectorate. For Harrington, the foundation of political liberty and independence was the armed free-holder. Only such a citizen could be counted on because as a property holder, he had a stake in preserving liberty. It was also his duty as a citizen to keep and bear arms in defense not only of his property but also of the public liberty.[5]

The militia loomed large in the thought of the American Founders, who not only drank deeply the draughts of classical republican thought,[6] but had experienced life under British troops before the Revolution. For them and most other Americans after the Revolution, a standing army was one of the most dangerous threats to liberty.

In thinking about the potential dangers of a standing army, the founding generation had before them the precedents of Rome and England. In the first case, Julius Caesar violated tradition by marching his provincial army into Rome, overthrowing the power of the Senate, destroying the republic, and laying the foundation of empire. In the second, Cromwell used the army to abolish Parliament and to rule as dictator. In addition, in the period leading up to the Revolution, the British Crown had forced the American colonists to quarter and otherwise support its troops, which the colonists saw as nothing more than an army of occupation.

But this image is not altogether true. For long stretches of time, dating from before the American Revolution, those who defended the frontier or who stood duty on the periphery of the American imperium were long-term soldiers far removed from the mainstream of American society. Indeed, they were often immigrants.[7]

Even before the Revolution, it was not the militia—free-holding citizens obligated, according to republican political thought, to keep and bear arms in defense not only of their property but also of the safety and liberty of the public—but "provincials," long-term enlistees mostly made up of the lowers rungs of society, that provided security for the British settlements on the frontier. Provincials conducted the expeditions against the Indians, Spaniards, and Frenchmen that posed the greatest threat. Reliance on such expeditionary forces represented a separation of citizenship and soldiering, violating the fundamental principle underlying the concept of the citizen-soldier.[8] This has been the norm during periods of what is now called "persistent conflict": times during which the American military performed service on the frontier, in support of "imperial policing," or other constabulary operations.[9]

Thus, in many respects, the concept of the militia as the embodiment of the citizen-soldier is a "myth," which according to Roland Barthes, is a cluster of ideas that have lost "the memory that they were ever made . . . . Myth does not deny things; on the contrary, its function is to talk about them; simply it purifies them, it makes them innocent, it gives them a natural and eternal justification, it gives them a clarity which is not that of an explanation but that of a statement of fact." The purpose of a myth, wrote Barthes, is to "organize a world which is without contradiction, because it is without depth, a world . . . [of] blissful clarity: things appear to mean something by themselves."[10]

Nonetheless, the militia myth persevered throughout the first part of the nineteenth century. However, the "obligated militia" envisioned by the American Founders—a true citizen-soldier in the tradition of Cincinnatus—was discredited by the militia's abysmal performance during the War of 1812. Although the militia tradition continued in the form of the "uniformed" militia, local volunteer units—usually artillery and cavalry—routinely equipped and supported by their own members, it was the several states that provided citizen soldiers—state volunteer units led by state-appointed officers—when it was necessary to expand the regular US Army. Accordingly, large numbers of state volunteers served during the Mexican War and the Civil War.[11] During World War I, the United States still called upon the states for volunteers, but conscripts provided by far the largest number of soldiers for that conflict. And of course, the United States conscripted soldiers during World War II and the Cold War. The draft ended in 1973.

With the end of the draft, the United States military has assumed a character closer to that of the long-term enlistee on the Western American frontier or serving in China and the Philippines during the early twentieth century than to the true citizen-soldier who serves during an emergency and then returns to civilian life.

But the myth of the citizen-soldier persists. Despite the fact that the character of the US military today is far different from that of the one that fought in World War II, many American service members see themselves as latter-day manifestations of the characters in the aforementioned *Saving Private Ryan*: reluctant warriors who serve in the military during a period of emergency but long for a return to civilian life. But for most of today's service members, military service *is* their life.

As noted earlier, today's American soldier is a citizen-soldier in the legal sense but lacks the three characteristics that have defined the traditional citizen-soldier. The first is his motivation for military service. According to Eliot Cohen, the true citizen-soldier emerges when

> the state is embarked upon some great crusade or adventure, and in the spirit of ancient Athens, citizens make the highest contribution to it by offering their service as soldiers. For the normal volunteer of today, neither motivation applies. Patriotism, a desire for personal challenge, monetary or career incentives—all mold the young man or woman who joins today. But in all cases (except perhaps that of patriotism), the link between citizenship and service is thin.[12]

The second characteristic of the true citizen-soldier is that he represents a cross section of the state as a whole. "The idea of military service as the great leveler is part of its charm in a democratic age, one of whose bedrock principles is surely the formal equality of all citizens. The voluntary military, by way of contrast, is very rarely representative."

The third characteristic is the maintenance of an identity that remains fundamentally *civilian*. "However much he may yield to the exigencies of military life, however much he may even come to enjoy it and become proficient in military skills, he is always, in the core of his being, a member of civil society. His participation in military life is temporary and provisional."[13]

Some have suggested ways to create a force that would include somewhat fewer professionals and somewhat more citizen-soldiers. The late Charles Moskos suggested a dual approach, in which some citizen-soldiers could serve for 2-year terms or, after a 6-month training period, join the reserves for an extended period. Expanding Reserve Officer Training Corps programs would increase the number of college graduates in the military. And expanding the National Guard, with its roots in the states and localities, would also increase the nonprofessional portion of the US military.[14]

The idea of a representative military that maintains a primarily civilian outlook plays a large role in concerns about a civil–military gap. Morris Janowitz and some of his followers saw (and see) military service as a means of ensuring "civic virtue." In this regard, military service is a positive obligation that, on the one hand, enhances one's citizenship and, on the other hand, improves democratic life.[15] For such writers, the central problem of civil–military relations is not the degree to which military elites follow the commands of civilian elites (civilian control), but how to maintain a military that sustains and protects democratic values.[16] Of course, this raises a second issue: to what extent does military effectiveness—Huntington's functional imperative—require an ethos at odds with a liberal democratic society?

The All-Volunteer Military and the Civil–Military "Gap"

With the end of the draft in 1973, observers raised a number of concerns. The most obvious of these was that the services would not be able to recruit and retain enough high-quality members. Observers also feared that the high cost of attracting recruits and retaining those on active duty would create budgetary problems. There were also concerns that an all-volunteer force would be overrepresented by minorities who, in the event of war, would suffer disproportionate casualties.[17]

In the 1990s, observers raised an additional new concern: that a dangerous and corrosive civil–military "gap"—a "nearly unbridgeable divide" between the military and American society, one fundamentally unhealthy for US democratic institutions—was emerging. This purported gap became a staple of the civil–military relations debate during that decade.[18]

In his 1997 book, *Making the Corps*, Thomas Ricks wrote that the US military "is extremely good today." Indeed, it is "arguably the best it has ever been and probably for the first time in history the best in the world."[19] But, argued Ricks, this excellence came at the cost of a US military that was increasingly alienated from American society and an officer corps that was abandoning its apolitical tradition and becoming both more conservative and more politically active than ever before.[20]

In many respects, the debate over the civil–military gap represents a conflict between the respective views of Huntington and Janowitz (Chapter 1). For the followers of Janowitz, the all-volunteer force was becoming too separated from civilian society, creating problems for civilian control. This separation manifested itself in three ways according to these observers. First, the military had become more politically conservative and more religious than the American mainstream. Second, it had also become increasingly alienated from and even hostile to civilian society. Third, it had resisted change, especially regarding the integration of women and homosexuals as well as reluctance to carry out the sort of constabulary operations that proliferated after the Cold War.[21]

The intellectual heirs of Huntington countered by charging that liberal civilian elites were attempting to obliterate differences between civilian society and military culture that are absolutely necessary to ensure the military's "functional imperative." They contended that the real "gap" was not between the military and American society at large but between the military and American society on the one hand and liberal elites on the other hand. The danger to an effective military, they argued, came from the indifference at best and hostility at worst of this liberal elite to military culture. They saw the attempts to impose liberal values on military culture as examples of Huntington's "extirpation."[22]

The alleged civil–military gap does not loom as large in the civil–military debate today as it did a decade ago, but the issue has not gone away. The military *is* different from civilian society; one danger is not that the military is necessarily partisan but that national civilian leaders may try to exploit those differences for partisan purposes.

As the civil–military bargain is renegotiated, certain questions must be addressed. What is the character of military service today and how does it differ from earlier times? Is the military a true profession? Is there indeed a gap between the military and the society the military is sworn to defend? Is there a distinct military ethos necessitated by what Samuel Huntington called the "functional imperative" to prevail in war? To what extent should Huntington's "societal imperative" govern the behavior of service members?

A Postmodern American Military?

One answer to these questions was provided by military sociologists, who developed the concept of the "postmodern military." "Postmodernism" as a concept has had a major impact on the study of society and institutions. In general, it has been seen as a reaction to the increasing uncertainty and complexity of society resulting from technological change and the like. The characteristics of postmodernism include the dissolution of old categories, the rejection of absolutes, and greater tolerance of difference and diversity, leading to changes in social patterns, e.g., the redefinition of the family, and to the disappearance of allegiances to units greater than the individual.[23]

Military sociologists have adapted the concept of postmodernism to the study of the military as a social institution. According to Charles Moskos and James Burk, the transition from modern certainty to postmodern uncertainty "about the meaning or purpose of central roles and institutions [and] various collective activities" is the central development relevant to changing military organization.[24]

Moskos has illuminated the contrast between today's military and militaries of earlier times. Moskos identified three distinct periods in tracing the evolution of the American military from the beginning of the twentieth century to the current era: the modern (pre–Cold War, 1900–1945); the late modern (Cold War, 1945–1990); and the postmodern (post–Cold War, 1990–present).[25] For each era, he posited a series of force variables: the perceived threat; force structure, i.e., the character of the force—mass conscript army vs. professional force; the major mission of the force; the dominant military professional "type"—combat leader, manager, "soldier-statesman;" the attitude of the public toward the military; media relations; the role of civilian employees; the role of women; the role of military spouses; the status of homosexuals; and the status of conscientious objectors (Table 4.1). John Allen Williams has expanded Moskos' framework (Table 4.2).

The postmodernists argue that the American military must be prepared to confront major subnational, international, and transnational threats, which include ethnic violence, terrorism, and insurgency, as opposed to state-on-state conventional or nuclear war, the perceived major threats of earlier eras.

In terms of force structure, the main character of the postmodern and hybrid US military is that it is a *professional* force with a *fully integrated reserve force*. This professional force came into being with the end of the draft in 1973. While larger than previous American standing armies, it is small in proportion to a population of 300 million.

The missions of the postmodern American military include the conduct of conventional war, counterinsurgency, counterterrorism, stability operations, peacekeeping operations, humanitarian relief, and state-building. In the 1990s, such tasks as peacekeeping and the like were often called "nontraditional" missions, but this term was ahistorical: in fact, US forces had conducted such tasks throughout American history.

For Moskos, the expertise of today's dominant professional transcends Huntington's "management of violence." Today's professional soldier is more properly described as a soldier-statesman, soldier-scholar, a soldier-constable or national security professional, a category that makes no distinction between soldiers and civilians.[26] This broader role of the soldier has led some to express concern about the growing influence of the military in areas beyond the strictly military, an issue addressed in chapter 2.

An important aspect of civil–military relations is the attitude of civilians, both the civilian elite and the public at large, toward the military. Presently, the public views the military favorably and is supportive of those who are fighting today's conflicts even if they oppose the war. This, of course, is a far cry from the days of Vietnam when war opponents often directed their disapproval of the war against service members.

Another manifestation of civilian attitudes toward the military is military–media relations. This relationship reached its nadir in the years after Vietnam but has since recovered. Both parties remain wary of each other, but there are a number of reporters and journalists who are trusted and respected by service members.

A major change in today's force compared to the past is the increasing role of civilian contractors. Many functions that were once carried out by soldiers are now privatized and outsourced.[27] This makes sense for functions associated with support, e.g., companies that run mess halls in Iraq, but becomes more problematic when contractors are doing things associated with the military mission itself. For instance, in Iraq, some civilian security firms were guilty of employing excessive force on several occasions. There were also instances of tensions between civilian security personnel and US troops.

Some of the most rancorous civil–military conflicts of the 1990s involved the twin issues of women in combat and service by open homosexuals. Since many specialties in all the services have been opened to women, the former issue has lost much of its salience. Nonetheless, most military occupations that involve close ground combat remain closed to women.

The homosexual issue is a different matter. At the present time, military service by open homosexuals is prohibited by law. Nonetheless, the Department of Defense during the Clinton presidency adopted a policy that prevents the services from asking recruits about their sexual orientation: "don't ask, don't tell." As a result, it is likely that there are a number of closeted homosexuals serving in the military. President Obama, of course, has vowed to end don't ask, don't tell. But if open homosexuals are to be permitted to serve, Congress must change the law now on the books. And as in the case of women in combat, herein lies the civil–military relations issue of military culture vs. American society.

Table 4.1 Armed Forces and Society in the Cold War Eras (*Source*: Orbis)

Forces Variable	Modern (Pre-Cold War – 1900–1945)	Late Modern (Cold War – 1945–1990)	Postmodern (Post-Cold War –since 1990)
Threat	Enemy invasion	Nuclear war	Subnational (e.g., ethnic violence, terrorism)
Major Mission Definition	Mass army, conscription Defense of homeland	Large professional military Support of alliance	Small professional military New missions (e.g., peacekeeping, humanitarian)

(*Cont'd*)

Forces Variable	Modern (Pre-Cold War – 1900–1945)	Late Modern (Cold War – 1945–1990)	Postmodern (Post-Cold War –since 1990)
Dominant Military Professional	Combat leader	Manager or technician	Soldier-statesman; soldier-scholar
Public Attitude Toward Military	Supportive	Ambivalent	Indifferent
Media Relations	Incorporated	Manipulated	Courted
Civilian Employees	Minor component	Medium component	Major component
Women's Role in Military	Separate corps or excluded	Partial integration	Full integration
Spouse and Military	Integral part	Partial involvement	Removed
Homosexuals in Military	Punished	Discharged	Accepted
Conscientious Objection	Limited or prohibited	Routinely permitted	Subsumed under civilian service

Table 4.2 Armed Forces and Society Beyond the Postmodern Era
    (*Source*: Orbis)

Forces Variable	Postmodern (1990–2001)	Hybrid (2001– ?)
Threat	Subnational (e.g., ethnic violence, terrorism)	
Force Structure	Small professional military	Professional military core Integrated reserve force
Major Mission Definition	New missions (e.g., peacekeeping, humanitarian)	Full spectrum of operations
Dominant Military Professional	Soldier-statesman Soldier-scholar	Soldier-warrior and manager Soldier-statesman and scholar Soldier-constable
Inter-Rank Relations (*new variable*)	(*Formal hierarchical*)	Informal flattened hierarchy

(*Cont'd*)

Table 4.2 Cont'd

Forces Variable	Postmodern (1990–2001)	Hybrid (2001– ?)
Public Attitude Toward Military	Indifferent	Supportive
Media Relations	Courted	Co-opted
Civilian Employees	Major component	**Civilian Role** (*more inclusive variable*) Integrated (operations & support) Privatization/outsourcing of functions
Women's Role in Military	Full integration (*Not by end of period*)	Full integration
Spouse and Military	Removed	**Military Family** (*more inclusive variable*) Dispersed/networked/nontraditional
Homosexuals in Military	Accepted (*Not by end of period*)	Full integration
Conscientious Objection	Subsumed under civilian service	**Recruitment Patterns** (*more inclusive variable*) Supplemented volunteerism

The Functional Imperative and the Nature of War

Postmodernism tends to reject categorical absolutes. The impact of this outlook on civil–military relations is significant, and it manifests itself primarily in its rejection of the idea that the military's functional imperative—success on the battlefield—requires a unique military ethos. Indeed, in a practical sense, the central civil–military relations debate for the past two decades has concerned the tension between the functional imperative and the social imperative—the belief that the military has to look more like American society as a whole, especially when it comes to the role of military women and military service by open homosexuals.

Those who support the idea that a distinct military ethos is necessary to protect liberal society point to a paradox: A military organization cannot govern itself on the basis of the same liberal principles that characterize the very society it defends. As Army Gen. Walter "Dutch" Kerwin, who helped pioneer the Army's shift from a conscript force to a volunteer force, once observed, "the values necessary to defend [liberal] society are often at odds with the values of the society itself. To be an effective servant of the people, the [military] must concentrate not on the values of liberal society, but on the hard values of the battlefield."[28]

Accordingly, they contend, behavior that is acceptable, indeed even protected, in civil society is prohibited in the military. The military restricts many freedoms that civilians take for granted. It restricts speech. It prohibits certain relationships among members, e.g., fraternization. It values virtues that many civilians see as brutal.

There are, of course, profound dangers for civil–military relations if the military is large, semiautonomous, and so different and estranged from society that it holds itself above society, and unaccountable to those it serves. The symptoms, pointed out by Richard Kohn and others, are disrespect and unresponsiveness on the part of the military to civilian leaders, elements that have in other countries led to military coups. At the societal level, such a phenomenon could result in a sense among the military and society in general that they have separate fortunes and are not entirely tied together. This was the German experience in 1806 when Prussian citizens saw the Army, and not Prussia or themselves, as defeated by Napoleon at Jena and Auerstadt.

The military must continuously answer to the society it serves in order to prevent these sorts of circumstances. But any gap that does exist between the military and American society is a functional gap, not one of diametrically opposed values and cultures. While the military must remain subordinate to civilian authority, it must also meet the hard requirements of the battlefield. Success on the battlefield is the military's *functional imperative*. To carry out its functional imperative, the military cannot govern itself in accordance with the principles of liberal society. The functional gap between society and the military must exist to some degree.[29]

This is especially so in a liberal society that has justified the existence of a military for one reason only—to provide for the common defense. As T. R. Fehrenbach wrote in *This Kind of War*, his classic study of the Korean conflict, "By the very nature of its missions, the military must maintain a hard and illiberal view of life and the world. Society's purpose is to live; the military's is to stand ready, if need be, to die."[30]

Those who advocate the necessity of maintaining a separate military ethos or culture and argue that the attempt to subordinate the military's functional imperative to the dictates of liberal society is dangerous contend that the distinct characteristics of military culture are the evolutionary response of human beings to the nature of war.[31]

No one has developed a more comprehensive theory of war than the nineteenth-century Prussian "philosopher of war," Carl Von Clausewitz.[32] He described the phenomenon of war as a violent clash of opposing wills, each seeking to prevail over the other, further complicated by the fact that the will of each adversary is directed at an animate object that reacts often in unanticipated ways. This cyclical interaction between opposing wills occurs in a realm of chance and chaos, constantly generating "friction . . . the only concept that more or less corresponds to the factors that distinguish real war from war on paper."[33]

In his magnum opus, *On War*, Clausewitz argues that war is a "remarkable trinity." The first part of this trinity is "primordial violence, hatred, and enmity," which Clausewitz calls the realm of the people. The second part is composed of "chance and probability within which the creative spirit is free to roam," which he calls the realm of the commander and his army. The third is the "element of subordination, as an instrument of policy, which makes [war] subordinate to reason alone," the realm of the government.[34]

Clausewitz makes the case that while the *character* of war is infinitely variable, the *nature* of war is basically immutable. It is first and foremost a violent clash between opposing wills, each seeking to prevail over the other. In Clausewitz's formulation, our will is directed at an *animate object that reacts* often in unanticipated ways. This cyclical interaction between opposing wills occurs in an environment dominated by chance and chaos.

Since war is a human enterprise, the human dimension is central to the proper understanding of the phenomenon. Accordingly, war involves intangibles that cannot be quantified. War is shaped by human nature, the complexities of human behavior, and the limitations of human mental and physical capabilities. Any view of war that ignores what Clausewitz called the "moral factors," e.g., fear, the impact of danger, and physical exhaustion, is fraught with peril. As the Prussian observed, "Military activity is never directed against material forces alone; it is always aimed simultaneously at the moral forces which give it life, and the two cannot be separated." Since the art of war deals with living and moral forces, it cannot attain anything approaching absolute certainty in things either large or small.[35]

War does not take place in a deterministic, predictable, or mechanistic world. Rather it is characterized by complexity, apparent randomness, and sensitivity to initial conditions. War is not a system that can be subjected to precise, positive control or synchronized, centralized schemes. Instead, it is a highly complex interactive system characterized by friction, unpredictability, disorder, and fluidity. Such systems are composed of numerous independent agents that interact with each other, coevolve from this interaction, and adapt. War is an open system interacting with its external environment (including the enemy) and characterized by complex feedback loops and nonlinear dynamics.

As the "new sciences" of complexity have demonstrated, nonlinear systems exhibit erratic behavior, arising from disproportionately small outputs or disproportionately large outputs relative to inputs and from "synergistic" interactions. An important branch of nonlinear dynamics is the so-called "chaos theory." "Chaos" is often observed when a system is nonlinear and sensitive to initial conditions. Immeasurably, small differences in input can produce an entirely different outcome, can follow various behavior routes, and exhibit characteristics of randomness. War seems to be such a system.[36]

Since "[w]ar is not the action of a living body on a lifeless mass . . . but always the collision of two living forces," war exhibits the sort of unpredictability observed in chaotic systems.[37] Military action does not produce a single reaction but a dynamic interaction, the very nature of which is bound to lead to unpredictability. This unpredictability inherent in war as a nonlinear system is magnified by three other phenomena that Clausewitz addresses in some detail: chance, uncertainty, and friction.

War takes place in the realm of chance and uncertainty, constrained by time, and always subject to friction. As Clausewitz observed, "No other human activity is so continuously and universally bound up with chance" as is war, and "Three-quarters of the factors on which action in war is based are wrapped in a fog of greater or lesser uncertainty."[38]

Uncertainty represents what we do not know or understand about a given situation. Practically, it is a doubt that threatens to block action. Uncertainty is not merely a lack of data that can be solved by gathering and processing more information, but the natural and inevitable product of the dynamics of war. In war, all actions generate uncertainty, and the ultimate requirement is to be able to operate effectively despite uncertainty.

Like uncertainty, friction in war also seems to be an intractable problem. As Clausewitz observes:

> . . . everything in war is simple, but the simplest thing is difficult. The difficulties accumulate and end by producing a kind of friction that is inconceivable unless one has experienced war. Countless minor incidents—the kind you can never really foresee—combine to lower the general level of performance, so that one always falls far short of the intended goal . . . . The military machine—the army and everything related to it—is basically very simple and therefore seems easy to manage. But we should keep in mind that none of its components is of one piece: each

part is composed of individuals, . . . the least important of whom may chance to delay things or somehow make them go wrong . . . . This tremendous friction, which cannot, as in mechanics, be reduced to a few points, is everywhere in contact with chance, and brings about effects that cannot be measured, just because they are largely due to chance.[39]

Clearly, apparently insignificant causes can be amplified in war until they produce unanticipated macroeffects.

Contending with the Nature of War: Military Culture or *Ethos*

In order to counter the effects of war, successful militaries have developed a distinct culture designed to mitigate the impact of chance, uncertainty, and friction, all multiplied by the impact of fear. Such a military culture places a premium on such factors as unit cohesion and morale; it stresses such martial virtues as courage, both physical and moral, a sense of honor and duty, discipline, a professional code of conduct, and loyalty. The military as an institution has developed its own codes of conduct, methods, procedures, and organizations for a reason. These characteristics of military culture are dictated by the requirements of a workplace that is foreign to most civilians.

Of all these factors, cohesion is perhaps the most important. While friction and the other characteristics of war that create uncertainty seem to be inherent to war itself, military organizations attempt to *reduce* these factors. Friction is countered by such means as training, discipline, cohesion, regulations, orders, and what Clausewitz calls "the iron will of the commander," i.e., what we think of as the components of the military *ethos*.

These are the factors that make it possible for American soldiers on battlefields in Iraq and Afghanistan to overcome the chaotic interaction of friction and chance that they have faced on battlefields throughout history. Success in war depends on selfless leadership of small-unit commanders and the discipline and courage of individual soldiers who continue to fight despite the most powerful emotion known to human beings—fear arising from the instinct of self-preservation. It depends on a military culture capable of transforming civilians into soldiers that makes the difference between ultimate success and failure on the battlefield.

Defenders of military culture contend that all too often, American political elites see military culture not as something that contributes to military effectiveness, but as a problem to be eradicated in the name of multiculturalism, sexual politics, and the politics of "sexual orientation." At a minimum, they say, elite opinion takes for granted that the military is obligated to adapt to contemporary liberal values, patterns of behavior, and social mores no matter how adversely they might affect the military's ability to carry out its functional imperative. These defenders of military culture argue that there is a more radical version, epitomized by former Rep. Pat Schroeder's claim during the Navy's Tailhook trauma that the Service's problems represented "the sound of a culture cracking," which seeks destruction of the culture, not its reform.[40]

Edgar Schein has defined an ethos or culture as a pattern of basic assumptions that are invented, discovered, or developed by an organization as it learns to cope with its problems of external adaptation and internal integration. This pattern has worked well enough to be considered valid and, therefore, is to be taught to new members as the "correct" way to perceive, think, or feel in relation to these problems.[41]

Based on Schein's definition, a culture is the "deep" structure of organizations that is rooted in the prevailing assumptions, norms, values, customs, and traditions that collectively, over time, have created shared individual expectations among the members.[42] Culture is what makes organizations a distinctive source of identity and experience.[43]

As James Burk observes, the central elements of military culture—and what makes military culture unique—derive from "an attempt to deal with (and, if possible, to overcome) the uncertainty of war, to impose some pattern on war, to control war's outcome, and to invest war with meaning and significance." It is "an elaborate social construction, an exercise of creative intelligence, through which we come to imagine war in a particular way and to embrace certain rationalizations about how war should be conducted and for what purposes."[44]

Military culture comprises four elements: discipline; a professional ethos; the ceremonial displays and etiquette that pervade military life; and cohesion and esprit de corps. Burk describes discipline as "the orderly conduct of military personnel, whether individually or in formation, in battle or in garrison, and most often prescribed by their officers in command" the purpose of which is to "minimize the confusion and disintegrative consequences of battle by imposing order on it with a repertoire of patterned actions that they may use on their own initiative, or in coordination with others, quickly to adapt and to prevail in battle."

The professional ethos, the second element of military culture, can be understood as a "set of normative self-understandings which for the members define the profession's corporate identity, its code of conduct and, for the officers in particular, its social worth." In order to provide legitimacy, society at large must also recognize and accept this ethos. In Huntington's words:

> People who act the same way over a long period of time tend to develop distinctive and persistent habits of thought. Their unique relation to the world gives them a unique perspective on the world and leads them to rationalize their behavior and role. This is particularly true where the role is a professional one. A profession is more narrowly defined, more intensively and exclusively pursued, and more dearly isolated from other human activity than are most occupations. The continuing objective performance of the professional function gives rise to . . . the values, attitudes, and perspectives which inhere in the performance of the professional military function and which are deducible from the nature of that function. The military function is performed by a public bureaucratized profession expert in the management of violence and responsible for the military security of the state. A value or attitude is part of the professional ethic if it is implied by or derived from the peculiar expertise, responsibility, and organization of the military profession.[45]

But the *quid pro quo* in the American case is that the US military ethos is also shaped by American society.[46] This creates a tension that, as noted earlier, has led to the most vociferous civil–military debates.

The third element of military culture consists of the ceremonial displays and etiquette that pervade military life. As Burk writes, "These ceremonies and etiquette make up an elaborate ritual and play the role that ritual typically plays in society: to control or mask our anxieties and ignorance; to affirm our solidarity with one another; and to celebrate our being, usually in conjunction with a larger universe."[47]

The fourth element of military culture is cohesion and esprit de corps, measures of a unit's morale and its willingness to perform a mission. Most observers understand cohesion to be a critical element of operational effectiveness. According to Burk,

> Military cohesion refers to the feelings of identity and comradeship that soldiers hold for those in their immediate military unit, the outgrowth of face-to-face or primary (horizontal) group relations. In contrast, esprit de corps refers to the commitment or pride soldiers take in the larger military establishment to which the unit belongs, an outgrowth of secondary (vertical) group relations. Both result to an important degree from structural factors of military organization, but they are primarily matters of belief and emotional attachment.

Behavioral studies since the Second World War have convincingly shown that, in the main, soldiers do not fight cohesively because of ideology or patriotism. As J. Glen Gray observed in his classic study of ground combat, *The Warriors: Reflections on Men in Battle*, while soldiers may first go to war for the defense of their country, political ideology, or religious convictions, these factors are not, in the long run, what sustains them. "When through military reverses or the fatiguing and often horrible experiences of combat, the original purpose becomes obscured, the fighter is often sustained solely by the determination not to let down his comrades." He continues:

Numberless soldiers have died, more or less willingly, not for country or honor or religious faith or for any other abstract good, but because they realized that by fleeing their posts and rescuing themselves, they would expose their companions to greater danger. Such loyalty to the group is the essence of fighting morale. The commander who can preserve and strengthen it knows that all other physical and psychological factors are little in comparison. The feeling of loyalty, it is clear, is the result not the cause of comradeship. Comrades are loyal to each other spontaneously and without any need for reasons.[48]

Burk confirms the Gray's observations, arguing that the basis of unit cohesion is loyalty to other members of the unit:

[It] was the capacity of the soldiers' immediate unit, their company and platoon, to meet their basic needs for food, shelter, affection and esteem. These factors increased in importance as war genuinely threatened soldiers' sense of security and recognition of worth as human beings. So long as these needs were met, soldiers believed themselves part of a powerful group and felt responsible, even empowered, to fight for their group's well being. However, when these needs were not met, soldiers felt alone and unable to protect themselves; the unit disintegrated and stopped fighting.

The issue of cohesion has often taken center stage in the debates over women in combat and military by open homosexuals. Advocates of both have tended to downplay cohesion, denying its importance or defining it down so that it could just as well apply to a civilian workplace. For instance, Robert MacCoun has made the case for "situational" or "task" cohesion in contrast to "social" cohesion. Looking primarily at fire and police departments, he argues that the common efforts and stresses of performing a task would generate cohesion and override any centrifugal tendencies—either homosexual or heterosexual in the case of women—among the personnel involved.[49]

But critics of this view observe that while there is some degree of commonality between public safety professionals on the one hand and the military on the other hand, the two cases are far from identical. What the police officer or firefighter must face on occasion is the norm for the soldier in combat. Even what the firefighter must face in terms of the danger of a fire is not the same as being manipulated by other human beings who are trying to kill him. Thus, unit cohesion in combat is far more than teamwork. Cohesion arises from the bond among disparate individuals who have nothing in common but facing death and misery together, a bond akin to what the Greeks called *philia*—friendship, comradeship, or brotherly love.[50]

The anthropologist Lionel Tiger has even suggested that the foundation of bonding among males is biological in nature. According to his hypothesis, such bonding is crucial within groups that must confront disruptions of the social order, e.g., politics and war.[51]

An excellent description of unit cohesion is found in the 1992 report of the *Presidential Commission on the Assignment of Women in the Armed Forces*. According to this report, cohesion refers to "the relationship that develops in a unit or group where (1) members share common values and experiences; (2) individuals in the group conform to group norms and behavior in order to ensure group survival and goals; (3) members lose their identity in favor of a group identity; (4) members focus on group activities and goals; (5) unit members become totally dependent on each other for the completion of their mission or survival; and (6) group members must meet all the standards of performance and behavior in order not to threaten group survival.[52]

Of course, not all cohesive military units will be combat effective. Cohesion is a *necessary* but not *sufficient* condition for success on the battlefield. But military effectiveness depends also on the technical and tactical competence of the unit's personnel, especially its leaders, and trust in and commitment to the chain of command.

Women in the Military

There are a number of personnel issues that have implications for civil–military relations because they transcend simply military affairs. In earlier times, one of these would have been the integration of African-Americans into the American military. But in fact such integration has taken place and, for the most part, is no longer an issue. The process of full integration into the military is now underway for two other groups: women and homo-sexuals. Advocates of both women and homosexuals claim the mantle of the earlier attempt to integrate blacks into the military. Opponents of opening all military specialties to women and to military service by open homo-sexuals take issue with this claim. They argue that the impetus for the full integration of blacks into the military was military effectiveness, not the quest for equal rights, and that military effectiveness should trump other considerations when it comes to both women and homosexuals.

The role of women in the American military has been renegotiated on a number of occasions. Before World War II, the participation of women in the military was marginal, but personnel shortages during that conflict led to the recruitment of women in order to free men for combat. During the Second World War, more than 350,000 women served in the US military.

On June 12, 1948, President Harry Truman signed the Women's Armed Services Integration Act, giving permanent status to women in the active and reserve branches of all services. However, the bill capped the percentage of each service's end strength made up of women at 2 percent. Women officers could advance no higher in grade than lieutenant colonel or Navy commander. In addition, the law barred women from all combat aircraft and all Navy vessels except hospital ships and transports.[53]

With the end of the draft in 1973, the civil–military bargain regarding women was renegotiated once again. In 1976, the service academies were opened to women, and in 1978, the Navy permitted women to serve on non-combatant ships for the first time. But in 1980, Congress rejected President Carter's proposal to require women to register for the draft, a decision that was upheld by the Supreme Court in 1981 when it ruled in *Rostker v. Goldberg* that a male-only draft does not violate the "equal protection" clause of the Constitution.

The decade of the 1990s brought many issues regarding women to the forefront of the civil–military relations debate. In 1990, a woman was given command of a Navy ship for the first time, and in 1991, Congress lifted the ban on women flying combat aircraft. Some believe this decision was facilitated by the "Tailhook" scandal of September 1991, during which a number of naval aviators, fresh from deployment in the Middle East and the First Gulf War, engaged in boorish behavior toward some women, including fellow officers.[54]

A number of other issues regarding women in the military followed during the 1990s. In 1995, Air Force Lt. Kelly Flinn, the first women to pilot a B-52, resigned her commission in order to avoid a court martial stemming from an affair she had carried on with a civilian spouse of an enlisted Air Force woman. And in 1996, female trainees at the Aberdeen Proving Grounds in Maryland alleged that they had been sexually harassed and in some cases raped by their drill sergeants.[55]

Currently, women constitute 14 percent of the uniformed military and 37 percent of the civilian work force of the Department of Defense. As of September 2007, the Army, Air Force, and Marine Corps each had one lieutenant general and the Navy had two vice admirals.[56] In June of 2008, Army Gen. Ann E. Dunwoody became the country's first female to achieve four-star rank when she took command of the US Army Materiel Command.[57] Within the civilian leadership of the Department of Defense, the number of high- and mid-level women is unprecedented.[58]

In addition, the sorts of jobs military women do have changed substantially. In 1972, the occupational distribution of enlisted women was as follows: clerical, 67 percent; health, 22 percent; technical, 8 percent; others, 2 percent. By 1990, the landscape for women in the military had changed: 38 percent of enlisted women served in a clerical capacity, 15 percent were in military health fields, and the percentage of women in technical fields had risen to 21 percent. During that period, the "other" occupation expanded substantially. In 1990, 11 percent of enlisted women were serving as craftsmen, 11 percent were working in the field of service and supply, and 4 percent were working in combat-related fields.[59]

At present, 90 percent of all military occupational specialties are open to women. The Navy has recently opened up service on submarines to women, meaning that only close ground combat and special operations remain closed to women, figures that support Moskos' claim that in the postmodern military, women are "fully integrated" into the force.[60] However, there is a great deal of debate over the remaining restrictions. This debate lies at the heart of US civil–military relations.

The current regulations regarding ground combat were established by then-Secretary of Defense Les Aspin. In a memorandum dated April 28, 1993, Secretary Aspin directed the services to open more specialties and assignments to women, but maintaining the ban on women in ground combat. In a second memo dated January 13, 1994, he announced a "ground combat" rule that dropped the previous "risk rule" that had been established in 1988 but clearly defined the remaining restrictions on women.

The rule reads: "All service members are eligible to be assigned to all positions for which they are qualified, except that women shall be excluded from assignment to units below the brigade level whose primary mission is to engage in direct combat on the ground . . ." Direct combat was defined as "engaging an enemy on the ground with individual or crew-served weapons, while being exposed to hostile fire and a high probability of direct physical contact with the hostile force's personnel. Direct ground combat takes place well forward on the battlefield while locating and closing with the enemy to defeat them by fire, maneuver, or shock effect."[61]

Those who oppose the idea of women in combat raise several issues. First, there are substantial physical differences between men and women that place the latter at a distinct disadvantage when it comes to ground combat. Second, in practice, these differences often lead to the generation of double standards that have a serious impact on morale and performance.[62] Third, women seem to possess less aptitude for the stresses of combat. Finally, men treat women differently than they treat other men. This can undermine the comradeship upon which the unit cohesion necessary to success on the battlefield depends.

Of course, although on average, women are weaker than men, there will always be some women who can physically outperform some men. Early in the debate over women in the military, even advocates of opening more military specialties to women drew the line at ground combat. For instance, one of the most vociferous advocates of increasing opportunities for military women, retired Air Force Maj. Gen. Jeanne Holm, testified before Congress that "women could fly jets, serve on combat ships, fire missiles and artillery, and do any job that requires skill rather than muscle . . . . I have great difficulty with ground combat where the number one concern is physical strength."[63]

But more recent advocates of women in combat argue that those who are physically qualified should be permitted to serve in ground combat units. In the words of Melissa Embser-Herbert, a professor of sociology, "If a woman demonstrates that she meets the requirements to perform a job, she should be allowed to do it. The requirements should include physical ability, and if this means that few women make the cut, so be it. Physical-fitness tests should be tied to the demands of one's military occupation, not one's sex."[64]

Regarding aptitude for ground combat, research suggests that men tend to be more aggressive than women. Men are much more likely to join the military because they want to fight. On the other hand, women typically join for career purposes rather than a desire to go to war.[65] But there is substantial disagreement about the etiology: are differences cultural or biological? In the words of Darlene Iskra, a sociologist at the University of Maryland, "everybody recognizes that women can kill. It's just not the cultural norm."[66]

Linda Grant de Pauw writes that "women have always been capable of killing." But most cultures, including our own, draw a veil over this reality.

"When combat serves as a puberty ritual for boys, girls cannot participate without destroying its meaning. If girls could qualify as both mothers and warriors, there would be no unique identity for boys."[67] The widely respected anthropologist, Margaret Mead, wrote that "the historical and comparative material at least suggests that it may be highly undesirable to permit women, trained to inhibit aggressive behavior, to take place in offensive war. Defensive warfare, on the other hand, does not have the same disadvantages, as it invokes the biological basis of defense of the nest and the young."[68]

Advocates of opening combat specialties to women point out that no matter what the restrictions may say, women have been exposed to combat in Iraq and Afghanistan.[69] Indeed, between May 2003 and April 2008, 120 female soldiers died in those two conflicts—66 of them killed in action.[70] But critics of women in combat argue that there is a difference between being "in harm's way" and directly attacking and destroying the enemy. In the latter case, research suggests "that female soldiers do not have an equal opportunity to survive or help others survive" in situations requiring them to "seek out the enemy."[71]

Opponents of opening combat specialties to women also make the case that the presence of women in combat units will result in increased friction and have an adverse impact on unit cohesion. In fact, the US military has had to contend with increased administrative and logistical problems arising from physical differences between men and women. These differences have led to the creation of double standards, undermining fairness and trust, which are fundamental to unit cohesion. Finally, the intermingling of women and men can result in the replacement of *philia* by *eros*.[72]

Those who make this argument contend that mixing the sexes introduces *eros* into an environment based on *philia*, creating the most dangerous form of friction in the military, which corrode the very source of military excellence itself. Unlike *philia*, *eros* is individual and exclusive. *Eros* manifests itself as sexual competition, protectiveness, and favoritism.[73] As James Webb observed several years ago, "there is no greater or more natural bias than that of an individual toward a beloved. And few emotions are more powerful, or more distracting, than those surrounding the pursuit of, competition for, or the breaking off of amorous relationships."[74]

The destructive impact of such relationships on unit cohesion should be obvious, say opponents of women in combat. Does a superior order his or her beloved into danger? If he or she demonstrates favoritism, what is the consequence for unit morale and discipline? What happens when jealousy rears its head? These are questions of life and death and also help to explain why open homosexuality and homosexual behavior traditionally has been prohibited in the service.

Advocates of opening combat specialties to women contend that these problems are overstated,[75] and to the extent they do exist, they can be eradicated by means of education and indoctrination.[76] But opponents contend that all the social engineering in the world cannot change the real differences between men and women and the fact that men treat women differently than they treat other men.[77] They point to the Israeli experience as a case in point.

During the period of the British Mandate for Palestine, Palestinian Jews formed an elite, semi-clandestine, volunteer Jewish youth organization called Palmach. The ideology of Palmach was egalitarian socialism, and according to the Israeli historian Martin van Creveld, the organization "was sexually integrated to an extent rarely attained by any armed force before or since."[78]

Palmach was essentially a militia made up of Palestinian Jews designed for self-defense against local Arab attacks. Van Creveld writes that before Israeli independence, Palmach women accompanied men on missions, especially "undercover missions that involved obtaining intelligence, transmitting messages, smuggling arms, and the like." During Israel's War of Independence, Palmach served as the core of Haganah, the forerunner of the Israel Defense Force (IDF).

Despite Palmach's ideological commitment to radical equality for women, the practical experience of the 1948 war, which involved coordinated, combined arms offensive actions, convinced the leaders of Israel and the IDF that the dangers of women in combat outweighed the benefits—including commitment to an abstract concept of equality between the sexes. According to former Israeli Defense Minister Moshe Dayan, women reduced the combat effectiveness of Haganah units because men took steps to protect them out of "fear of what the Arabs would do to [the] women if they captured them."

In any event, the American people seem to have accepted the idea that women's military roles should be expanded. As Admiral Mike Mullen, Chairman of the Joint Chiefs, wrote to the Senate Armed Services Committee in support of opening submarine service to women, "as an advocate for improving the diversity of our force . . . one policy I would like to see changed is the one barring [the service of women] aboard submarines."[79]

But critics wonder if "diversity" is an appropriate goal when lives are at stake, as they are in combat. They are also concerned that there is a disconnect between efforts to protect women from sexual abuse while at the same time pushing them into dangerous combat roles. As Elaine Donnelly has observed, "Many officials in Congress, the Pentagon, and the service academies are eager to establish ubiquitous 'victim advocate' offices, staffed by professionals who vow to protect military women from the slightest form of harassment, real or imagined" while "simultaneously [promoting] the deliberate exposure of military women to extreme abuse and violence in close, lethal combat, where females do not have an equal opportunity to survive."[80]

In addition, she contends, there are indications "that many female recruits are not being informed, prior to enlistment, that regulations no longer exempt women from assignments known to involve a 'substantial risk of capture' . . . Nor are recruits being told that the 'job description' might involve involuntary placement in ground-combat-collocated units, despite regulations requiring those units to be coded for men only."[81]

Nonetheless on the whole, military women have performed well since 9/11. Supporters of opening the remaining military specialties still closed to women observe that the worst fears of opponents have not come to pass. They point out that like soldiers before them, military women are just "doing their job" and that to the extent they do, their male comrades are willing to accept them. Not all do of course. But the record seems to indicate that as long as military women act professionally and perform their jobs well, their male counterparts will treat them with respect.[82]

The question of opening ground combat specialties to women will continue to be negotiated. For better or worse, American society seems to have accepted a more expansive role for women in the military. Critics of opening more military specialties will argue that the presence of women will undermine the unique ethos necessary to fulfill the military's functional imperative. Supporters will maintain that as long as women maintain their professionalism, the military ethos will not suffer.

Homosexuals in the Military

During his 2010 State of the Union Address, President Obama pledged to "work with Congress and our military to finally repeal the law that denies gay Americans the right to serve the country they love because of who they are," reaffirming his campaign pledge to end the military's policy of "don't ask, don't tell," which on the one hand, prevents military recruiters from asking about a recruit's sexual orientation and, on the other hand, permits homosexuals to serve in the military as long as they remain closeted.[83] But the president's remarks and media coverage of the "don't ask, don't tell" issue indicate an ignorance of the facts at hand. In fact, contrary to most accounts of the issue of open homosexuals in the military, there is a difference between the *law* regarding homosexuals in the military on the one hand and the "don't ask, don't tell" *policy* adopted by the Clinton administration—and still in effect—on the other hand.

The law, passed in 1993 by a veto-proof margin in a Democratic-controlled Congress, codified regulations in effect before President Clinton's inauguration. This law (section 654 of title 10, *United States Code*, included in the *National Defense Authorization Act for Fiscal Year 1994, Public Law 103–160*, November 30, 1993, and accompanying Senate and House report language) makes the historical prohibition against military service for homosexuals a matter of statute law.

Some have suggested that the president has the authority to lift the ban by executive order pursuant to his authority to suspend statutory policies regarding the retention of military personnel during periods of "national emergency."[84] But as Secretary of Defense Robert Gates observed in June 2009, "What we have is a law, not a policy or regulation. And as I discovered when I got into it, it is a very prescriptive law. It doesn't leave a lot to the imagination or a lot of flexibility."[85]

The "don't ask, don't tell" policy was the result of a compromise between the president, who had failed in his attempt to lift the ban on homosexuals serving openly in the military, and the Joint Chiefs of Staff and key members of Congress, who adamantly opposed lifting the ban. The subject policy does not have the force of law and could be repealed at the stroke of a pen.

However, the reverse is not the case. Since Article I, Section 8 of the Constitution, gives Congress the exclusive power to "raise and support Armies, . . . provide and maintain a Navy, [and] . . . make Rules for the Government and Regulation of the land and naval Forces," the president cannot unilaterally declare that homosexuals are now permitted to serve openly in the military. The law would have to be changed as well.

The only modification of previous regulations codified in the 1993 law was suspension of the long-standing policy of asking recruit candidates if they were homosexuals before entering service. This small change has been the source of the false claim that the 1993 law embodied the "don't ask, don't tell" compromise.

In fact, the law *requires* that homosexuals, identified on the basis of acts or self-admission, *must* be separated from the service. Supporters of the ban observe that the reason for this has nothing to do with equal rights or

freedom of expression. According to the law on the books, there is no constitutional right to serve in the military. The findings of Congress as expressed
in the legislation and report language include the following points:

- Success in combat depends on military units characterized by high morale,
  good order and discipline, and unit cohesion.
- Military life is fundamentally different from civilian life. Because of the
  unique conditions service members face and the unique responsibilities
  that military service entails, the military community constitutes a specialized society governed by its own laws, rules, customs, and traditions,
  including restrictions on personal behavior that would be unacceptable
  in civilian society. Standards of conduct apply to military members at
  all times, whether on or off duty, whether on or off base.
- "The presence in the armed forces of persons who demonstrate a propensity or intent to engage in homosexual acts would create an unacceptable
  risk to the high standards of morale, good order and discipline, and unit
  cohesion that are the essence of military capability."[86]

There are clearly parallels between the issue of military service by open
homosexuals and the issue of women in combat. But as the language above
illustrates, the key objection to service by openly homosexual members
centers on unit cohesion. As in the case of women in combat, opponents of
service by open homosexuals argue that unit cohesion will be affected.[87]
Opponents vociferously deny the claim. They argue that the integration of
open homosexuals in the military is merely a manifestation of the quest for
equal civil rights that began with African-Americans after World War II.
Furthermore, the separation of homosexuals from the military deprives the
country of some critical personnel, e.g., Arabic language specialists. They
also argue that other Western countries have lifted their bans on open service by homosexuals without suffering adverse effects.[88]

Proponents of permitting homosexuals to serve openly in the military
often invoke President Truman's executive order after World War II that
integrated the US military. In *Boston Globe* column on January 11, 1993,
James Carroll wrote that "today's soldiers **and sailors** reluctant to serve
shoulder to shoulder with homosexuals **are the progen**y of racist and sexist
soldiers and sailors who were told to get **over it or get out**."

But opponents of service by open homosexuals argue that the similarities
between opposition to permitting homosexuals to serve openly in the military today and opposition to racial integration of the services five decades
ago are superficial. Testifying before Congress in 1993, then-Chairman of

the Joint Chiefs of Staff, Gen. Colin Powell said, "I think it would be preju-
dicial to good order and discipline to try to integrate gays and lesbians in the
current military structure." In response to his testimony, Congresswoman
Pat Schroeder, then a Democrat representing Colorado, quoted a 1942
government report and claimed that the same arguments used then against
racial integration in the military were being used against gays today. In his
memoirs, Gen. Powell wrote: "She had her logic wrong. I responded, 'Skin
color is a benign, nonbehavioral characteristic. Sexual orientation is perhaps
the most profound of human behavioral characteristics. Comparison of the
two is a convenient but invalid argument'."

Powell noted the mixed reaction among African-American groups to the
linking of gay rights and the civil rights movement. "The Congressional
Black Caucus favored removing the ban on homosexuals in the armed
services. But other leaders were telling me that they resented having the civil
rights crusade hijacked by the gay community for its ends."[89] (Powell has
since concluded that the policy should be reevaluated.)

Others agreed. Testifying before a Senate Committee hearing on this
issue on April 29, 1993, Lt. Gen. Calvin A. H. Waller, a highly respected
African-American military leader, responded to a query by the Chairman
of the Senate Armed Services Committee, Democratic Senator Sam Nunn
of Georgia, concerning whether he agreed with equating homosexual rights
and civil rights for racial minorities. Waller replied, "We are talking about
the lifestyle or the sexuality of a person who wants to be open with their
sexuality or with their lifestyle into a force or into the Armed Forces where
I think that is detrimental to readiness and to good law and order and discipline." Waller further commented that he strongly disagreed with the racial
analogy. "I am opposed to that. I do not like that analogy. I do not think it is
the same in any respect." Charles Moskos, testifying on the same day, suggested that the black/white analogy vis-à-vis homosexuals/heterosexuals
was less appropriate than the male/female analogy.[90]

In response to the claim, advocates of service by open homosexuals
observe that other countries, e.g., France, Israel, and Germany, permit
homosexuals to serve openly in their militaries; those who support the continued ban contend that such militaries still discriminate. According to
Moskos, with the exceptions of the Netherlands and the Scandinavian
countries, "there is no country in Europe, much less Israel, that American
advocates of gay rights would find a suitable model."[91]

In response to the claim that military readiness is being hurt by the
discharge of homosexuals from the military, supporters of the ban observe
that such separations constitute only a small proportion of all discharges.

From 2004 until 2008, discharges for homosexuality averaged one-third of 1 percent (0.32 percent) of all discharges. For instance, in 2008, there were 5,627 discharges for drugs, 3,817 for serious offenses, 4,555 for failure to meet weight standards, 2,353 for pregnancy, 2,574 for parenthood, and 634 for homosexuality.[92]

While the Chairman of the Joint Chiefs of Staff, Admiral Mike Mullen, has called for ending the ban, the uniformed military leadership has tended to support maintaining it, or at least moving slow on the issue. The most outspoken of the service chiefs was General James Conway, then Commandant of the Marine Corps, who explicitly rejected lifting the prohibition. His successor, General James Amos, argued that this is not the time to change the law. "This is not a social thing. This is combat effectiveness," he said.[93] Retired Air Force General Merrill McPeak, former chief of staff of that service, also came out in favor of maintaining the ban.[94]

Nonetheless, there are currently a number of proposals in Congress to change the law.[95] Perhaps the most prominent member of Congress to introduce such legislation is Sen. Joseph Lieberman, an Independent from Connecticut, a supporter of the war in Iraq. On March 3, 2010, he, along with 22 cosponsors, introduced S. 3065, "A bill to amend title 10, United States Code, to enhance the readiness of the Armed Forces by replacing the current policy concerning homosexuality in the Armed Forces, referred to as 'Don't Ask, Don't Tell', with a policy of nondiscrimination on the basis of sexual orientation."

In September of 2010, proponents of lifting the ban attempted to attach an amendment to the Defense Authorization Bill. However it was defeated on a procedural point as Sen. Harry Reid, the Senate majority leader, was unable to get the 60 votes necessary to ensure passage of the bill with the amendment.[96] The result left the future of legislatively repealing the homosexual ban in doubt.

However, in October of 2010, the issue returned to the fore when a federal district judge in California ruled that the federal law governing homosexuals in the military violates substantive due process and First Amendment speech rights. The judge, Virginia A. Phillips, ruled that the plaintiff organization was entitled to a permanent injunction against the law, which she issued shortly thereafter, rejecting the government's argument that such an injunction would harm military readiness.[97]

Secretary Gates denounced the injunction, arguing that an abrupt end to the law would have "enormous consequences" for the troops. "This is a very complex business. It has enormous consequences for our troops," Gates said. "As I have said from the very beginning, there should be legislation, and that legislation should be informed by the review we have underway." Nonetheless, the Pentagon indicated that it would, of course, comply with the injunction. Meanwhile, the Obama administration asked the judge to stay the injunction, a request that was granted and indicated that it would appeal the decision.[98]

While advocates of repeal rejoiced, opponents argued that the decision represented the worst sort of judicial interference in military affairs. They also suggested that the decision would not withstand Supreme Court scrutiny, especially since the 1993 law was an example of Congress' powers under Article I, Section 8, of the Constitution.

Clearly President Obama is committed to repealing the restrictions on military service by open homosexuals and even a new Congress may still modify the current law. But renegotiating this element of the civil–military bargain requires the participation of the American people. There is considerable debate concerning what that attitude is on the one hand and what the response of current service members would be to changing the law on the other. The answer depends a great deal on how the question is asked.[99]

There is no doubt that the push for open homosexual military service will continue to be a contentious civil–military relation issue for the foreseeable future. Even if the ban is lifted, the debate will continue—as has been the case with women in the military—as both sides attempt to prove that the bad or good that they had predicted had in fact come to pass. But such debate is the essence of the continuous renegotiation of the civil–military bargain.

Religious "Diversity"

The issue of homosexuals openly serving in the military will no doubt continue to be the main focus of the debate regarding who serves. However, there is another issue that may become increasingly divisive: the question of religious "diversity."

For instance, some have expressed concern about the increasing influence of evangelical Christians in the US military. Ann Loveland has traced this trend, arguing that between the end of World War II and the beginning of the 1990s, American evangelicals steadily grew in importance within the military structure. At the close of the 1940s, evangelical denominations were a minority within the American religious community and the military chaplains were dominated by mainline Protestant denominations. However, steady proselytizing led to an increase in the numbers of evangelicals within the military throughout the 1950s.

According to Loveland, the real change began during the Vietnam conflict. While many mainline Protestant churches had actively opposed the Vietnam War—and by extension, those who fought it—conservative Protestants in general and evangelicals in particular had tended to support it.

Many evangelicals saw the military as a place congenial to their beliefs. But many observers of the US military are concerned that while military ministries in the past have had a strong tradition of tolerance to a wide variety of faiths, the evangelical impulse is to seek new converts.[100]

In 2005, the Air Force created a task force to investigate the Air Force Academy for religious proselytizing and intolerance. Among the allegations were that cadets were frequently pressured to attend chapel and take religious instruction, particularly in the evangelical Christian faith; that prayer was a part of mandatory events at the academy; and that in at least one case a teacher ordered students to pray before beginning their final examination.[101]

According to the subsequent report, "a perception of religious intolerance" did exist among some at the academy. "The root of this problem is not overt religious discrimination, but a failure to fully accommodate all members' needs and a lack of awareness over where the line is drawn between permissible and impermissible expression of beliefs."[102] In 2007, seven officers, including two Air Force and two Army generals, were disciplined for appearing in uniform in a fundraising video for a Christian evangelical organization.[103]

The flip side of the problem of religious diversity arises with respect to service by religious minorities. In the past, the main issues have concerned uniform regulations: yarmulkes for Orthodox Jews and turbans for Sikhs. But recent efforts to recruit and retain service members who profess Islam have created a more troubling dilemma.

On the one hand, the military has been making a concerted effort to recruit Muslims. As the *Christian Science Monitor* reported in 2006,

> An underlying goal is to interest more Muslims in the military, which needs officers and troops who can speak Arabic and other relevant languages and understand the culture of places like Iraq and Afghanistan. The effort is also part of a larger outreach. Pentagon officials say they are striving for mutual understanding with Muslims at home and abroad and to win their support for US war aims.[104]

On the other hand, several recent events have raised the issue of possible conflicted loyalty on the part of American Muslim service members.

In 2003, on the eve of the US invasion of Iraq, a US soldier who had converted to Islam rolled a fragmentation grade into three tents at a camp in Kuwait, killing an officer and wounding 16 others, three seriously. One subsequently died. Sergeant Asan Akbar, an engineer from the 326th Engineer Battalion, part of the 101st Air Assault Division, also reportedly opened fire with his weapon. One Pentagon spokesman stated that "he's a Muslim, and it seems he was just against the war."[105] At his trial, he admitted carrying out the attack because he believed that American soldiers would kill Muslims and rape Muslim women in Iraq. He also claimed that he was religiously harassed before the incident, but the defense did not present any testimony to this effect at the trial. He was convicted of murder and sentenced to death.

In November 2009, a Muslim Army officer opened fire at a processing center at Fort Hood, Texas, killing 13 and wounding 30 others. The perpetrator, Maj. Nidal Malik Hasan, an American of Palestinian Arab descent, had, according to reports, previously expressed radical Islamist beliefs and been in e-mail contact with Anwar al-Awlaki, a radical imam. Many commentators expressed concerns that Hasan had not been disciplined or discharged because of "political correctness" and a desire for diversity. According to a report in the *Boston Globe*,

> Army superiors were warned about the radicalization of Major Nidal Malik Hasan years before he allegedly massacred 13 soldiers at Fort Hood, Texas, but did not act in part because they valued the rare diversity of having a Muslim psychiatrist, military investigators wrote in previously undisclosed reports.
>
> . . . .
>
> Examples of Hasan's radical behavior have previously been disclosed in press accounts based on interviews with unnamed Army officials, including his defense of suicide bombings and assertions that Islamic law took priority over his allegiance to the United States.
>
> . . . .
>
> "Major Hasan's military superiors did not apply correct regulatory standards to evaluate and act on statements that may have been contrary to his oath of allegiance to the Constitution of the United States," according to the findings. "As military officers, Major Hasan's superiors had a duty to determine whether Major Hasan's stated loyalties were compatible with continued military service."
>
> New details also emerge of Hasan's pattern of radical behavior, the first signs of which were detected in 2005, according to at least four officers who worked with him at the time and spoke to the FBI and Pentagon investigators.[106]

The volatility of this issue was illustrated by reaction to comments by the Chief of Staff of the Army, Gen. George Casey, who said after the shootings at Fort Hood, "Speculation could potentially heighten backlash against some of our Muslim soldiers and what happened at Fort Hood was a tragedy, but I believe it would be an even greater tragedy if our diversity becomes a casualty here. It's not just about Muslims, we have a very diverse army, we have very diverse society and that gives us all strength. But again we need to be very careful about that."[107]

Supporters of Muslims in the service make the obvious point that it is unfair to generalize about disloyalty by Muslims based on only a handful of violent incidents. But the issue is unlikely to go away since the current wars in which the United States is involved are being conducted against coreligionists of American Muslims. As one report put it right after the Fort Hood shootings,

> The push to boost Muslim representation has proven to be a double-edged sword for the military, which desperately needs the Muslim soldiers for their language skills and cultural knowledge, but also worries that a small percentage of those soldiers might harbor extremist ideologies or choose to turn their guns on their fellow soldiers.[108]

At present, the Muslim population within the military remains small. As of April 2008, there were 3,409 Muslims on active duty. But the issue will constitute part of the renegotiation of the civil–military bargain, not only within the services but also within the American Muslim community.[109]

Conclusion

Maintaining an effective and robust military is critical to the security of the United States. Despite an ongoing war, military retention and recruiting have remained relatively robust.[110] Some have suggested that this is the result of a weak economy, but in fact, both retention and recruiting were high when the economy was strong and when casualty rates in Iraq were on the rise. There was a surge in enlistments after 9/11 that reflected a patriotic fervor and the continuing high levels of recruitment and retention suggest that this fervor has not ebbed, despite a force that is under stress as a result of continuous action in Iraq and Afghanistan.

Indeed, stress on the force has been the main issue since the beginning of the wars in Iraq and Afghanistan. Repeated deployments cause numerous problems that not only have an impact on morale and discipline now, but may have long-term consequences that are not yet visible, from posttraumatic stress disorder to various medical maladies that will only manifest themselves in the future. These problems will extend as well to the reserve components. The fact is that, for the most part, the reserves are not structured to constantly deploy and redeploy. Observers have noted that deployments by the reserves affect the civilian sector as well. Deployments mean that employers who hire members of the reserve will lose their services during the period of deployment. For this reason, some may choose not to hire reservists. This does not seem to have happened yet, but it could in the future.

It is also the case that the issues of women in combat, military service by open homosexuals, and the accommodation of religious minorities by the services will continue to fuel the debate. But although the concept of a "postmodern" military may be new and the true "citizen-soldier" may be a thing of the past, the question of "who serves" remains since 9/11 and the wars in Iraq and Afghanistan what it always has: a central component of the constantly renegotiated civil–military bargain in America.

Notes

1   Eliot Cohen, "Twilight of the Citizen Soldier," *Parameters*, 31(2), Summer 2001, p. 24.
2   Thom Shanker, "US Troops Wonder: Is There a Home Front?" New York Times, July 26, 2005, http://www.nytimes.com/2005/07/25/world/americas/25iht-troops.html?_r=1.
3   Andrew Bacevich, *The New American Militarism: How Americans Are Seduced by War* (New York: Oxford University Press, 2005), p. 2.
4   Niccolo Machiavelli, *The Prince*, Leo Paul de Alvarez, ed. and trans. (Irving, TX: University of Dallas Press, 1980), p. 84 (Chapter XIII).
5   James Harrington, *The Commonwealth of Oceana*, ed. J. G. A. Pocock (Cambridge: Cambridge University Press, 1992).
6   Caroline Robbins, *The Eighteenth-Century Commonwealthman: Studies in the Transmission, Development, and Circumstance of English Liberal Thought from the Restoration of Charles II Until the War with the Thirteen Colonies* (Indianapolis: Liberty Fund, 2004 [first published in 1959 by Harvard University Press]).
7   For an excellent treatment of the American Army from the time of the Revolution to the eve of World War II, see Edward M. Coffman, *The Old Army: A Portrait of the American Army in Peacetime, 1784–1898* (New York: Oxford University Press, 1986) and Coffman, *The Regulars: The American Army 1898–1941* (Cambridge: The Belknap Press of Harvard University Press, 2004).
8   Lawrence Delbert Cress, *Citizens in Arms: The Army and Militia in American Society to the War of 1812* (Chapel Hill: The University of North Carolina Press, 1982). For other treatments of the militia myth, see James

Kirby Martin and Mark Edward Lender, *A Respectable Army: The Military Origins of the Republic, 1763–1789* (Wheeling, IL: Harlan Davidson, 1982), pp. 1–6. Cf. Charles Royster, *A Revolutionary People at War: The Continental Army and American Character, 1775–1783* (New York: Norton, 1979).

9 In addition to Coffman, note 7 supra, see Max Boot, *The Savage Wars of Peace: Small Wars and the Rise of American Power* (New York: Basic Books, 2002).

10 Roland Barthes, *Mythologies* (London: Jonathan Cape, 1956), p. 143. It is useful to remember that the word "myth" is derived from the Greek *mythos*, which means simply a "story."

11 Cress, *Citizens in Arms*; John C. Pinheiro, *Manifest Ambition: James K. Polk and Civil-Military Relations During the Mexican War* (Westport, CT: Praeger, 2007); William B. Skelton, "The Army in the Age of the Common Man, 1815–1845," in Kenneth J. Hagan and William R. Roberts, eds., *Against All Enemies: Interpretations of American Military History from Colonial Times to the Present* (New York: Greenwood Press, 1986).

12 Eliot Cohen, "Twilight of the Citizen Soldier," p. 24. On the citizen-solider and the idea of military obligation, see the articles in a special symposium on the topic in this issue of *Parameters*, the professional journal of the United States Army War College: James Burk, "The Military Obligation of Citizens Since Vietnam," pp. 48–60; Peter Karsten, "The US Citizen-Soldier's Past, Present, and Likely Future," pp. 61–73; and Charles Moskos, "What Ails the All-Volunteer Force: An Institutional Perspective," pp. 29–47.

13 Cohen, "Twilight of the Citizen Soldier," p. 24.

14 Charles Moskos, *A Call to Civic Service: National Service for Country and Community* (New York: Free Press, 1988); Moskos, "Time to Bring Back the Draft?" *The American Enterprise*, December 2001, pp. 16 and 17; Eliot A. Cohen, "The Civil-Military Balance," in *The Demilitarization of the Military*, Report of a Defense Task Force Chaired by Hon. John F. Lehman, Jr. and Dr. Harvey Sicherman (Philadelphia: Foreign Policy Research Institute, March 1997), pp. 31–38.

15 Morris Janowitz, "Civic Consciousness and Military Performance," in Morris Janowitz and Stephen D. Wesbrook, eds., *The Political Education of Soldiers* (Beverly Hills, CA: 1983), pp. 55–80, esp. 74–76. Cf. James Burk, "Theories of Democratic Civil-Military Relations," *Armed Forces and Society*, 29(1), Fall 2002 and Rebecca Schiff, *The Military and Domestic*

Politics: A Concordance Theory of Civil–Military Relations (London: Routledge, 2009).

16 Burk, "Theories of Democratic Civil-Military Relations," pp. 7 and 8.

17 Morris Janowitz and Charles Moskos, "Racial Composition of the All-Volunteer Force," *Armed Forces and Society,* 1(3), November 1974, pp. 109–123; Martin Binkin and Mark J. Eitelberg, *Blacks in the Military* (Washington, DC: Brookings, 1982).

18 For a useful historical overview of the issues, see Lindsay Cohn, "The Evolution of the Civil-Military 'Gap' Debate," TISS Project Paper, http://www.poli.duke.edu/civmil/cohn_literature_review.pdf.

19 Thomas E. Ricks, *Making the Corps* (New York: Scribners, 1997), p. 19.

20 Thomas E. Ricks, "The Widening Gap Between the Military and Society," *The Atlantic Monthly,* July 1997, pp. 66–70, 72–74, and 76–78. For a less alarmist view, see James Kitfield, "Standing Apart," *National Journal,* June 13, 1998, pp. 1350–1358; Mackubin Thomas Owens, "American Society and the Military: Is There a Gap?" *Providence Journal,* March 27, 1998; and Owens, "Gaps, Real and Imagined: American Society vs. Military Culture," *Washington Times,* November 1, 1999. The most comprehensive treatment of the gap can be found in Peter D. Feaver and Richard H. Kohn, eds., *Soldiers and Civilians: The Civil-Military Gap and American National Security* (Cambridge: MIT Press, 2001).

21 Andrew Bacevich and Richard Kohn, "Grand Army of the Republicans: Has the US Military Become a Partisan Force?" *The New Republic,* December 8, 1997; James McIsaac and Naomi Verdugo, "Civil-Military Relations: A Domestic Perspective," in Don Snider and Miranda Carlton-Carew, eds., *US Civil-Military Relations* (Washington, DC: Center for Strategic and International Studies, 1995); Thomas Ricks, "Duke Study Finds Sharp Rightward Shift in Military," *The Wall Street Journal,* November 11, 1997, p. A20; Ricks, "The Widening Gap"; Peter Maslowski, "Army Values and American Values," *Military Review,* April 1990, pp. 10–23; Keith Hutcheson, "The Discipline Crisis," *Armed Forces Journal International,* March 1996; Elizabeth Kier, "Homosexuals in the US Military: Open Integration and Combat Effectiveness," *International Security,* Fall 1998.

22 John Hillen, "The Military Ethos," *The World & I,* July 1997; Hillen, "The Civilian-Military Gap: Keep It, Defend It, Manage It," US Naval Institute *Proceedings,* October 1998; James Kitfield, "The Pen and the Sword," *Government Executive,* April 2000; Charles Maynes, "The Perils of (and for) an Imperial America," *Foreign Policy,* Summer 1998; James

Webb, "The War on Military Culture," *The Weekly Standard*, January 20, 1997; Webb, "Military Leadership in a Changing Society," Speech at the Naval War College Ethics Conference, November 16, 1998; Webb, "Interview: James Webb," US Naval Institute *Proceedings*, April 2000; Sam Sarkesian, "The Military Must Find Its Voice," *Orbis*, Summer 1998.

23 Pauline N. Rosenau, *Postmodernism and the Social Sciences: Insights, Inroads, and Intrusions* (Princeton: Princeton University Press, 1992); Francis Fukuyama, *The Great Disruption: Human Nature and the Reconstitution of the Social Order* (New York: Simon and Schuster, 2000).

24 Charles C. Moskos and James Burk, "The Postmodern Military," in James Burk, ed., *The Adaptive Military Armed Forces in a Turbulent World* (New Brunswick, NJ: Transaction, 1998), p. 168.

25 Charles C. Moskos, "Toward a Postmodern Military: The United States as a Paradigm," in Charles Moskos, John Allen Williams, and David R. Segal, eds., *The Postmodern Military: Armed Forces After the Cold War* (New York: Oxford University Press, 2000). Cf. also Bradford Booth, Meyer Kestenbaum, and David R. Segal, "Are Post-Cold War Militaries Postmodern?" *Armed Forces and Society*, 27(3), Spring 2001, pp. 319–342 and Gregory D. Foster, "The Postmodern Military: The Irony of 'Strengthening' Defense," *Harvard International Review*, 23(2), Summer 2001, pp. 24–29. Moskos' colleague John Allen Williams has added a new category dating from 2001, which he calls a "hybrid" military. "The 'Hybrid' label tries to capture the idea that the range of threats faced today combines threats of earlier eras, from nuclear attack to large-scale conventional war to low-intensity conflict against non-state actors to subnational threats within country." John Allen Williams, "The Military and Society: Beyond the Postmodern Era," *Orbis*, 52(2), Spring 2008, p. 202.

26 See also David R. Segal and Karin De Angelis, "Changing Conceptions of the Military as a Profession," in Suzanne C. Nielsen and Don M. Snider, eds., *American Civil-Military Relations: The Soldier and the State in a New Era* (Baltimore: The Johns Hopkins University Press, 2009), pp. 194–212.

27 Deborah D. Avant, *The Market for Force: The Consequences of Privatizing Security* (New York: Cambridge University Press, 2005).

28 Mark Thompson, "Walter Kerwin," *Time*, July 28, 2008, http://www.time.com/time/magazine/article/0,9171,1826297,00.html.

29 John Hillen, "The Civilian-Military Gap: Keep It, Defend It, Manage It," pp. 2–4.

30 T. R. Fehrenbach, *This Kind of War: A Study in Unpreparedness* (New York: Pocket Books, 1964), p. 467.

31 Mackubin Thomas Owens, "Technology, Friction, the RMA, and Future War," *Strategic Review*, Spring 1998. See also Owens, "Reflections on the Nature of War and Its Implications for Women in Combat and Gender-Integrated Training," Testimony Before the Congressional Commission on Military Training and Gender-Related Issues, December 21, 1998. *Final Report of the Congressional Commission on Military Training and Gender-Related Issues*, July 1999.

32 Clausewitz, *On War*, Michael Howard and Peter Paret, eds. and trans. (Princeton: Princeton University Press, 1976).

33 Ibid., p. 119.

34 Ibid., p. 89.

35 Ibid., p. 132.

36 Alan Beyerchen, "Clausewitz, Nonlinearity, and the Unpredictability of War," *International Security*, 17(3), Winter 1992/1993.

37 Clausewitz, *On War*, p. 77.

38 Ibid., pp. 85 and 101.

39 Ibid., pp. 119 and 120. See also Barry D. Watts, *Clausewitzian Friction and Future War*, McNair Paper 52 (Washington, DC: National Defense University Press, 1996).

40 Cf. John Hillen, "The Military Ethos," pp. 34–39; Hillen, "Must Military Culture Reform?" *Orbis*, Winter 1999, pp. 43–57 and Don Snider, "An Uniformed Debate on Military Culture," *Orbis*, Winter 1999. For an example of the "elite" attack on military culture, see Madeline Morris, "By Force of Arms: Rape, War, and Military Culture," *Duke Law Journal*, February 1996, pp. 651–781.

41 Edgar Schein, "Organizational Culture," *American Psychologist*, February 1990, p. 110.

42 Don Snider, "An Uniformed Debate on Military Culture," p. 13.

43 Bernard Bass, *A New Paradigm of Leadership: An Inquiry Into Transformational Leadership* (Alexandria: U.S. Army Research Institute for the Behavioral and Social Sciences, February 1996).

44 James Burk, "Military Culture," in Lester Kurtz, ed., *Encyclopedia of Violence, Peace and Conflict* (San Diego, CA: Academic Press, 1999). The other citations attributed to Burk in this section are also from this article.

45 Samuel P. Huntington, *The Soldier and the State* (Cambridge: Harvard University Press, 1957), p. 61.

46 Anthony E. Hartle, *Moral Issues in Military Decision Making*, Second Revised Issue, (Lawrence: University Press of Kansas, 2004), pp. 33 and 34.

47   See also Martin Van Creveld, *The Culture of War* (New York: Ballantine, 2008).

48   J. Glenn Gray, *The Warriors: Reflections on Men in Battle* (New York: Harcourt, Brace and Company, 1959). For a fascinating sociological analysis of the dichotomy between the Argentine and British military cultures operating in the 1982 Falklands War, see Nora Kinzer Stewart, *Mates and Muchachos: Unit Cohesion in the Falklands/Malvinas War* (Washington, DC: Brassey's, 1991).

49   Robert MacCoun, "What is Known About Unit Cohesion and Military Performance," in MacCoun, *Sexual Orientation and US Military Personnel Policy: Optinos and Assessment* (Santa Monica: RAND National Defense Research Institute, 1993); Cf. Elizabeth Kier, "Homosexuals in the U.S. Military" and Kier, "Discrimination and Military Cohesion: An Organizational Perspective," in Mary Fainsod Katzenstein and Judith Reppy, eds., *Beyond Zero Tolerance: Discrimination in Military Culture* (Lanham, MD: Rowman and Littlefield, 1999).

50   On behavior in combat, see the classic study by Samuel Stouffer et al., *The American Soldier: Combat and Its Aftermath*, vol. 2 (Princeton: Princeton University Press, 1949); William Darryl Henderson, *Cohesion: The Human Element in Combat* (Washington, DC: National Defense University Press, 1985); and Charles Moskos, *The American Enlisted Man: The Rank and File in Today's Military* (New York: Russell Sage Foundation, 1970).

51   Lionel Tiger, *Men in Groups* (London: Thomas Nelson, 1969); Tiger, "Male Dominance? Yes, Alas. A Sexist Plot? No." *New York Times Magazine*, October 25, 1970.

52   Presidential Commission on the Assignment of Women in the Armed Forces, *Women in Combat: A Report to the President* (Washington, DC: Brassey's, 1993), commission findings 2.5.1.

53   Jeanne Holm, *Women in the Military: An Unfinished Revolution*, revised edition (Novato, CA: Presidio Press, 1992), p. 120.

54   US Department of Defense, Office of the Inspector General, *The Tailhook Report: The Official Inquiry into the Events of Tailhook '91* (New York: St. Martin's, 1993); William McMichael, *The Mother of All Hooks* (New Brunswick: Transaction, 1997).

55   Elaine Sciolino, "B-52 Pilot Requests Discharge That Is Honorable," New York Times, May 18, 1997, p. A1; Bradley Graham, "Army Leaders Feared Aberdeen Coverup Allegations," *Washington Post*, November 11, 1996, p. A1.

56 Department of Defense, Active Duty Military Personnel by Rank/Grade, September 30, 2007 (Women Only) http://siadapp.dmdc.osd.mil/personnel/MILITARY/rg0709f.pdf.

57 Rachel L. Swarns, "Commanding Role for Women in the Military," *New York Times*, June 30, 2008, p. A17.

58 Ann Mulrine, "A Woman's Place is in the Pentagon: The Ranks of Women in the Defense Field Continue to Grow," *US News and World Report*, November 1, 2009, p. 75.

59 Data from the Defense Manpower Data Center, cited in Martin Binkin, *Who Will Fight the Next War? The Changing Face of the American Military* (Washington, DC: The Brookings Institution, 1993), p. 10.

60 Moskos, "Toward a Postmodern Military: The United States," pp. 22 and 23.

61 The Aspin memo is available at http://cmrlink.org/CMRNotes/LesAspin%20DGC%20DefAssign%20Rule%20011394.pdf.

62 Stephanie Gutmann, "Sex and the Soldier," *The New Republic*, February 24, 1997, pp. 18–22; Gutmann, *The Kinder, Gentler Military: Can America's Gender-Neutral Fighting Force Still Win Wars?* (New York: Scribner, 2000); Brian Mitchell, *Women in the Military: Flirting with Disaster* (Washington, DC: Regnery, 1998); Mackubin Thomas Owens, "It's Time to Face the Gender Paradox," US Naval Institute *Proceedings*, July 1998. The title on the submitted manuscript was "The Military *Ethos*, 'Friction,' and Women in Combat."

63 Holm, p. 342.

64 Melissa Embser-Herbert, "Should Military Combat Roles be Fully Opened to Women? Yes," *CQ Researcher*, November 13, 2009, p. 973.

65 Kingsley Browne, *Co-Ed Combat: The New Evidence that Women Shouldn't Fight the Nation's Wars* (New York: Penguin, 2007, p. 115).

66 Cited in *CQ Researcher*, November 13, 2009, p. 963.

67 Linda Grant de Pauw, *Battle Cries and Lullabies: Women in War from Prehistory to the Present* (Norman: University of Oklahoma Press, 2000), p. 12.

68 Margaret Mead, "A National Service System as a Solution to a Variety of National Problems," in Sol Tax, ed., *The Draft: A Handbook of Facts and Alternatives* (Chicago: University of Chicago Press, 1967). For an instance supporting her thesis see Lionel Tiger and Joseph Shepher, *Women in the Kibbutz* (New York: Harcourt Brace Jovanovich, 1975), esp. p. 186.

69 Erin Solaro, *Women in the Line of Fire: What You Should Know About Women in the Military* (Berkeley, CA: Seal Press, 2006).

70 Hannah Fischer et al., *American War and Military Operations Casualties: Lists and Statistics*, Congressional Research Service, May 2008.
71 Elaine Donnelly, cited in *CQ Researcher*, November 13, 2009, p. 963. Donnelly and her Center for Military Readiness have been consistent critics of opening combat specialties to women. See http://www.cmrlink.org/.
72 Owens, "It's Time to Face the Gender Paradox."
73 Mackubin Thomas Owens, "The Eros of Women in the Military," *Washington Times*, February 6, 1997.
74 James Webb, "The War on Military Culture," http://www.theweekly-standard.com/Content/Public/Articles/000/000/008/443hngrd.asp?pg=2.
75 Margaret C. Harrell and Laura L. Miller, *New Opportunities for Military Women: Effects upon Readiness, Cohesion, and Morale* (Santa Monica: RAND National Defense Research Institute, 1997).
76 Donna McAleer and Erin Solaro, "Full Participation by Our 'Sisters in Arms,'" *Washington Post*, December 12, 2009, http://www.washingtonpost.com/wp-dyn/content/article/2009/12/11/AR2009121103271.html.
77 Anna Simons, "Women in Combat Units: It's Still a Bad Idea," *Parameters*, Summer 2001, pp. 89–100.
78 Martin van Creveld, *The Transformation of War* (New York: Free Press, 1991), p. 184.
79 "Mullen Wants Females on Subs," *Defense Tech*, September 24, 2009, www.defensetech.org. See also Andrew Scutro and Mark D. Faram, "Female Sailors Could Join Sub Crews by 2011," *Navy Times*, October 12, 2009, www.navytimes.com.
80 Elaine Donnelly, "Constructing the Co-Ed Military," *Duke Journal of Law and Gender Policy*, June 18, 2007, p. 931.
81 Ibid., p. 931.
82 Kirsten Holmstedt, *Band of Sisters: American Women at War in Iraq* (Mechanicsburg, PA: Stackpole Books, 2008); Solaro, "Women in the Line of Fire."
83 Christine Simmons, "Obama's HRC Speech: 'I Will End Don't Ask, Don't Tell,' Says President Obama," *Huffington Post*, October 10, 2009, http://www.huffingtonpost.com/2009/10/10/obama-says-he-will-end-do_n_316524.html.
84 Aaron Belkin et al., "How to End 'Don't' Ask, Don't Tell': A Roadmap of Political, Legal, Regulatory, and Organizational Steps to Equal Treatment," *Palm Center Report*, May 2009.

85   Donna Miles, "General Counsel Looking into 'Don't Ask, Don't Tell,' Gates Says," *American Forces Press Service*, June 30, 2009, http:// www.globalsecurity.org/military/library/news/2009/06/mil-090630- afps04.htm.

86   Section 654 of Title 10, *United States Code*, http://www.law.cornell.edu/ uscode/10/654.html. For a useful summary of the policy changes effected in 1993, see David F. Burrelli, "An Overview of the Debate on Homosexuals in the US Military," in Wilbur J. Scott and Sandra Carson Stanley, eds., *Gays and Lesbians in the Military: Issues, Concerns, and Contrasts* (New Brunswick, NJ: Aldine Transaction, 1994), pp. 17–31.

87   Mackubin Thomas Owens, "The Case Against Gays in the Military," *Wall Street Journal*, February 3, 2010, p. A17; James Bowman, "Don't Change 'Don't Ask, Don't Tell'," *Weekly Standard*, October 12, 2009, http://www.weeklystandard.com/Content/Public/Articles/000/000/ 017/032hubhb.asp?pg=1.

88   Aaron Belkin and Geoffrey Bateman, eds., *Don't Ask, Don't Tell: Debating the Gay Ban in the Military* (Boulder: Lynne Rienner, 2003); Randy Shilts, *Conduct Unbecoming: Gays and Lesbians in the US Military* (New York: St. Martins Griffin, 2005); Nathaniel Frank, *Unfriendly Fire: How the Gay Ban Undermines the Military and Weakens America* (New York: Thomas Dunne Books, 2009). Elisabeth Burmiller, "Gay Soldiers Don't Cause Disruption, Study Says," *New York Times*, February 22, 2010, p. 7. The cited report is Nathanial Frank, *Gays in Foreign Militaries: A Global Primer* (Santa Barbara: The Palm Center, 2010).

89   Colin Powell, with Joseph Persico, *My American Journey* (New York: Random House, 1995), p. 533.

90   *Policy Concerning Homosexuality in the Armed Forces*. Hearings Before the Committee on Armed Services, U.S. Senate, 103rd Congress, 2nd Session. Senate Hearing 103–845 (1993), pp. 399–404 and 424.

91   Ana Puga, "Ex-General Sees Gays Hurting Military: Quality Would Fall, He Says," *Boston Globe*, April 30, 1993, p. A3.

92   David F. Burrelli, "Don't Ask, Don't Tell: The Law and Military Policy on Same-Sex Behavior," Congressional Research Service, August 14, 2009, Report 7–5700 R40782, pp. 5–10.

93   Ed O'Keefe, "Military Leaders Seek More Data On Repeal Of 'Don't Ask, Don't Tell,'" *Washington Post*, February 24, 2010, p. 11; Thom Shanker, "2 Generals Wary About Repealing Gay Policy," *New York Times*, February 24, 2010; Julian E. Barnes, "No 'Half Measures' On Gays, Chiefs Say," *Los Angeles Times*, February 25, 2010, p. 9; Julian E. Barnes, "Marine Corps Leader Stands Against Gays In Military: Gen. James T. Conway

tells the Senate Armed Services Committee that he thinks 'don't ask, don't tell' works as it is," *Los Angeles Times*, February 26, 2010, p. 16; Elliot Spagat, "Marine commandant: 'don't ask' should not be over-turned now," Washington Post, November 8, 2010.

94   Merrill McPeak, "Don't Ask, Don't Tell, Don't Change," *New York Times*, March 5, 2010, p. 27.

95   HR 1246, offered by former Democratic Rep. Marty Meehan of Massachusetts, HR 1283 offered by Democratic Rep. Patrick Murphy of Pennsylvania, and HR 4180 offered by Democratic Rep. Alcee Hastings of Florida.

96   Ed O'Keefe, "Senate fails in attempt to repeal 'don't ask, don't tell,'"*Washington Post*, Sept 21, 2010 http://voices.washingtonpost. com/federal-eye/2010/09/dont_ask_dont_tell_vote_set_fo_1.html? hpid=topnews&wpisrc=nl_natlalert. Accessed, Sept 22, 2010.

97   Jerry Markham and Ed O'Keefe, "Judge halts 'Don't ask don't tell' policy," *Washington Post*, October 13, 2010. http://www.washington-post.com/wp-dyn/content/article/2010/10/12/AR2010101206145. html?hpid=moreheadlines

98   Craig Whitlock and Scott Wilson, "Gates says that abrupt end to 'don't ask' would have 'enormous consequences,'" *Washington Post*, October 13, 2010. http://www.washingtonpost.com/wp-dyn/content/article/ 2010/10/13/AR2010101304121.html

99   Brendan McGarry, "Troops Oppose Repeal of 'Don't Ask': But Most Troops Would Stay in if Ban Ends," *Military Times*, December 29, 2008, http://www.militarytimes.com/news/2008/12/122908_military_ poll_DADT/.

100   Anne C. Loveland, *American Evangelicals and the U.S. Military 1942– 1993* (Baton Rouge: Louisiana State University Press, 1997).

101   Mike Mount, "Air Force Probes Religious Bias Charge at Academy," *CNN.com*, May 5, 2005, http://edition.cnn.com/2005/US/05/03/airforce. religion/index.html.

102   "Air Force Academy Faulted Over Religion," *CNN.com*, June 23, 2005, http://edition.cnn.com/2005/US/06/22/airforce.religion/.

103   Josh White, "Officers' Roles in Christian Video Are Called Ethics Breach," *Washington Post*, August 4, 2007; Louis Hansen, "Langley General Could be Punished for Role in Christian Video," *The Virginian-Pilot*, August 8, 2007.

104   Richard Whittle, "Uncle Sam Wants US Muslims to Serve," *Christian Science Monitor*, December 27, 2006, http://www.csmonitor.com/2006/ 1227/p03s01-usmi.html.

105 Tim Reid, "US Muslim Soldier Kills Officer and Wounds 16," *Times Online*, March 24, 2003, http://www.timesonline.co.uk/tol/news/world/iraq/article1122736.ece.

106 Bryan Bender, "Ft. Hood Suspect was an Army Dilemma: His Extreme Views Possibly Overlooked in Favor of Diversity," *Boston Globe*, February 22, 2010, p. 1.

107 ABC News, http://blogs.abcnews.com/george/2009/11/ft-hood-gen-casey-doesnt-rule-out-terrorism.html.

108 Yochi Dreazen, "Muslim Population in the Military Raises Difficulties," *Wall Street Journal*, November 7, 2009.

109 See "Should American Muslims Join the American Armed Forces?" Muslims for a Safe America Website, November 5, 2009, http://muslimsforasafeamerica.org/?p=5.

110 Michele A. Flournoy and Alice E. Hunt, *The State of the U.S. Ground Forces* (Washington, DC: Center for a New American Security, 2008); Stephen J. Lofgren, "Retention During the Vietnam War and Today," US Army Center of Military History Information Paper, US Army, Washington, DC, February 2008.

CHAPTER FIVE

Renegotiating the US Civil–Military Bargain into the Future

As the previous chapters have attempted to demonstrate, American civil–military relations have been under a great deal of stress since 9/11. Given trends in both the domestic and international realms, these tensions may well increase in the future. There are a number of issues that will influence the way in which the American civil–military bargain continues to be negotiated in the future.

In light of these recent examples of civil–military tensions, what does the future bode? What should the parties to the American civil–military bargain take into account as they continue to renegotiate it in the future? Are the problems likely to arise between civilian policy makers and the uniformed military indicative of a "crisis" or are they merely the manifestation of yet another search for a new equilibrium based on changing factors?[1] Will the kind of officer required to conduct military operations in the future make civilian control of the military more difficult? What is the future of the "normal" theory of civil–military relations? What are the prospects for balanced, harmonious, and effective civil–military relations in the future?

The answer to these questions will depend a great deal on the interplay of the domestic and international environments. Domestically, political polarization continues to run deep, even after the election of President Barack Obama, who, many believed, would restore some semblance of harmony to American politics. Concerns over the economy, health care reform, and energy are likely to dominate the domestic political landscape for the foreseeable future.

Internationally, the unprecedented character of the 9/11 attacks on the US homeland, the character of the wars in Iraq and Afghanistan, the concomitant rise of Chinese power, and disagreements between the United States and other states in the international political system, especially our friends and allies, have created a particularly volatile international environment that is likely to continue into the future.

The Domestic Political Context of the Future Civil–Military Bargain

Since the civil–military bargain is negotiated in the context of US domestic politics, those who look at civil–military relations cannot ignore the political realm. As noted above, health care, the economy, and energy will most likely dominate domestic agendas, perhaps pushing civil–military relations and international affairs to the back burner. But there is one aspect of domestic politics with significant implications for future civil–military relations that has not been addressed to the extent that it should be. This is the issue of post-Iraq "narratives," both "failure" and "success" narratives, as well as the role of returning veterans, both officers and enlisted, and both active duty and reserve. As two Air Force Academy professors have noted in one article that does raise the issue, these competing narratives of the Iraq War may have an impact on how Americans think about the military and vice versa. "As the public debate about Iraq unfolds, there is a risk that the currently cordial relations between civil and military society may be threatened."[2]

After both Vietnam and the American Civil War, military veterans were vocal participants in the postwar debates and helped to shape the political culture of the United States for years. The past is instructive.

Consider the case of the Peace Democrats or "Copperheads,"[3] who rhetorically condemned Abraham Lincoln, the Republicans, the war, and often Union troops themselves. Rhetoric is one thing, but the Copperheads also actively interfered with recruiting and encouraged desertion. Indeed, they generated so much opposition to conscription that the Army was forced on several occasions to divert resources from the battlefield to the hotbeds of Copperhead activity to maintain order.[4]

However, in the long run, the Democratic Party was badly hurt by the Copperheads. Their actions radically politicized Union soldiers, turning into stalwart Republicans many who had strongly supported the Democratic Party's opposition to emancipation as a goal of the war. Indeed, many Union soldiers came to despise the Copperheads more than they disdained the Rebels. In the words of an assistant surgeon of an Iowa regiment, "it is a common saying here that if we are whipped, it will be by Northern votes, not by Southern bullets. The army regard the result of the late [fall 1862] elections as at *least* prolonging the war."[5]

It is certain that the Union soldiers tired of hearing from the Copperheads that the Rebels could not be defeated. They surely tired of being described by the Copperheads as instruments of a tyrannical administration trampling the legitimate rights of the Southern states. The soldiers seemed to understand fairly quickly that the Copperheads preferred Lincoln's failure to the country's success. They also recognized that the Copperheads offered no viable alternative to Lincoln's policy except to stop the war.

As a result, Union soldiers voted overwhelmingly for Lincoln in 1864, abandoning the once-beloved George McClellan because of the perception that he had become a tool of the Copperheads. And as the Democrats were reminded for many years after the war, the Copperheads had made a powerful enemy of the Union veterans.[6]

A similar dynamic was at work after Vietnam. "Many Vietnam veterans felt betrayed when they returned home amid controversy over the war" and believed that "antiwar protests at home led to restrictions on the use of force that tied the hands of the military and caused South Vietnam to fall to the communists."[7] It was also the case that the Vietnam antiwar movement's "willingness to concede the American flag to supporters of the war sharpened these perceptions. Indeed, the burning of the American flag remains an enduring symbol of opposition to Vietnam War policy."[8]

Whether true or not, these perceptions were largely to blame for the "Republicanization" of the military as many members of the US military came to believe that the Democratic Party had treated them the way the Copperheads had treated Union soldiers after the Civil War. The substantial opposition among Vietnam veterans to the candidacy of John Kerrey during the 2004 election was driven largely by his 1973 testimony before the Senate Foreign Affairs Committee, which many veterans perceived as accusing them of being war criminals.

While perceptions about Vietnam affected domestic politics by shifting the party affiliations, they also had a more direct impact on civil–military relations. Among them were the emergence of the Weinberger/Powell Doctrine, the military's insistence on the "normal" theory of civil–military relations, which grants a realm of military autonomy when it comes to the conduct of war, and the Abrams Doctrine, which many believe, by placing much of the Army's force structure in the National Guard and reserve, had the practical effect of limiting the discretion of the president to employ military force.

A similar "culture" war over the legacy of Iraq and Afghanistan is likely to accelerate in the future as more veterans return to civilian life. "The repeated, lengthy deployments, the hardships of service members and their families, and of course, the casualties, motivate many members to see the sacrifices they and their families have made in an unerringly positive light. American Soldiers are willing to sacrifice, but for a noble purpose—no one wants to waste their lives and livelihoods on a moral mistake."[9]

Of course, today's veterans do not constitute a monolithic community any more than Vietnam veterans did. But how today's veterans perceive the debate over the Iraq War narrative will shape civil–military relations in the years to come. Fortunately, today's antiwar movement has, at least for the most part, focused its anger about the wars in Iraq and Afghanistan on the Bush administration rather than on the soldiers who fought those wars. Accordingly, it may be possible to avoid the worst features of the sort of divisive struggle over the legacy of this war that characterized the post-Vietnam period.

One other aspect of the future domestic environment as it relates to civil–military relations is worth noting: the possibility that a high-ranking officer will enter politics based on his record in the Iraq and Afghan wars. One such possibility is Gen. David Petraeus, whom many consider to be the architect of the dramatic turnaround in Iraq after 2007 who was then elevated to command US Central Command (CENTCOM), the theater command that includes both Iraq and Afghanistan and was recently tasked to oversee the US effort in Afghanistan. Although he has not indicated any interest in politics or an inclination to enter the political arena, others have mentioned him as a possibility.

Although such a foray is possible, precedent does not favor the success of generals in American politics. The refusal of Gen. Colin Powell to throw his hat into the presidential ring when many Republicans wanted him to do so and the failure of Gen. Wesley Clark, the Supreme Allied Commander in Europe during the Balkans operations, to gain the presidential nomination of the Democratic Party in 2004 are only the latest examples. Several prominent generals and admirals, including Gen. Leonard Wood, a former Chief of Staff of the Army; Admiral George Dewey, the victor of Manila Bay; and Gen. John. J. Pershing, the supreme commander of US troops in Europe during World War I have entered politics, but the only general to achieve electoral success since the post–Civil War era has been Dwight D. Eisenhower.

Thinking About the Future International Security Environment

America's engagement in world affairs ensures that healthy civil–military relations will still be a major concern. There are bound to be many areas of contention that will bring these concerns to the fore. The character of the future security environment and future conflict will have a great deal of impact on the character of American civil–military relations.

What will the future security environment look like? How will the future security environment differ, if at all, from what it is today? What will future conflict look like and how should we shape our military services? To envision the future is akin to "looking through a glass darkly." In attempting to answer these questions, it is important to recognize that planners do not have a stellar record when it comes to predicting the future.[10] Indeed, the United States has suffered a major strategic surprise on the average of once a decade since 1940.

A case in point is the consensus that emerged two decades ago in the wake of the Cold War's end and Operation Desert Storm, the first Gulf War of 1991. During the decade of the 1990s, some argued the United States was the only real global power in a unipolar world, having reached the "end of history." With the collapse of the Soviet Union, went the argument, communism, the last ideological competitor to liberalism, had been discredited. A true liberal world order was now possible and the age of war had finally come to an end.[11]

These "international optimists" claimed that globalization and increasing interdependence of the international system had converged with the recognition of the destructiveness of modern war to render the idea of large-scale, interstate conflict more or less unthinkable. They contended that while small-scale strife remained a possibility, it could be curbed by means of preventive diplomacy and cooperative structures based on liberal principles. This view prevailed during much of the Clinton administration.

The argument of the "international optimists" was supplemented by that of the "technological optimists" who believed that the United States could maintain its dominant position in the international order by exploiting the "revolution in military affairs" (RMA). In the words of Colin Gray, these individuals believed that they had discovered a technological El Dorado, a "golden city of guaranteed strategic riches."[12]

The rapid coalition victory over Saddam Hussein that drove Iraqi forces out of Kuwait in 1991 led some influential defense experts to argue that emerging technologies and the RMA had the potential to transform "the very nature of war." One of the most prominent advocates of this position was the former Vice Chairman of the Joint Chiefs of Staff, Admiral William Owens, who contended that these emerging technologies and "information dominance" would eliminate "friction" and the "fog of war," providing the commander and his subordinates nearly perfect "situational awareness," thereby promising "the capacity to use military force without the same risks as before."[13]

Owens argued that "technology could enable US military forces in the future to lift the 'fog of war' . . . battlefield dominant awareness—the ability to see and understand everything on the battlefield—might be possible." Furthermore, "if you see the battlefield, you will win the war."[14]

A publication of the National Defense University fleshed out this claim. "In short," it said, "we will move from a situation in which decision making takes place under uncertainty, or in the presence of incomplete and erroneous information, to a situation in which decisions are made with nearly 'perfect' information."[15]

The Chief of Staff of the Air Force at the time echoed this view, saying, "In the first part of the 21st century, you will be able to find, fix or track, and target—in near real-time—anything of consequence that moves or is located on the face of the Earth. Quite frankly, I can tell you we can do most of that today. We just can't do it in real-time."[16]

Thus, the 1990s were a period of strategic optimism. Analysts concluded that because of its edge in emerging technologies, especially information technologies, the United States' position in the world was unassailable for the foreseeable future. At the same time, there was no "peer competitor" on the horizon capable of replacing the Soviet Union as an existential threat to the United States.

This apparent national security situation led US planners in many cases to adopt simplified—if not simplistic—defense planning assumptions:

- Challenges to US security would arise primarily from regional powers and involve regional/theater contingencies featuring conventional major combat operations.
- These likely adversaries would be smaller, less capable versions of the USSR.
- The US monopoly in strike, information technology, and stealth would constitute a barrier to entry for adversaries and would continue into the foreseeable future

These assumptions led to major changes in US force structure, including the "conventionalization" of the US strategic bomber force and a shift in the focus of space and C3I programs from the strategic level to the operational/ technological level. Planners assumed that since future wars would be short, "strategic speed" had become critical. Thus, joint planners stressed such concepts as "rapid halt," "rapid decisive operations," and "shock and awe." One consequence of perspective was a lack of focus on "Phase V" operations: security, stabilization, transformation, and reconstruction. This was, of course, the view that Donald Rumsfeld brought with him to the Pentagon. As was argued in Chapter 3, this outlook had an adverse impact on civil–military relations during the Bush administration and led to serious problems in the conduct of the Iraq War.

Of course, all of these optimistic assumptions about a liberal world order came crashing down with the Twin Towers of the World Trade Center on September 11, 2001. There was indeed a downside to globalization: international optimism blinded us to the rise of Islamic extremism. After all, Osama bin Laden issued *fatwahs* against the United States, essentially declaring war many years before most Americans had ever heard his name.

Similarly, 9/11 and the subsequent difficulties that US military forces faced in Iraq and now continue to face in Afghanistan have served to seriously undermine the views of the technological optimists of the 1990s. Contrary to much of their argument during that decade, the technological edge of the United States did not make the country invulnerable.

But some wonder if the pendulum has not swung too far in the other direction. As the United States continues to deal with Iraq and Afghanistan and to prepare primarily for "small" or "irregular" wars in the future, is it possible that our ability to conduct high-tech conventional wars against rising powers will atrophy?[17]

But even as we continue to win "the wars we are in," disagreements between the uniformed military and the civilian leadership are bound to continue. For instance, the former commander of US forces in Iraq stated that continuing problems in Iraq might require American combat troops to remain in that country after the June 2011 date that President Obama set as the deadline for the exit of all US combat formations. It is also the case that many military officers believe that any success resulting from the US "surge" in Afghanistan and the concurrent application of a population-based counterinsurgency in that country was seriously undermined by an "exit date" announced by the president at the same time.

The Future Security Environment[18]

As critics of the technological optimists of the 1990s predicted and events such as 9/11, Iraq, and Afghanistan have demonstrated, adversaries have adapted to American power by adopting "asymmetric" responses to US advantages. The result has been the emergence of trends that undermine the older US planning assumptions and require rethinking the character of future war.

Driving Forces and Areas of Future Military Competition

Several years ago, Peter Schwartz outlined a methodology for thinking about the future.[19] He suggested that planners can best understand the emerging security environment by positing scenarios based on an assessment of *driving forces, predetermined elements*, and *critical uncertainties*. The first category—assessing future trends—is really the key to the methodology.

What are the dominant emerging trends in the security environment? They include—but are not limited to—the proliferation of militarily useful technology; unlimited access to information technologies, including light-weight movie cameras, cell phones, portable laptop computers, and satellite modems that ensure that everyone—including adversaries—has the capa-bility to deliver images of conflict in real time; and aspects of globalization that permit terrorists and other armed groups to employ cheap means to achieve costly effects by exploiting the vulnerabilities of advanced, especially liberal, societies.

Indeed, the changing cost equation may be the most consequential trend of all. During the Cold War, the United States possessed a decided cost advantage in its competition with the Soviet Union. The Reagan administra-tion exploited this by adopting an asymmetric and cost-incurring strategy to exploit the mismatch between the large and growing US economy and the much smaller Soviet economy. This cost-incurring strategy forced the USSR to expend resources its economy could not afford. The combination of the US defense buildup, support for anti-Soviet forces in Afghanistan, and such programs as the Strategic Defense Initiative, which threatened to render obsolescent or even obsolete the Soviet nuclear arsenal, was more than the USSR could withstand.[20]

As former Secretary of Defense Donald Rumsfeld acknowledged in 2003, this advantage has dissipated. "The cost-benefit ratio is against us! Our cost is billions against the terrorists' cost of millions."[21] In fact, Rumsfeld may have substantially understated the cost ratio. John Robb contends that on 9/11, "a $250,000 attack was converted into an event that cost the United States over $80 billion (some estimates are as high as $500 billion)."[22]

An important aspect of thinking about the future is making an educated guess about the types of military competition that may take place in the future. Examples of such areas of future military competition include power projection vs. antiaccess strategies; "hider" vs. "finder;" and precision strike vs. active defense.[23] We can also expect greater competition in space and cyberspace. Indeed, adversaries will seek the capability to launch difficult-to-detect electronic or information attacks from great distance.

Another emerging military competition involves countering the threat of attack on the homeland from either a large peer competitor or terrorists who are able to wield much greater destructive power than in the past. To deal with the former, the United States must be prepared to counter such threats as ballistic and cruise missile attack, which may occur with substantially less warning than was anticipated only a few years ago. Addressing the latter requires the capability to counter terrorists or other armed groups who may well gain access to chemical and biological weapons.

Changing Character (Not Nature) of War

As noted above, it was not unusual during the 1990s for planners to claim that emerging technologies had changed "the very nature of war." But it seems clear that the nature of war remains constant. Clausewitz reminds us that war is a violent clash between opposing wills, each seeking to prevail over the other. In war, the will of one combatant is directed at an *animate object that reacts*, often in unanticipated ways. This cyclical interaction between opposing wills occurs in a realm of chance and chaos. He also identified the following enduring characteristics of war: the persistence of "general friction" as a structural component of combat, the seeming impossibility of eliminating uncertainty from war and the critical importance of the "moral factors" in war.[24]

On the other hand, the "character" of war is infinite. Thus a weaker adversary can adopt various modalities of war to engage and defeat a stronger power. Success in war has traditionally gone to the most adaptive side that can bear the costs of the conflict relative to what Clausewitz called "the value of the object." Accordingly, the record shows that the materially weaker side has prevailed in a conflict a surprisingly large number of times: around 40 percent of the time since World War II.

As Philip Bobbitt has observed, for five centuries it has taken the resources of a state to destroy another state. Only states could muster the huge revenues, conscript the vast armies, and equip the divisions required to threaten the survival of other states. Indeed, meeting such threats *created* the modern state. In the past, every state knew that its enemy would be drawn from a small class of nearby potential adversaries with local interests. But because of globalization, global reach, advances in international telecommunications, rapid computation and methods of mass destruction, this is no longer true.[25]

The Emerging Security Environment and the Character of Future War

The present and still evolving security environment exhibits a number of characteristics that currently affect the character of war—and will most likely continue to do so in the future. These include such phenomena as expanded global interdependence, which, although seen as a boon to prosperity also permits terrorists and other violent ideologues to inflict damage at a very low cost and risk to themselves. In the words of Shamil Basayev, a Chechen commander and mastermind of the Beslan massacre, "we are not bound by any circumstances, or to anybody, and will continue to fight as convenient and advantageous to us and by our rules."[26]

Citing this passage, John Robb observes that "this new method of warfare . . . offers guerrillas the means to bring a modern nation's economy to its knees and thereby undermine the legitimacy of the state sworn to protect it. Furthermore, it can derail the key drivers of economic globalization: the flow of resources, investment, people, and security." Those who adopt this form of warfare, says Robb, are not really terrorists, but *global guerrillas*, who represent "a broad-based threat that far exceeds that offered by terrorists or the guerrillas of the past."[27]

Such global guerrillas are able to exploit the dissonance caused by "spikey" economic development and urbanization, the diffusion of and impact of technology, especially information technology, and the dislocation caused by globalization and demographic bulges. They are able to effect "systems disruption" in advanced economies, by causing "cascading" failures in the system. "If attackers can disrupt the operations of the hubs of a scale-free infrastructure network, the entire network can collapse in a cascade of failure."[28]

Because of interdependence, failures within a single network can cause the failure of others. In a tightly interconnected infrastructure, not only do the transportation network, the water network, and the fuel network depend on the electricity network, but also the electricity network depends on the fuel and transportation networks. "Global guerrillas have proven to be increasingly adept at using these interconnections to cause cross-networks of failure."[29]

Categories of War—Multidimensional Conflict

While the categorization of war by the 2004 Defense Strategy and subsequent QDR—Traditional, Irregular, Catastrophic, and Disruptive—represents an advance in thinking about future war, it implied that adversaries would focus on only one of the other categories. But war, properly understood, is always *multidimensional*.

In a past dominated by state-on-state warfare, the traditional or conventional category was central, but combatants also pursued strategies to exploit irregular capabilities, e.g., guerrilla warfare and insurgency, or disruptive attempts to undermine an enemy's public support for the war, e.g., by acts of terrorism. But a particular form of multidimensional warfare may constitute the most demanding challenge to American planners in the future: "complex irregular warfare" (CIW).[30]

One characteristic of CIW is the likelihood that future adversaries will be "hybrids." These hybrid threats will seek to raise the potential cost of US military action by adopting aspects of all of the warfare categories.[31]

An example of a prototype hybrid is Hezbollah. During the 2006 war with Israel, Hezbollah exhibited both state-like capabilities—long-range missiles, antiship cruise missiles, sophisticated antiarmor systems, armed UAVs, and SIGINT—while still skillfully executing guerrilla warfare. Such a hybrid has the potential to complicate future US military planning and execution.

Hezbollah was able to stand up to the Israel Defense Force (IDF) because it was able to skillfully adapt to the particular circumstances that it faced. For instance, unlike US forces, which must be prepared to fight in a variety of environments and under various conditions, Hezbollah was able to tailor its forces specifically to counter the IDF. Since Hezbollah did not have to organize for offensive operations, it was able to concentrate on defense in depth.

> With decades of experience in low-intensity conflict with the IDF, Hezbollah understood its enemy's strengths and vulnerabilities. The IDF's ground forces remain structured for swift, conventional thrusts toward Damascus or Cairo. So Hezbollah leaders didn't attempt to build traditional brigades or battalions equipped with armored vehicles—the classic Arab error. Instead, they concentrated on stockpiling the most sophisticated defensive weapons they could acquire, such as the Kornet, a lethal late-generation Russian anti-tank missile, as well as a range of rockets, from long-range, Iranian-made weapons to man-portable point-and-shoot Katyushas. Thanks to the Katyushas, an Arab military force was able to create a substantial number of Israeli refugees for the first time since 1948.[32]

Hezbollah exhibited flexibility by fielding modular units and adopting mission-type orders. It was effective in its innovative use of weapons. Although most Hezbollah fighters did not seek death, the organization was willing to accept casualties. Hezbollah was perfectly willing to accept a loss ratio of about five Hezbollah fighters to one IDF soldier. Hezbollah's intelligence performance was surprisingly effective. As Ralph Peters observed,

"Israel fought as a limping stepchild of Clausewitz. Hezbollah fought as Sun Tzu's fanatical son."

As suggested above, the sort of hybrid threats generated by CIW and illustrated by Hezbollah may well constitute the most probable, most demanding, and potentially most costly type of future conflict. Implications of wars against hybrid threats include the likelihood that they will be extremely lethal and protracted and that since they will often take place in contested urban zones (feral cities), they will be manpower intensive. They will be widely distributed by distance, complexity, and mission. In most cases, these hybrid threats will seek to win the war of perceptions, waging a "conflict among the people." To prevail against such a threat requires "cultural intelligence" and exploitation of the "human terrain."

The operational environment in such conflicts very likely will be characterized by close encounters between friendly forces and an enemy that seeks to blur the distinctions between the conventional and the unconventional and between combatants and noncombatants, between conflict and stability operations, and between the physical and the psychological. After all, hybrid war is a competition for influence and legitimacy in which perceptions are paramount. As the current conflict in Iraq illustrates, in the battle for legitimacy, religious identity may trump or negate better governance and economic benefits.

In general, hybrid foes utilizing CIW will attempt to exploit the political effects of a conflict, seeking to undermine the legitimacy of US military actions. Thus, these enemies will try to leverage "lawfare," the use of "law as a weapon, law as a tactical ally, law as a strategic asset, an instrument of war."

> Once a bit player in military conflict, law now shapes the institutional, logistical and physical landscape of war . . . . If war remains, as Clausewitz taught us, the continuation of politics by other means, the politics continued by warfare today has itself been legalised . . . . Law can often accomplish what we might once have done with bombs and missiles: seize and secure territory, send messages about resolve and political seriousness, even break the will of a political opponent.[33]

One way to do this is to use the rules of warfare against the United States (while ignoring these rules themselves), by, e.g., taking refuge among the civilian population in an attempt to maximize civilian casualties.

In turn, adversaries employing CIW will take advantage of the fact that such casualties are magnified by the proliferation of media assets on the battlefield. CIW is, above all, a battle of perceptions. As Lawrence Freedman has observed, "In irregular warfare, superiority in the physical environment is of little value unless it can be translated into an advantage in the information environment... Our enemies have skillfully adapted to fighting wars in today's media age, but for the most part we, our country, our government, has not."[34]

Preempting Preemption

The best way to counter such threats is through preemption. To do so, the United States needs to establish favorable conditions for access, including a flexible forward basing posture and the adoption of effective means to counter the asymmetric antiaccess strategies that hybrid opponents are likely to adopt. Such strategies are designed to undermine the cornerstone of US global military power: the ability to project and sustain substantial military forces at great distances from CONUS. In general, there are four points at which an adversary may attempt to derail US power projection.

First, as the United States is deciding to project power, an adversary may attempt to deter it, by threatening actions that would make the cost of power projection too high, e.g., attacking targets in the US homeland in order to undermine public support for an overseas intervention. Second, as the United States is deploying its forces to ports and airfields, an adversary may attempt to disrupt the deployment by means of terrorist attacks and sabotage of transportation means and the like. Such attacks in both of these phases would force the United States to use some of its forces, intended for power projection, to defend against attacks at home.

Third, as the United States is transporting its forces to the theater of action and attempting to debark, an adversary may try to deny entry to the US force by military and political means, e.g., attacks and threats against US allies in the region. And finally, as US forces establish a lodgment and begin offensive operations, an adversary will seek to defeat US forces.

In the past, adversaries have focused their efforts on the last two points, denial and defeat. But in the future, an adversary's most cost-effective actions may be to deter and disrupt the projection of US forces. This possibility is the result of another emerging characteristic of future conflict: "360 degree warfare."

Past wars have usually been characterized by the existence of "fronts" and secure "rear areas," whether at the strategic, operational, or tactical level. Of course, airpower provided a means of attacking the enemy's rear and long-range airpower and missiles threatened to extend the ability to attack the rear to the homeland. Nonetheless, actual attacks against the strategic rear of both sides were deterred by the likelihood of mutual destruction.

While guerrillas, insurgents, terrorists, and other armed groups have sought to wage a "war without fronts," the strategic emergence of true 360 degree warfare is a recent development. 9/11 indicated that the ability of the United States to deter attacks against its homeland is no longer assured. Iraq and Afghanistan illustrate that our adversaries have adopted this approach at the operational and tactical levels of war as well.

Thus, multidimensional war in the future is likely to be characterized by distributed, weakly connected battlefields; unavoidable urban battles and unavoidable collateral damage exploited by adversary's strategic communication; and highly vulnerable rear areas. On such battlefields, friends and enemies are commingled and there is a constant battle for the loyalty of the population. All this is exacerbated by the proliferation of militarily useful technology, including nuclear weapons and delivery systems.

A Large Peer Competitor?

As noted earlier, many believe that the US intelligence community during the 1990s and the early 2000s was so focused on the rise of China to great power status that it was blind to the threat that manifested itself on September 11, 2001. But many are now concerned that the pendulum may have swung too far to the other extreme. Are we now so fixated on counterinsurgency and terrorism that we will not take the steps necessary to counter the military of a "large peer competitor?"

The leading candidate for the role of future peer competitor is China. According to the Department of Defense's 2007 annual report to Congress on Chinese military power,

> much uncertainty surrounds the future course China's leaders will set for their country, including in the area of China's expanding military power and how that power might be used. The People's Liberation Army (PLA) is pursuing comprehensive transformation from a mass army designed for protracted wars of attrition on its territory to one capable of fighting and winning short-duration, high intensity conflicts against high-tech adversaries—which China refers to as "local wars under conditions of informatization." China's ability to sustain military power at a distance, at present, remains limited but, as noted in the 2006 *Quadrennial Defense Review Report*, it "has the greatest potential to compete militarily with

the United States and field disruptive military technologies that could over time offset traditional U.S. military advantages."[35]

The report states that the China's economic growth has permitted it to accelerate the pace and scope of its military transformation. "The expanding military capabilities of China's armed forces are a major factor in changing East Asian military balances; improvements in China's strategic capabilities have ramifications far beyond the Asia Pacific region." China has enhanced its strategic strike capabilities and pursued a robust counter-space program, "punctuated by the January 2007 successful test of a direct-ascent, anti-satellite weapon." Thus, its continued pursuit of area denial and antiaccess strategies has expanded from "the traditional land, air, and sea dimensions of the modern battlefield to include space and cyber-space."

The case of China illustrated that hybrid warfare is not only a phenomenon associated with the "low end" of the spectrum of conflict. There is no reason that a future peer competitor would restrict military competition with the United States to only the "traditional" category. It would logically also try to confront the United States asymmetrically in those areas where the United States is perceived to be less capable than in the traditional category. The publication in China several years ago of *Unrestricted Warfare* indicates the potential of hybrid CIW at the "upper end" of the spectrum of conflict.[36]

The Future of Future War

As the foregoing discussion illustrates, any future adversary, no matter his preferred mode of warfare, will, at a minimum, attempt to employ all the dimensions of warfare to asymmetrically counter critical US military capabilities in such areas as conventional warfare, force projection, C4ISR, including space operations, and precision strike.

In the area of irregular warfare, opponents will attempt to impose untenable costs on the United States by using time-tested techniques against superior force, threatening a protracted war of attrition to undermine domestic public support, raising the level of violence and brutality, and expanding and escalating the conflict by targeting the US homeland and that of its key allies.

In the area of power projection, opponents will attempt to raise the cost of access by increasing the risk to the United States of naval and air operations by expanding the area of a "contested zone," seeking to destroy high-value assets, e.g., aircraft carriers, dissuading allies and partners from providing bases and other forms of support to US forces, and degrading the ability of the United States to deploy forces into an area of interest.

In the area of C4ISR, adversaries will attempt to "bring down the network" by attacking US space assets, degrading US information systems, disrupting command and control, denying US surveillance and reconnaissance, and deceiving US intelligence.

In the area of precision strike, the enemy will seek to reduce US standoff range, spoof US guidance systems that enable precision attack, and disperse targets, to include interspersing them in populated areas. All these methods have already been employed by adversaries and represent manifestations of the changing cost equation that will likely make it more difficult for the United States to use military force in the future.

The best way to think about the future is not to try to *predict* it but to project a number of *plausible alternative futures* against which to test strategies and force structures. To do so, US planners must develop a representative—not exhaustive—set of plausible contingencies that encompass the principal challenges the US military might encounter over the planning horizon. This approach is particularly relevant to the United States, which, given its global responsibilities, must be prepared for a variety of contingencies across the entire range of military operations.[37]

In 2005, Andrew Krepinevich suggested a useful methodology for addressing areas of future military competition by reintroducing the concept of "color plans" similar to those the United States employed during the interwar period.[38] His scenarios include the following:

- China (Disruptive Peer) (Plan Yellow)
- North Korea (Nuclear Rogue) (Plan Red)
- Pakistan (Failed Nuclear State) (Plan Green)
- Radical Islam (Plan Purple)
- Global Energy Network Defense (Plan Black)
- Global Commons Defense (Plan Orange)
- Nuclear/Biological Homeland Attack (Plan Blue)

These illustrative scenarios seek to identify a representative array of contingencies encompassing the principal military challenges US planners may confront over the "planning horizon" (15–20 years). As such, they presumably enable US strategists and force planners to "hedge" against uncertainty by testing concepts of operations and force structures against plausible alternatives—not the most familiar or the contingencies believed to be the most likely—permitting planners to realistically assess the potential impact of a range of possible futures on relative military effectiveness.[39]

Gen. James Mattis, USMC, recently the commander of US Joint Forces Command, pointed out the difficulty of "predicting" the future. "We are not likely to get the future right," he remarked. "We just need to make sure we don't get it too wrong." The question is: what will such a future mean for civil–military relations?

Civil–Military Realignments

In light of these possible developments in US domestic politics and the international security environment, what does the future bode for healthy civil–military relations in the United States? As noted above relations, "tense" at best during the Rumsfeld years, seem to have improved during the tenure of his successor, Robert Gates. But the pattern of civil–military relations seems to matter more than personalities when it comes to maintaining a balance between the military and the civilians. And these patterns have varied depending on the circumstances.

Two recent works noted in Chapter 1 have attempted to place the realignment of civil–military patterns in historical context. In the first, Thomas Langston examined the civil–military adjustments that have taken place in the past as the United States has made the transition from war to peace.[40]

According to Langston, following Huntington, the source of the civil–military conflict in peacetime is that the military prefers to reform the military for the next war (the military's "functional imperative") while civilians would rather "tame" the military in order to serve the goals of the civilian elites (imposing a "societal imperative"). As noted in Chapter 1, Langston argues that "the inevitable conflicts of civil–military relations . . . are best resolved when neither the civilianizers nor their opponents [the military reformers] win a complete victory."[41]

The period after the end of the Cold War seems to validate Langston. As Huntington predicted, Congress sought to cut military force structure substantially in order to acquire a "peace dividend" that members argued would result from a reduction in defense spending. This was not pure extirpation, but as Huntington argues, that is only an ideal type. And falling short of extirpation, the civilianizers fell back on transmutation.

Foremost among these were the efforts to open military specialties to women and to permit military service by open homosexuals, episodes discussed in Chapter 4. But the Clinton administration also committed the military to a number of missions that became known as "military operations other than war" (MOOTW). The military, as Langston's framework suggests, resisted—as described in Chapters 2 and 3—contending that such missions detracted from the need to prepare for the next large-scale war.

The outcome of this struggle is a classic example of renegotiating the civil–military bargain and validates Langston's view that the best outcome for healthy civil–military relations is when neither party gets all of what it seeks. In the first case—enforcing the "societal imperative" at the cost of the military's "functional imperative"—the civilianizers achieved part of their goals in that some military specialties were opened to women. However, the military leadership was able to keep some closed and its resistance to service by open homosexuals led Congress to ban such service. In the second case—the civilianizers preference for using armed forces for what the military leadership contends are nonmilitary purposes—the military did conduct a number of MOOTW, but defense budgets were not cut so much that the military's emphasis on planning for large-scale war had to be cut back. This dynamic is likely to continue as the civil–military bargain is renegotiated in the future.

Charles Stevenson has proposed a similar framework for examining the different patterns emerging from the civil–military bargain as negotiated at different points in the history of the United States. While Langston looks at various periods of transition from war to peace, Stevenson breaks his examination of peace down into two different categories: the challenge of rearmament or "preparation for war"; and the challenge of transformation while also looking at civil–military relations during wartime.[42]

As Stevenson observes, wartime provides the greatest challenge to civil–military relations by forcing agonizing choices on both civilians and the military. And the longer the conflict in pursuit of an elusive victory, "the more the friction builds between warriors and politicians."

When the United States has been rearming for war, civil–military relations have been stressed in different ways. This period "requires a strategic judgment that conflict is approaching and then strong leadership to persuade the people and their representatives to shift resources from peacetime pursuits to military requirements. The military, too, must be responsive to the new situation and willing to undertake different ways of dealing with the expected threat."

Military modernization places more stress on the armed forces than on the strategic judgments of the civilian policy makers. ". . . History has shown that military institutions tend to make radical changes only in response to defeats, and that successful militaries are slow to change what they believe provided past victory. When outsiders try to impose their own vision of a modern military, they tend to confront tough resistance from the officer corps—unless they make strategic alliances with those mavericks who advocate major innovation."[43]

In fact, all three of these challenges came together in an unprecedented way after 9/11. As observed earlier, the original focus of the George W. Bush administration was to "transform" the military. As in the case of earlier outside reformers, Secretary of Defense Donald Rumsfeld faced institutional resistance to his efforts. After the 9/11 attacks, the United States undertook offensive military operations against al Qaeda and the Taliban in Afghanistan and later against Saddam Hussein in Iraq. During this period, Rumsfeld's Pentagon continued its transformational efforts despite a substantial war effort. As discussed in Chapter 3, the rancor that Rumsfeld created over his transformation agenda before 9/11 generated civil–military tensions that affected the conduct of the war, particularly with regard to strategic assessment.

While there was considerable support for the post 9/11 retaliatory offensive against al Qaeda in Afghanistan, the public was divided over the subsequent war in Iraq. This meant that while the United States was simultaneously fighting a war and transforming its military, the president had to convince the American people that his strategic judgment in leading the country into the Iraq War was correct and that they needed to continue to support the allocation of resources to the war effort. Maintaining healthy and balanced civil–military relations is difficult enough when the parties only have to face one challenge. Doing so when a country faces all three challenges at the same time is nearly impossible.

President Bush belatedly recognized the magnitude of this civil–military challenge when he threw his support behind Gen. Petraeus in Iraq and later as commander of CENTCOM and when he replaced Rumsfeld with Gates. The focus of the Pentagon noticeably shifted away from transformation and toward more emphasis on current operations.

The Future of American Civil–Military Relations

The emerging security environment, the changing character of warfare, an expanded conception of military professionalism, and the imperatives of American politics all have implications for future US civil–military relations. On March 3, 2010, Admiral Mike Mullen, the Chairman of the Joint Chiefs of Staff, provided an indication of what this will entail when he delivered a speech at Kansas State University outlining three principles regarding the use of force.[44]

First, he argued, military power should not necessarily be the last resort of the state:

> Military forces are some of the most flexible and adaptable tools to policymakers. We can, merely by our presence, help alter certain behavior. Before a shot is even fired, we can bolster a diplomatic argument, support a friend or deter an enemy . . . .
>
> And we can do so on little or no notice. That ease of use is critical for deterrence. An expeditionary force [can provide] immediate, tangible effects. It is also vital when innocent lives are at risk. So yes, the military may be the best and sometimes the first tool; it should never be the only tool.
>
> . . .
>
> Defense and diplomacy are simply no longer discrete choices, one to be applied when the other one fails, but must, in fact, complement one another throughout the messy process of international relations.
>
> . . .
>
> In fact, I would argue that in the future struggles of the asymmetric counterinsurgent variety, we ought to make it a precondition of committing our troops, that we will do so only if and when the other instruments of national power are ready to engage as well.

This principle creates a civil–military issue because it seemingly conflicts with the perspective of the State Department. As Secretary of State Hillary Clinton said during her confirmation hearing, "We will lead with diplomacy because it's the smart approach. But we also know that military force will sometimes be necessary, and we will rely on it to protect our people and our interests when and where needed, as a last resort."[45]

The second point he raised in his speech was that "force should, to the maximum extent possible, be applied in a precise and principled way."

> Though it can never lessen the pain of such loss, precisely applying force in a principled manner can help reduce those costs and actually improve our chances of success. Consider for a moment ongoing operations in Marja in Afghanistan, Gen. McChrystal chose to move into this part of Southern Afghanistan specifically because it was a hub of Taliban activity. There, they had sway over the people; there, they were able to advance their interests to other places in the country. It wasn't ground we were interested in retaking so much as enemy influence we were interested in degrading.

This principle represents a rejection of the Weinberger/Powell Doctrine, which holds that when policy makers do decide to use force, it should be applied in an overwhelming manner.

His third principle, the idea that "policy and strategy should constantly struggle with one another," is a rejection of the "normal" theory of civil–military relations, the drawing of a distinct line that separates the military sphere from the policy sphere.

> Some in the military no doubt would prefer political leadership that lays out a specific strategy and then gets out of the way, leaving the balance of the implementation to commanders in the field. But the experience of the last nine years tells us two things: A clear strategy for military operations is essential; and that strategy will have to change as those operations evolve.
>
> In other words, success in these types of wars is iterative; it is not decisive. There isn't going to be a single day when we stand up and say, that's it, it's over, we've won. We will win but we will do so only over time and only after near constant reassessment and adjustment. Quite frankly, it will feel a lot less like a knock-out punch and a lot more like recovering from a long illness.
>
> The worst possible world I can imagine is one in which military commanders are inventing or divining their strategies, their own remedies, in the absence of clear political guidance, sometimes after an initial goal or mission has been taken over by events. That's why we have and need political leadership constantly immersed in the week-to-week flow of the conflict, willing and able to adjust as necessary but always leaving military commanders enough leeway to do what is expected of them.
>
> . . .
>
> Contrary to popular imagination, war has never been a set-piece affair. The enemy adapts to your strategy and you adapt to his. And so you keep the interplay going between policy and strategy until you find the right combination at the right time. What worked well in Iraq will not necessarily work in Afghanistan. What worked well today will not necessarily work tomorrow. The day you stop adjusting is the day you lose. To quote one of war's greatest students, Winston Churchill, you can always count on Americans to do the right thing after they've tried everything else. Trying everything else is not weakness. It means we don't give up. It means we never stop learning, and in my view if we've learned nothing else from these two wars of ours, it is that a flexible, balanced approach to

using military force is best. We must not look upon the use of military forces only as a last resort, but as potentially the best, first option when combined with other instruments of national and international power.

We must not try to use force only in an overwhelming capacity, but in the proper capacity, and in a precise and principled manner. And we must not shrink from the tug of war—no pun intended—that inevitably plays out between policymaking and strategy execution. Such interplay is healthy for the republic and essential for ultimate success. For Churchill also noted that in war, as in life, and I quote, "It is often necessary, when some cherished scheme has failed, to take up the best alternative, and if so, it is folly not to work with it with all your might."

Mullen's approach represents a step toward the likely renegotiation of the civil–military bargain. This renegotiation takes into account the changing security environment, the character of military professionalism and the new realities of American politics.

Trends in American Civil–Military Relations: The Changing Concept of Military Professionalism

In an era of complex irregular and hybrid wars, the professional soldier will continue to shift from being a "manager of violence" to a true "national security professional" in the broadest sense. If, indeed, complex irregular and hybrid wars are truly "political" conflicts, the soldier of the future will, more often than not, be required to act as a diplomat as well as a war fighter.[46] This has certainly been a lesson of fighting insurgencies in Iraq and Afghanistan. These conflicts have demonstrated the need for officers able to switch with speed and agility from warfighting to governance.[47]

The United States has usually chosen to conduct military operations, including counterinsurgencies, within a coalition or as part of a multinational framework. This complicates the life of a military officer who has to coordinate a variety of civilians from the US government, intergovernmental organizations, and nongovernmental organizations. In the absence of anything approaching a "chain of command," these individuals are often working at cross-purposes. If, indeed, the wars we will be fighting for the foreseeable future are what Huntington once called "permanent campaigns," the requirement to go far beyond the "management of violence" will have to become a part of the military profession. This applies as well to that other category of eminently political–military operations, stability operations.[48]

The Expertise of the Military Professional

This reality means that several important components of civil–military relations as understood and practiced in the United States will have to be reexamined. One of these is the meaning of military professional expertise. It has been understood for sometime that Huntington's description of the military's expertise as the management of violence is too narrow. While the culture of the services would prefer that this not be the case, the fact is that since the end of the Cold War, the US military has been engaged in complex contingency operations and irregular conflicts rather than the conventional wars that it would prefer to fight.

The military expertise necessary to conduct a population-centered counterinsurgency is different than that required to fight a conventional war. While a counterinsurgency may require the killing and capture of insurgents, the ability to do so is not sufficient for success. It is also necessary to provide security for the people at large and often to provide basic services such as clean water and electricity.

Sam Sarkesian, John Allen Williams, and Stephen Cimbala describe the military mind-set necessary to prevail in a counterinsurgency:

> An effective force structure responding to unconventional conflicts cannot be wedded to conventional hierarchy or command systems . . . It demands individuals with the requisite military skills who also understand and are sensitive to the cultural forces and nationalistic desires of foreign systems—especially those in the less developed world. They must be self-reliant individuals capable of operating for long periods in small groups isolated from the US environment. It will require patience, persistence, political–psychological sophistication, and the ability to blend in with the indigenous political–military system to prevail.[49]

As many observers have pointed out, the increase in troop strength in Iraq in 2007 was not the main cause of the improved situation there. More important was the change in the approach brought to bear by Gen. David Petraeus that helped to improve an uncertain security situation.

While the expertise of the military professional has been broadened far beyond the "management of violence," even his monopoly on said management has been eroded by two developments that are likely to continue into the future. The first of these is the expansion of the role of lawyers in the planning and execution of war at the tactical, operational, and strategic levels in response to the rise of "lawfare" noted above. Military lawyers in many cases now have a say—often the final say—in whether and under what circumstances a strike may be carried out or an attack launched. Thus, even when it comes to the concept that once defined the officer's very identity, he now must share it with the lawyer.[50]

The military officer's monopoly on the management of violence has also been undermined by increasing reliance on private security companies.[51] Such entities did not exist in Huntington's time and even as late as the Gulf War of 1991, they played only a marginal role. Now firms such as Blackwater, a security company that is now named Xe Services, play a major role in combat zones, often causing problems ranging from creating friction with US troops to charges of corruption and misconduct.[52]

Both the increasing role of the military lawyer and the rise of private security firms are likely to increase civil–military tensions created, but other potential problems arising from the shift from "kinetic" to nonkinetic capabilities should also be recognized. First, at a time when defense spending is sure to decrease, the new nonkinetic capabilities that the civilian leadership is likely to prefer will have to be paid by decreasing investment in the traditional combat capabilities necessary to fight and win conventional conflicts. This is likely to cause friction between the civilian leadership and that of the military. It is also probable that such a shift will generate interservice and even intraservice rivalry as "bill-payers" will have to fund the shift.

Second, the propensity of civilian policy makers to see the military as an all-purpose instrument of foreign and even domestic policy is also likely to generate civil–military friction. In foreign policy, the issue of "mission creep" emerged as a major concern during the Clinton era. As Chairman of the Joint Chiefs of Staff, Gen. Colin Powell was concerned about mission creep and the overuse of the military, typified by a question put to him by Clinton's secretary of state, Madeline Albright: "What's the point of having this superb military you're always talking about if we can't use it?"[53] And as we saw in Chapter 3, many lawmakers and others have not hesitated to call for an increased military role in domestic affairs.

Third, the expansion of the meaning of military expertise will have an impact on professional military education (PME), training, and organization. As Suzanne Nielsen and Don Snider ask, "is it possible to define a professional identity to help shape the development of professionals who are equally capable of practicing both kinetic and nonkinetic forms of warfare? Or does the way ahead for America's armed forces involve greater specialization of roles for officers and the units they lead?"[54] Both the Army and Congress previously have indicated interest in this topic.[55]

General Petraeus has called the new kind of officer required by the emerging security environment the "Pentathlete Leader." These are "individuals who, metaphorically speaking, are not just sprinters or shot putters but can do it all. We need officers comfortable not just with major combat operations but with operations conducted throughout the middle- and lower-ends of the spectrum of conflict, as well."[56]

The Future of the "Normal" Theory of Civil–Military Relations

Given the central role of professionalism in the theory and practice of American civil–military relations, the redefinition of professional military expertise will necessarily affect other aspects of the US civil–military bargain. One of these is the whole concept of professional military autonomy, the prerequisite for Huntington's "objective control" of the military and its corollary, the "normal" theory of civil–military relations.

To recap, Huntington argued that "objective civilian control" would simultaneously maximize military subordination and military fighting power. The key to objective control is "the recognition of autonomous military professionalism," i.e., respect for an independent military sphere of action. Interference or meddling by civilian policy makers in military affairs undermines military professionalism and so undermines objective control.[57]

Objective control constitutes a bargain between civilians and soldiers. On the one hand, civilian authorities, while deciding issues of policy and strategy, grant a professional officer corps autonomy in the realm of military affairs: operations and tactics. On the other hand, "a highly professional officer corps stands ready to carry out the wishes of any civilian group which secures legitimate authority within the state."[58] For Huntington, obedience to legitimate civilian authority is the very definition of professionalism.

But as one of Huntington's most accomplished students, Eliot Cohen, argued in his book, *Supreme Command*, this military autonomy, the basis of what Cohen calls the "normal" theory of civil–military relations, has often been violated, especially in liberal democracies at war. And as argued in Chapter 2, it did not hold during US military operations after 9/11 either. As Andrew Bacevich has observed, in practice, the civilians do not command the military establishment so much as cajole it, negotiate with it, and, as necessary, appease it.[59] If this has been the case in the past, how likely is the normal theory to hold in the future when the emerging military professional is Petraeus' "pentathlete leader?"

The Normal Theory of Civil–Military Relations and the US Strategy Deficit

But there is another reason to rethink the normal theory as currently understood. As noted in Chapter 3, US strategy making has left a great deal to be desired. In Colin Gray's words, cited in that chapter, "All too often, there is a black hole where American strategy ought to reside." The failure of American civil–military relations to generate strategy can be attributed to the confluence of three factors. The first of these is the continued dominance within the American system the normal theory.

The second factor, strongly reinforced by the normal theory of civil–military relations, is the influence of the uniformed services' organizational cultures. As discussed in Chapter 3, each military service is built around a "strategic concept," which according to Samuel Huntington constitutes "the fundamental element of a military service," the basic "statement of [its] role . . . or purpose in implementing national policy." A clear strategic concept is critical to the ability of a service to organize and employ the resources that Congress allocates to it.

As previously noted, the organizational culture of a service in turn exerts a strong influence on civil–military relations, frequently constraining what civilian leaders can do and often constituting an obstacle to change and innovation. In Iraq, the Army, focused as it was on the "operational level of war," was slow to respond to the emerging insurgency that almost brought the American effort in that country to naught.

The Army was able to continue on its preferred path because of the prevalence of the normal theory despite the fact that the conditions were different from the ones that had been assumed at the start of the war. The combination of the dominant position of the normal theory of civil–military relations in the United States and the US military's focus on the nonpolitical operational level of war meant that in the case of Iraq there was a disjunction between operational excellence in combat and *policy*, which determines the reasons for which the war was fought.

The third factor contributing to the American strategic deficit was an unintended consequence of the Goldwater–Nichols Department of Defense Reorganization Act of 1986. The act increased the authority of the chairman of the Joint Chiefs of Staff while reducing that of the Joint Chiefs themselves and increased the authority of the theater commanders. Congress expected that such reorganization would, among other things, improve the quality of military advice to policy makers.

The Joint Chiefs of Staff are responsible for integrating theater strategy and national policy. But if they are marginalized, as they were during much of the time during the Bush administration, and if there is acceptance of the idea of an autonomous realm of military action within which civilians have no role, such integration does not occur. The result of such a disjunction between the military and political realms is that war plans may not be integrated with national policy and that strategy, despite lip service to its importance, in practice becomes an orphan. And in the absence of strategy, other factors rush to fill the void, resulting in strategic drift. This seems to have been the case in Iraq.

Thomas Ricks described the failure of this dysfunctional system in his book *The Gamble*:

> The irony of all of this was that policy formulation was following the prescribed method, with the hierarchy being observed and all the correct bureaucratic players involved, but the system wasn't really working. That it looked good but it wasn't leading to a robust discussion by top officials of the necessary strategic questions. Nor were leaders held accountable and quizzed on their failures. It was only months later, when the prescribed system was subverted and the chain of command bypassed, that a rigorous examination of the American strategy in the Iraq War would get underway.[60]

Civil–Military Relations and Professional Military Education

As Sir Michael Howard once observed, the military profession is not only the most demanding of all the professions physically but the most demanding intellectually.[61] A major goal of professional military education (PME) is to address the problems discussed above by producing officers with the intellectual ability to rectify the "strategy deficit." While an important component of PME is to produce operational excellence, an exclusive focus on the operational level of war leads to the inability to think strategically, i.e., to relate military means to political ends. An officer who understands strategy must understand politics without becoming partisan.[62]

As suggested above, the distinction between the military and civilian realms in national security affairs has become blurred. Both civilian policy makers and military officers are national security professionals. As such, officers are required to understand and evaluate the judgments of political leaders and vice versa. Officers have an obligation to participate in the national security process by bringing to the table their best strategic judgment.

PME must produce more than a narrowly focused operator, who may know how to launch an airstrike, command a carrier battle group, or maneuver a brigade on the battlefield, but does not understand how to develop a strategy for counterinsurgency. It must produce an officer who understands the strategic nexus where operations and policy are integrated.

As Williamson Murray argues, because civilian leaders often lack the level of military experience of our adversaries, "it is essential that they receive nuanced, perceptive advice from their military adviser. Whether they take it or not is another matter, but an intelligent dialogue between political leaders and their military advisors, based on deep historical knowledge is essential for successful civil–military relations in coming decades."[63]

For many years, PME institutions paid insufficient attention to civil–military relations because of the consensus that US military officers had internalized the concept of civilian control. Since there was no threat of a military coup in the United States, why spend time on civil–military relations? Civil–military relations were also ignored because of the dominant view that the military should focus on its professional expertise and operational excellence and stay out of politics.

But as argued above, this view is mistaken. The conduct of war and the political ends for which it is fought are inextricably linked. The officer who ignores this connection does so at his peril and the peril of the military institution.

To prepare officers for the future, PME institutions need to ensure that their graduates understand a number of points raised previously. First, civil–military relations do not have to result in a coup to be "bad." There are a number of patterns and activities falling short of a coup, which indicate unbalanced or unhealthy civil–military relations. Attempts by the military to undercut policy decisions by means of leaks to the media or foot-dragging threaten the civil–military bargain.

Second, civil–military relations transcend the simple issue of civilian control of the military. The focus on civilian control by American students of civil–military relations has obscured the fact that different patterns of civil–military relations are necessary for different security challenges and that a pattern applicable in one situation may be dysfunctional in another.

Third, the "normal" theory of civil–military is not universally applicable. Many other countries with successful civil–military relations, e.g., Israel, do not have anything approaching the military autonomy that constitutes the cornerstone of the normal theory. Indeed, as we have seen, the normal theory does not seem to apply anymore—if it ever did—in the United States.

Healthy civil–military relations in the United States will depend on placing PME at the center of the personnel policies of the services. Only serious PME can ensure that officers can meet the intellectual challenges of integrating policy, strategy, and operations in the service of US interests. Yet the services continue to undervalue PME, as retired Army Major General Robert Scales observes in the *US Naval Institute Proceedings*.[64] This is certainly a problem that needs to be rectified in the interest of improved civil–military relations and rectifying the strategy deficit that has hampered US military performance since 9/11.

Conclusion

Part of renegotiating the civil–military bargain in the future is to ensure that the dysfunctional confluence that has created America's strategic deficit is not repeated. Rectifying this situation requires that both parties to the civil–military bargain adjust the way they do business. On the one hand, the military must recover its voice in strategy-making while realizing that politics permeates the conduct of war and that civilians have a say, not only concerning the goals of the war but also how it is conducted. On the other hand, civilians must understand that to implement effective policy and strategy requires the proper military instrument. They must also insist that soldiers present their views frankly and forcefully throughout the strategy-making process.

The future security environment and the reality of American politics suggest the need to shift from the outdated normal theory of civil–military relations to one more historically grounded, a model that accounts for the overlapping and reciprocal interrelationships of ends, ways and means necessary for strategic success. This means the establishment of new norms for creating a decision-making climate that encourages candid advice and the rigorous exchange of views and insights.

It is important to remember that civil–military relations entail more than merely civilian control, as important as that may be. Civilian control is constitutionally grounded in the United States, and the principle is accepted without question in the officer corps. The more important questions of American civil–military relations concern how to ensure effective strategies for the employment of the military instrument. To ensure this outcome to the benefit of US security requires discipline, a deliberate process, and a continuous dialogue between the civilian leadership and the military.

Notes

1   Richard Kohn, "Coming Soon: A Crisis in Civil-Military Relations," *World Affairs,* Winter 2008, http://www.worldaffairsjournal.org/2008% 20-%20Winter/full-civil-military.html.

2   George Mastroianni and Wilbur Scott, "After Iraq: The Politics of Blame and Civil-Military Relations," *Military Review,* July–August 2008, p. 55.

3   Jennifer L. Weber, *Copperheads: The Rise and Fall of Lincoln's Opponents in the North* (New York: Oxford University Press, 2006).

4   Robert W. Coakley, *The Role of Federal Military Forces in Domestic Disorders, 1789–1878* (Washington, DC: Center of Military History, United States Army, 1988), pp. 227–267.

5   Cited in Weber, p. 69.

6   Mackubin Thomas Owens, "When Dissent Becomes Obstruction," *Christian Science Monitor,* March 30, 2007, http://www.csmonitor.com/ 2007/0330/p09s01-coop.html?page=3.

7   Mastroianni and Scott, p. 56.

8   Ibid., p. 58.

9   Ibid., p. 56.

10 Stephen Biddle, *Military Power: Explaining Victory and Defeat in Modern Battle* (Princeton: Princeton University Press, 2004), pp. 198–199.

11 Francis Fukuyama, *The End of History and the Last Man* (New York: Free Press, 1992) and John Mueller, *Retreat From Doomsday: The Obsolescence of Modern War* (New York: Basic Books, 1989).

12 Colin Gray, *Modern Strategy* (Oxford: Oxford University Press, 1999), p. 6.

13 Admiral William Owens, "System-of-Systems: US' Emerging Dominant Battlefield Awareness Promises to Dissipate 'Fog of War'," *Armed Forces Journal International,* January 1996, p. 47.

14 The first quote is from Thomas Duffy, "Owens Says Technology May Lift 'Fog of War': Breakthroughs Could Give Forces Total Command of Future Battlefield," *Inside the Navy,* January 23, 1995, p. 5. The second is from Owens' speech before the Navy RMA Roundtable, Center for Naval Analyses, May 5, 1997. Cf. also Arnold Beichman, "Revolution in the Warfare Trenches," *Washington Times,* January 31, 1996, p. 17.

15 David Alberts, "The Future of Command and Control with DBK [Dominant Battlespace Knowledge]," in Stuart E. Johnson and Martin C. Libiki, eds., *Dominant Battlespace Knowledge* (Washington, DC: National Defense University Press, 1995), p. 93.

16 Ronald R. Fogelman, "Information Technology's Role in 21st Century Air Power," *Aviation Week & Space Technology,* February 17, 1997, p. 17.

17   Qiao Liang and Wang Xiangsui, *Unrestricted Warfare: China's Master Plan to Destroy America* (Los Angeles: Pan American Publishing Company, 2002). Cf. James Kraska, "How the United States Lost the Naval War of 2015," *Orbis*, Winter 2010.

18   This section is based on Mackubin Thomas Owens, "Reflections on Future War," *Naval War College Review*, Summer 2008. A number of points developed by the author here were also incorporated into the final report of the "Future of War" panel of the 2007 Defense Science Board Summer Study on which he served.

19   Peter Schwartz, *The Art of the Long View: Planning for the Future in an Uncertain World* (New York: Currency Doubleday, 1991).

20   Mackubin Thomas Owens, "The 'Correlation of Forces' Then and Now," February 2004, http://www.ashbrook.org/publicat/owens/04/cof.html.

21   Donald Rumsfeld, "War on Terror Memo," *USA Today*, October 16, 2003.

22   John Robb, *Brave New War: The Next Stage of Terrorism and the End of Globalization* (Hoboken: Wiley, 2007), p. 31.

23   Michael Vickers, *Warfare in 2020: A Primer* (Washington, DC: Center for Strategic and Budgetary Assessments, 1996), p. ii.

24   Carl von Clausewitz, *On War*, Michael Howard and Peter Paret, eds. and trans., (Princeton: Princeton University Press, 1976) passim; Alan Beyerchen, "Clausewitz, Nonlinearity, and the Unpredictability of War," *International Security*, Winter 1992/1993; Barry D. Watts, *Clausewitzian Friction and Future War*, McNair Paper 52 (Washington, DC: National Defense University Press, 1996); and Mackubin Thomas Owens, "Technology, the RMA, and Future War," *Strategic Review*, Spring 1998.

25   Philip Bobbitt, *The Shield of Achilles: War, Peace, and the Course of History* (New York: Alfred A. Knopf, 2002), p. xxi.

26   Cited in Robb, p. 14.

27   Ibid., pp. 14–15.

28   Ibid., p. 102.

29   Ibid., p. 103.

30   See, for example, Frank Hoffman, "Complex Irregular Warfare: The Next Revolution in Military Affairs," *Orbis*, Summer 2006.

31   Col. Doug King, USMC, "Hybrid War," A Presentation to the Defense Science Board, May 24, 2007.

32   Ralph Peters, "Lessons from Lebanon: The New Model Terrorist Army," *Armed Forces Journal*, October 2006.

33   David Kennedy, "Law Has Become a Military Instrument," *Times Online*, October 25, 2006, http://www.timesonline.co.uk/tol/comment/

article613078.ece. Cf. David Kennedy, *Of War and Law* (Princeton: Princeton University Press, 2006); Benjamin Wittes, *Law and the Long War: The Future of Justice in the Age of Terror* (New York: Penguin, 2008); James Kraska and Brian Wilson, "China Wages Maritime Lawfare," *ForeignPolicy.com*, March 11, 2009; and William H. Taft, IV, "The Law of Armed Conflict After 9/11: Some Salient Features," *28 Yale Journal of International Law*, 2003.

34 Cited in King, "Hybrid War," briefing to the DSB (supra, note 31).

35 Office of the Secretary of Defense, *Military Power of the People's Republic of China, 2007*, Annual Report to Congress, 2007, p. I.

36 Liang and Xiangsui, op. cit.

37 Mackubin Thomas Owens, "The Logic of Force Planning," A Briefing to the 2007 Defense Science Board Summer Study "Future of War" Panel, April 24, 2007.

38 See *Stephen Ross, American War Plans, 1890–1939* (London: Routledge, 2002) and Edward Miller, *War Plan Orange: The U.S. Strategy to Defeat Japan, 1897–1945* (Annapolis: US Naval Institute Press, 1991).

39 Andrew F. Krepinevich, *The Quadrennial Defense Review: Rethinking the US Military Posture* (Washington, DC: Center for Strategic and Budgetary Assessments, 2005), pp. 56–59. In 2009, Krepinevich updated his scenarios in *7 Deadly Scenarios: A Military Futurist Explores War in the 21st Century* (New York: Bantam, 2009).

40 Thomas S. Langston, *Uneasy Balance: Civil-Military Relations in Peacetime America Since 1783* (Baltimore: Johns Hopkins University press, 2003), p. 6.

41 Langston, p. 6.

42 Charles A. Stevenson, *Warriors and Politicians: US Civil-Military Relations under Stress* (New York: Routledge, 2006).

43 Ibid, pp. 8–9.

44 Admiral Mike Mullen, Landon Lecture Series, Manhattan, Kansas, March 3, 2010; Thom Shanker, "Mullen Recalibrates the Use of Force," *New York Times*, March 4, 2010; and Julian E. Barnes, "A Call for a New Type of U.S. Warfare: The Chairman of the Joint Chiefs Says Precision, Not Force, Is What the Future Holds," *Los Angeles Times*, March 4, 2010, p. 12.

45 Hillary Clinton, Statement before the Senate Foreign Affairs Committee, January 13, 2009.

46 Michele Flournoy, ed., *Beyond Goldwater-Nichols Phase Two Report* (Washington DC: Center for Strategic and International Studies, 2005) and Derek Reveron and Kathleen Mahoney-Norris, "Military-Political

Relations: The Need for Officer Education," *Joint Forces Quarterly*, Issue 52, First Quarter 2009.

47 David Kilcullen, *The Accidental Guerilla: Fighting Small Wars in the Midst of a Big One* (New York: Oxford University Press, 2009); Brent C. Bankus and James Q. Kievit, "Reopen a Joint School of Military Government and Administration?" *Small Wars and Insurgencies*, March 2008; and Michael Metrinko, *The American Military Advisor: Dealing with Senior Foreign Officials in the Islamic World* (Carlisle: Strategic Studies Institute, 2008).

48 Nadia Schadlow and Richard Lacquement, "Winning War, Not Just Battles: Expanding the Military Profession to Incorporate Stability Operations," in Suzanne Nielsen and Don Snider, eds., *American Civil-Military Relations: The Soldier and the State in a New Era* (Baltimore: Johns Hopkins University Press, 2009), pp. 112–132.

49 Sam C. Sarkesian, John Allen Williams, and Stephen J. Cimbala, *US National Security: Policymakers, Processes, and Politics*, 4th ed. Boulder: Lynne Rienner, 2008), p. 43.

50 Kelly D. Wheaton, *Strategic Lawyering: Realizing the Potential of Military Lawyers at the Strategic Level* (Carlisle: US Army War College Strategic Studies Institute, 2006); Geoffrey Corn, "Developing Warrior Lawyers: Why It's Time to Create a Joint Service Law of War Academy," *Military Review*, May–June 2006; Harvey Rishikof, "Judicial Warfare: The Neglected Legal Element," *Joint Forces Quarterly*, January 2008.

51 Deborah Avant, *The Market for Force: The Consequences of Privatizing Security* (Cambridge: Cambridge University Press, 2005); Peter Singer, *Corporate Warriors: The Rise of the Privatized Military Industry* (Ithaca: Cornell University Press, 2005).

52 AFP, "Pentagon Concerned Over Blackwater's Work in Afghanistan," March 6, 2010, http://news.yahoo.com/s/afp/20100306/pl_afp/afghanistanunrestuspoliticscongress.

53 *Michael Dobbs*, "With Albright, Clinton Accepts New U.S. Role," *Washington Post*, December 8, 1996, p. A01, http://www.washingtonpost.com/wp-srv/politics/govt/admin/stories/albright120896.htm.

54 Nielsen and Snider, "Conclusion," in Nielsen and Snider, pp. 297–298.

55 Bradley Graham, "Pentagon Considers Creating Postwar Peacekeeping Units," *Washington Post*, November 24, 2003, p. A16; Andrew Feickert, "Does the Army Need a Full-Spectrum Force or Specialized Units? Background and Issues for Congress," Congressional Research Service, January 2008, Report RL 34333.

56 David H. Petraeus, "Beyond the Cloister," *The American Interest*, July–August 2007, http://www.the-american-interest.com/ai2/article.cfm?Id=290&MId=14.

57 Huntington, *The Soldier and the State: The Theory and Politics of Civil-Military Relations* (Cambridge: The Belknap Press of Harvard University Press, 1957), p. 83.

58 Ibid., p. 84.

59 Andrew Bacevich, "Discord Still: Clinton and the Military," *The Washington Post*, January 3, 1999, p. C1.

60 Thomas Ricks, *The Gamble: General David Petraeus and the American Military Adventure in Iraq, 2006–2008* (New York: Penguin, 2009), p. 43.

61 Michael Howard, "The Use and Abuse of Military History," in Howard, *The Causes of War* (Cambridge: Harvard University Press, 1984).

62 Williamson Murray, "Professionalism and Professional Military Education," in Nielsen and Snider, pp. 133–148.

63 Ibid., p. 148.

64 Robert H. Scales, "Too Busy to Learn," US Naval Institute *Proceedings*, February 2010.

Index

Page numbers in **bold** denote tables.